A Commentary on the Gospel of

MARK

A Commentary on the Gospel of
MARK

Thomas H Glover

AMBASSADOR INTERNATIONAL
Greenville, South Carolina • Belfast, Northern Ireland

A Commentary on the Gospel of Mark
Simple and Sublime

NB. Unless otherwise stated, Bible text and quotations are from the New International Version, 1984.

ISBN 978-1-84030-197-7

Ambassador Publications
a division of
Ambassador Productions Ltd.
Providence House
Ardenlee Street,
Belfast,
BT6 8QJ
Northern Ireland
www.ambassador-productions.com

Emerald House
427 Wade Hampton Blvd.
Greenville
SC 29609, USA
www.emeraldhouse.com

DEDICATION

In memory of my late father-in-law James H Capie.
A true servant of God, who was my 'best friend and spiritual father' for over forty years.

ACKNOWLEDGEMENTS

I am indebted to the following people for their contribution towards the writing of this Commentary.

- My wife Dorothy and my family for their continual support and encouragement.

- Dr William Thomson, past Professor of Societal Theology who oversaw this Commentary. I am indebted to him for his wisdom, literary skills and encouragement. His input has been invaluable.

- Margaret Maxwell, a member of my Congregation at Largo Baptist Church for her studious proof reading and encouragement.

Author's Preface

Although Mark is the shortest of all four gospels, it is rich in simplicity, directness and detail. It is a gospel waiting to reward those who read and understand it. Being the first gospel to be written, and without the influence of the other gospels, Mark bears witness to what he had seen and heard in a straightforward, uncluttered way.

The author's aim is to present a Commentary which is very 'readable and understandable' and was written with a wide readership in mind. Those seeking to learn more about the life and ministry of the historical Jesus should find value in this book. For the student of God's Word who seeks a wider and deeper understanding of many of the truths and themes introduced in Mark's gospel, footnotes should be read and references from Old and New Testament pursued.

The study of parallel passages in the Synoptics would also be most rewarding. Reading this Commentary with an open Bible at hand is to be encouraged.

At the very outset of this gospel, Mark informs the reader of his subject in chapter 1:1 *'The beginning of the gospel, about Jesus Christ, the Son of God.'*

The gospels (including Mark), have proved pivotal for many who have sought an understanding of the person of Jesus

Christ, the Son of God. This was certainly true for the late C.S. Lewis.

In her biography of C.S. Lewis,[1] Anne Arnot writes, *'Over the years he had become an expert in literary criticism, and in the study of myths. By now he was too experienced in literary criticism, he said, to regard the Gospels as myth. Nothing else in all literature was like them, and the Person they depicted was unique. Christ was this person: and Jack (C.S.) Lewis slowly came to see that he appeared in the narrative accounts as if he were 'lit by a light from beyond the world'. Slowly he accepted that this was not just a picture of a god, but God. Here, and here only, God was made man. The myth had become fact, and the Everlasting Word had become flesh for him.'*

The gospels were instrumental in his journey that took him from Atheism > Theism > conversion to Christ.

The author's aim may be summarised in three ways:-

- To explain the text in a readable and understandable way.
- To inform and encourage.
- To exalt the person of Christ.

---

1. The Secret Country of C.S. Lewis. Anne Arnot. Published by Hodder and Stoughton 1974. Quote from p94-95.

ANALYSIS OF THE GOSPEL OF MARK

THE GOSPEL OF MARK
Introduction

It is difficult to read the gospel of Mark without being caught up in the swiftness of pace and the rapid change from one subject to the other. The impression given is that Mark's mind and heart are racing ahead to bring testimony to what he has seen and heard – he just has to get it out! His opening words – *'The beginning of the gospel about Jesus Christ, the Son of God'* present us with a sweeping statement that bridged 400 years of silence when no word of prophecy had been heard. Spiritual darkness was the experience of the nation of Israel and spirituality was at a low ebb. Following this period known as the 'Intertestamental period' (between testaments), Mark wastes no time in introducing Jesus Christ as the Son of God. Throughout this gospel the activity and ministry of Jesus clearly established His deity.[1]

Of the first three gospels Mark's is the shortest in length. From the earliest days Scholars have endeavoured to answer questions such as:-

---

[1] 'This picture of the Messiah sent from God is made even more compelling by the demonstrations, beyond words of preaching, in the miracles Jesus performed. For the first eight chapters of this gospel there is a quite breathless presentation of one work of power after another'. BST The Message of Mark. Donald English p16 IVP 1992

- Where does Mark's gospel come in order of writing, before or after Matthew and Luke?
- Was Mark influenced by other sources?
- Why does Mark exclude material common to the other two?

These and other questions have been discussed and debated under what is known as the 'Synoptic Problem'. A brief introduction to this subject might be helpful.

The Synoptic Problem.

Most Christians when presented with the possibility of a 'Synoptic Problem' would say, 'What problem?' Laymen, to a large extent, are unaware that such a concept exists. Although it would be difficult for the average reader, or even student of the 'Synoptic' gospels, to go into all the intricacies of this subject, no one should be left in ignorance that such a problem exists and all should have some awareness of the subject matter.

The first three gospels, as we have them in the New Testament, are Matthew, Mark and Luke. These are known as the 'Synoptic Gospels' because they survey the life of Christ from a common viewpoint (sun = with: opsis = seeing). In these gospels we have both resemblances and differences and the problem consists in the harmonizing of these and attempting to determine the relation of the synoptics to one another. How to account for these resemblances and differences has been the basis for much investigative study and research by scholars, both past and present.

The earliest serious attempt to resolve the problem of unity and diversity goes back to Tatian (110-172 AD).[2] As a pupil of Justin Martyr he wrote his famous 'Diatesseron' around 150 AD. In his work he sought to deal with the four gospels, aiming at producing one single comprehensive text. When finished he had reduced the 3,780 verses of the four gospels to 2,769. Tatian's 'Diatesseron' is the earliest example of what has been

[2] Christian apologist and Gnostic who came to Rome about 150 AD, was converted and later became a pupil of Justin Martyr. Like his master he engaged in the defence of the faith against pagan misrepresentation.

called a 'harmony of the gospels'. His influence can be seen throughout the centuries that followed in the works of many others who addressed the problem. These have included one of the most famous of all time – Andreas Osilander's 'Harmoniae Evangelicae' which was published in Basel in 1537. Also of note was the most famous of the historical parallel harmonies by John Calvin which was published in Geneva in 1555.

Throughout the years scholars, in their attempt to produce answers to the seeming variations, have investigated the subject from different directions. These have often, but not exclusively, come under the banners of Literary, Form and Redactive Criticism.[3] In their investigations scholars had to account for:-

- What was common to all three gospels?
- What was common to any two of them?
- What was peculiar to each?

There were also other considerations. Were other sources used in the writings of the gospels? Was Mark the first to be written, and did Matthew and Luke use Mark as a source? To what extent did oral tradition and knowledge contribute?

Scholars have studied the gospels literally as single contributions and, by comparison, looking at grammar, composition, areas of emphases, and by classifying areas of parallel agreement. It might be helpful to have a brief glimpse at some of the main hypotheses.

1. The Oral Tradition Hypothesis.

This theory assumes that each of the three Evangelists wrote independently of each other and derived the substance of this writing not from written sources, but from oral narratives of sayings and doings of Jesus which had become, through repetition, a relatively fixed form. This oral tradition would have had its rise in Jerusalem, and would be the teaching given

[3] For further and more comprehensive understanding of these, see. The 'Synoptic Problem'. Robert H Stein – Baker Book House –1992.

in catechetical schools until written editions appeared; the truth would be entrusted to the trained memories of Christian men. Whether or not the theory solves the 'Synoptic Problem', there can be no doubt that such catechetical schools existed.

2. The Mutual Use Hypothesis.

This is the view that the problem can be accounted for by assuming that the authors of these gospels used each other's writings, but there never has been agreement as to who the borrowers were, each in turn was regarded as a borrower of others. There are six possible permutations and this theory has few advocates today.

3. The Documents Hypothesis.

This is the most commonly held theory among present day scholars, with varying opinions as to how many such documents there were. Most scholars are agreed on two sources:- 1) Mark's gospel 2) A non-extant document called 'Q'.[4] Critics are not agreed on the content of Q and there is no general agreement as to how much of this hypothetical document was used by each of the three Evangelists. However, it seems difficult to account for so many non-Markan parallels in Matthew and Luke without assuming such a document.

Mark the man.

It is generally accepted that this is the oldest written account of the life and ministry of Jesus which we possess. Although this gospel contains no reference to its author, it has to be noted that there is no matter less disputed among New Testament scholars than that it was written by one whose name was Mark. Scholars generally accept that Peter's eye witness account of the life of

[4] This document is designated 'Q' from the German 'Quelle' which means 'source'.

Christ was also a source for Mark. It was written around 30 years after the death of Jesus by John Mark, probably in Rome, with gentile readers in mind, in particular the Romans.[5] Mark was his Roman surname and John his Hebrew name. He was the son of a wealthy lady of Jerusalem whose name was Mary, and whose house was a meeting place of the early Church **(Acts 12:12)**. From Mark's earliest days he came under the influence of a godly home which was the centre for Christian fellowship.

Mark was also the nephew of Barnabas, and when Paul and Barnabas set off on their first missionary journey they took him with them **(Acts 12:25).** These two godly men must have been a tremendous influence on this young man. However, this journey proved to be most unfortunate for Mark for we read in **Acts 13:13** *'John (Mark) left them to return home.'*

There may have been several reasons for his departure. He may have been afraid to face the dangers of that particularly perilous part of the world. It may be that he feared for the way ahead, both physically and spiritually.

The fact remains that he turned back, and in so doing, failed Paul and Barnabas at a time of crisis that caused the severance of two friends. We find that as Paul and Barnabas proposed to set out on their second missionary journey, Barnabas was anxious to take Mark with them, but Paul refused because he had previously turned back.[6]

In Mark's failure we see his truly human side, yet it was not the end, but proved to be a valuable learning experience for him. For a number of years Mark disappeared from history. Tradition has it that he went to Egypt where he founded the Church of Alexandria, but we cannot be certain. When Mark re-emerges it is by the most unexpected discovery that, when Paul writes his letter to the Colossians from prison, Mark is there with him. *'My fellow-prisoner Aristarchus sends you*

---

[5] 'Here too this Gospel, though nowhere definitely indicating and proving its place of origin, confirms the statements of Eusebius, Clement of Alexandria, Irenaeus, etc,. that it was written in Rome and for the Romans' William Hendriksen, NTC Banner of Truth Trust. 1976 p13

[6] Acts 15:37-40

greetings, as does Mark, the cousin of Barnabas. (You have received instructions about him; if he comes to you, welcome him) (**Col 4:10**). In Philemon also, Paul mentions Mark as a fellow-worker (**v24**). Again in **2 Tim 4:11** Paul writes *'Get Mark and bring him with you, because he is helpful to me in my ministry.'*

What a remarkable testimony is given of Mark His failure did not have the final say, but the transforming power of God is seen at work in his life, that same power which Mark unfolds in vivid form throughout his gospel. As he introduces his reader to the life and ministry of Jesus, he does so in a way that resembles the journalist giving his eyewitness account, telling the facts of Jesus' life in the simplest and most dramatic way.

Mark leaves his readers in no doubt as to what he believed Jesus to be – Jesus Christ, the Son of God.[7] It is worth pointing out that Mark, just like John, does not use his own name in his gospel.

Though Mark is the shortest of the gospels it is rich in its content and, included in its seventy different sections (according to the English Bible) it covers even more subjects, moving from one to the other as though they were 'hot off the press'. The fact that Mark seems at times merely to mention an incident then move swiftly on is not necessarily a disadvantage.

For example, in the short section in chapter one from **vv9-13**, Mark, having focussed on the baptism of Jesus, immediately turns his attention to the Spirit sending Jesus out into the desert. Yet he only mentions three things: firstly, that He was in the desert for forty days; secondly, that He was with the wild animals; and thirdly, that the angels attended Him. There is no elaboration in this part of the narrative, no further detail given. While this is obviously how Mark, inspired by the Spirit of God, intended it to be, there is nothing to stop the reader widening the search and, where suitable comparing with the other gospels.

---

[7] To Mark, Jesus was not simply a man among men; he was God among men, ever moving them to a wondering amazement with his words and deeds.' William Barclay. Daily Study Bible. St Andrews Press 1975. p6

1

Although all four gospels present the life and ministry of Jesus, the Son of God, they all begin with a different starting point. **Matthew** begins his story with an account of the ancestry, conception, birth, and naming of Jesus. **Luke** begins with a personal affirmation of the reliability of his gospel, he then moves into the narrative relating to the birth of John the Baptist, providing the background leading up to his mother Elizabeth's pregnancy. **John** immediately leads straight into deep truths, pointing to the pre-existence and deity of Christ. As already noted, **Mark** wastes no time with any preliminaries, he launches the gospel and person of Christ in the opening sentence; then, without a breath, turns to John the Baptist, who in turn points to Christ.[1]

The dawning of a new age. 1:1

> *'The beginning of the gospel about Jesus Christ, the Son of God'.*

[1] We are all accustomed to call the first books of the New Testament the Four Gospels. Before the fourth century, however, the whole fourfold collection was usually called 'the Gospel' – the one and only Gospel of Christ – and the four components of the collection were distinguished by the addition 'according to'. The New Bible Commentary, Inter-Varsity Fellowship. March 1961. Prof F.F. Bruce. p58

There could be no finer or more comprehensive statement to introduce Mark's gospel than this sentence, for it immediately points, in a descriptive way, to the central person of the entire gospel. This opening verse is probably intended by Mark as a title to the whole book.

The beginning of the gospel.

Mark points towards the new start that God was making possible for mankind – here is the beginning of 'good news' that would change the world by the inner transformation of humankind, referred to by Jesus and the apostles as a 'new birth'.[2] Four hundred years of spiritual darkness were about to come to an end. During that period, the voice of the prophets had not been heard and spiritual life was at an all time low. This four hundred year period is referred to as the 'Inter-testamental period', the time-span between Old and New Testament writings.

Although Mark is proclaiming a new message, he is careful to link up what he is saying with the Old Testament, because he knows that his hearers are familiar with these writings. It was their Scripture. To create a link between the Old and New Testaments, in **vv2-3** he quotes from the Old Testament.[3]

About Jesus Christ, the Son of God.

The gospel or 'good news' is all about a person, the person of Jesus Christ. In Jesus Christ the 'dawning of a new age' would come, a new way for people to approach God, know God, and live in the power of God for His glory. The key to this new life is found in Jesus Christ – it's about Him!

But why does Mark use the title '*Jesus Christ the Son of God*'? What is the significance of this? All that Mark has to

---

[2] See John 3:1-8. 2 Corinthians 5:17. 1 John 5:1. 1 Peter 1:3
[3] Isaiah 40:3 Malachi 3:1

write hinges on our understanding of this title. Never before had anyone been introduced in such a way, this was not just 'another prophet' sent from God – here was God, in human flesh! The exalted title given here is significant, for the name 'Jesus' was given at His birth because He was to be a Saviour. According to **Matthew 1:21** *'She will give birth to a son, and you will give him the name Jesus, because he will save his people from their sins'.*

Furthermore, by using the word 'Christ', Mark affirms that Jesus the Saviour was the Messiah as prophesied in the Old Testament. The name, Christ, was the Greek equivalent of the Hebrew *Messiah,* meaning *Anointed.* This was the One for whom the Jewish nation had waited for many years, eagerly longing for Him, especially in the days of oppression by others, in particular under Roman occupation as was their present experience.

To conclude his description Mark adds 'the Son of God'.[4] By doing this he links the humanity and deity of Christ together, both of which were essential for the salvation of mankind and the fulfilment of the eternal purpose of God. This was to be 'the dawning of a new age' through Jesus Christ, the Son of God.

John the Baptist prepares the way for Jesus. 1:2-8

> *'It is written in Isaiah the prophet: I will send my messenger ahead of you, who will prepare your way – a voice of one calling in the desert, Prepare the way for the Lord, make straight paths for him.' And so John came, baptising in the desert region and preaching a baptism of repentance for the forgiveness of sins. The whole Judean countryside and all the people of Jerusalem went out to him. Confessing their sins, they were baptised by him in the Jordan River.*

[4] Some manuscripts do not have the Son of God.

> *John wore clothing made of camel's hair, with a leather belt round his waist, and he ate locusts and wild honey. And this was his message: 'After me will come one more powerful than I, the thongs of whose sandals I am not worthy to stoop down and untie. I baptise with water, but he will baptise you with the Holy Spirit.'*

Mark now introduces the one who would be the messenger of God, whose responsibility was to prepare the way for Jesus the Messiah. What is known about this unusual man?

His ministry was one of preparation.

All that he would say and do was not an end in itself – it was a preparation for someone greater; he was just a signpost that pointed away from himself to Jesus. His job was to challenge his hearers to look within their own hearts, and in the light of Old Testament Scripture, see themselves as they really were – to take a good look at themselves. If only they could do this, they would understand with greater clarity the significance of Jesus' message; hence **v3** '.....*Prepare the way for the Lord'*. When John says *'make straight paths for him'* he is telling them to get everything and anything out of the way that would hinder them from responding in obedience to what Jesus would say.[5] Domestically, it conveys the idea of cleaning out the house because the arrival of a guest is awaited.

There must have been enormous crowds listening to John's preaching for they not only travelled from around all Judea but also from Jerusalem.

His ministry was not easy on the ears.

John challenged his hearers to repent. What did he mean by

[5] Heb 12:1 '....let us throw off everything that hinders and the sin that so easily entangles...'

using the word repentance? The Greek word for repentance is METANOEO, and means to *'change one's mind or purpose, a turning around.'* The challenge to repent, either then or today, can never be easy, for it calls for inner searching, honesty and a willingness to change. The evidence that his audience had repented was seen by their willingness to be baptised. This was the practical outworking of their decision to confess their sins. There was no place to hide, confessing their sins and seeking forgiveness meant being baptised in public. It was a public testimony to the change that had taken place within their hearts. His message was incredibly effective because it was this truth that struck home in the multitudes that heard.

His character was an example.

Here was a man who had spent most of his life living in the obscurity and isolation of the desert. His primitive clothing and simple diet typified his simplistic and self-effacing lifestyle. In the most positive way, he was obsessed by his own insignificance and did not want his hearers to focus on him. He is referred to as just a voice. The Greek word for voice is PHONE, meaning 'a single sound', not stereo, not quadraphonic but just a sound – a mere noise.[6] The stamp of genuine humility is seen in John's life and by referring to himself as just a voice, tells us that he could not think any less of himself.

Pointing again to Jesus as the One more powerful than himself, he says in **v7** *'....the thongs of whose sandals I am not worthy to stoop down and untie.'* In ancient times this was the mark of servanthood, carried out by the servant or slave for his master following his return from a wearing journey. John stands as a glorious example for all who would seek to take up the challenge of discipleship and follow Jesus. In **Jn 3:30** John summarises his attitude to Jesus when he says – *'He must become greater; I must become less'.* [7]

---

[6] See John 1:19-23.

[7] John's more complete testimony is found in Jn 3:22-36

A contrast of baptisms.

John describes the baptism which he performed as 'a baptism with water'. This was a baptism of total immersion, for the Greek word for baptism is BAPTIZO, and means 'to completely submerge'. This same word was used at that time for the dyeing of a garment which had to be totally covered by the colouring liquid. We may also note that in **Jn 3:23** John was baptising there *'because there was plenty of water'*.

In contrast to this water baptism John says *'but he (Jesus) will baptise you with the Holy Spirit.'*[8] Repentance and baptism is something that man must do. Now in **v8** he points to something that only God can do – 'baptise you with the Holy Spirit.'[9]

From the time of Pentecost in **Acts 2** the Holy Spirit was given to all who repented, believed and followed Christ. This may be referred to as the moment of 'spiritual birth'. When Jesus, in **John 3**, is teaching Nicodemus about being 'born again' he speaks of it as being 'born of the Spirit' **(v8)**. We may also note that it is the receiving of the Holy Spirit that brings about the believer's entrance into the Kingdom and family of God. With great clarity the apostle Paul writes in **Rom 8:9** *'And if anyone does not have the Spirit of Christ, he does not belong to Christ'* and in **v15** *' received the Spirit of sonship'*.

The baptism of Jesus. 1:9-11

> *'At that time Jesus came from Nazareth in Galilee and was baptised by John in the Jordan. As Jesus was coming up out of the water, he saw heaven being torn*

[8] 'We must not assume that this is an easy verse to understand. It helps to hold firmly in mind that the fact that the prime contrast is between two persons – John the Baptist and Jesus – rather than two kinds of baptisms'. BST The Message of Mark. IVP Donald English p34.

[9] Ephesians 4:5 '.... one Lord, one faith, one baptism'

open and the Spirit descending on him like a dove. And a voice came from heaven: You are my Son, whom I love; with you I am well pleased'.

This passage raises the all important question; why should Jesus be baptised by John in the Jordan, when such a baptism was associated with repentance and forgiveness of sins?

Since Jesus was the Son of God Incarnate and therefore without sin, why the need to be baptised?[10] We find in Matthew's account of Jesus' baptism **(3:13-17),** that John the Baptist tried to stop Him being baptised, in fact, John says in **v15** *'I need to be baptised by you, and do you come to me?'* John cannot understand why Jesus should come to him. Numerous suggestions have been offered as reasons for Jesus' baptism.

- That it was his first act of public **obedience** to his Father's will.
- That it was a wonderful act of **humility**.
- That we have an **example** for others to follow.
- That it was the seal of his Father's **approval**.

In these suggestions there are undoubtedly commendable thoughts, and truth within them, yet it is necessary to examine a far greater and more profound reason for His baptism.

Although Jesus was entirely sinless, there would come a time when on the cross He would lay down His own life as a sacrifice for sin. On the cross Jesus not only laid down His life for sinners, but also paid the price for sin – in doing so HE ACTUALLY BECAME THAT SIN.

Beyond human understanding this most assuredly is, yet, Jesus would identify with the personal sin of each one by becoming that sin. Peter writes in **1 Peter 2:24** *'He himself bore our sins in his body on the tree.....'.* This is helpful in

[10] 1 Peter 2:22 'He committed no sin, and no deceit was found in his mouth'.

understanding why His Father in heaven had to look away as His one and only Son offered up His life on the cross, for during that period of darkness His Father could not look upon sin.[11] Jesus responded to this by calling out *'My God, my God, why have you forsaken me?' (***Mtt 27:46***)*.

It was therefore with a view to the cross that lay ahead of Him that Jesus was baptised. His baptism was 'symbolic' with the sin of others in mind. On the cross Jesus would identify with the sin of all mankind and not His own, for He was without sin.

The baptism of Jesus, then, was with the sin of others in mind. It symbolised the time when He would be immersed in suffering for the sin of others. Bearing in mind how Jesus responded to John's reservation in **Matthew 3:15** also introduces a meaning that takes into account the whole ministry of Jesus, including His finished work on the cross, *'Jesus replied, Let it be so now; it is proper for us to do this to fulfil all righteousness.'*

The baptism of Jesus has further significance for it brings two things into focus:-

1) His heavenly anointing by the Holy Spirit.

As Jesus was coming up out of the water He received a special anointing by the Holy Spirit. The account asserts that He (Jesus) saw heaven being torn open; what a breathtaking thought! This can only be imagined! The words 'torn open'[12] seem to be another way of saying 'unveiling' or 'opening out', for the Greek word used for 'open' is ANAPTUSSO, meaning 'to unroll'. With heaven opened up before His eyes, the Spirit descended on Him like a dove.

It may be noticed that Mark writes 'like' a dove; though there is no reason to doubt the reality of an actual dove, it is possible that he is thinking about the manner in which the Spirit

---

[11] Habakkuk 1:13 'Your eyes are too pure to look on evil; you cannot tolerate wrong'.
[12] The words 'torn open' was a common Jewish expression used to introduce a divine revelation. BST. Message of Mark. Donald English p39.

descends, rather than the shape. However, the picture of a dove reminds us of gentleness, peacefulness and graciousness.

Whatever form it takes, the Holy Spirit is bringing that 'special anointing' - equipping Jesus for His ministry that lay ahead. The question may be asked, 'Why, if Jesus is the Son of God did He need this anointing?' It is here that it must be re-affirmed that, although Jesus was fully divine, He was also fully human; therefore as a man His anointing was necessary. If such an anointing was necessary for the Son of God, surely it raises the importance of God's anointing upon all who seek to serve Him and minister in His name.

2) The affirmation of his deity and the approval of His Father.

Not only did heaven pour out the Spirit upon Jesus but the voice of His Father is also heard, declaring the deity of His Son, His pleasure in His obedience and the fullness of His love. To those who may consider Jesus just to be the best of men or simply the greatest of human prophets, here is a word of Divine rebuke, for the reality is contained in the words of the Father in heaven *'You are my Son'*.

In this passage we also witness the doctrine of the Holy Trinity in action, for here Jesus is the central figure, coming up out of the water, and immediately being anointed by the Holy Spirit, followed by the voice of the Father, and what does He do? He affirms the deity of Jesus his Son.

The Temptation of Jesus. 1:12-13

> *'At once the Spirit sent him out into the desert, and he was in the desert for forty days, being tempted by Satan. He was with the wild animals, and angels attended him'.*

No sooner had the glory of His baptism passed, when the battle of the temptation arrived. The same Spirit who anointed Him was now sending Him into the wilderness to engage in spiritual warfare. Surely this is typical of Christian experience; times of blessing are often followed by times of temptation or trial. Christians do well to remember the outcome of this - victory!

It is perhaps impossible for us to contemplate Jesus the Son of God being tempted. Since God cannot be tempted **(James 1:13)**, it can only be assumed that His temptations were targeted towards the human nature of Jesus. That the temptation of Jesus actually happened cannot be in dispute, since not only do Matthew and Luke record it, but also in **Hebrews 4:15** we have a reference to it. Typical of Mark, his narrative is very brief; not surprisingly **v12** begins with '*At once the Spirit sent him out into the desert..*'.

Under the guidance of the Spirit of God He is directed to the place of confrontation, where He would engage with his enemy Satan, and would spend forty days. Mark provides us with no actual detail with regard to the nature of the temptations as do Matthew and Luke.[13] However, it should be noted that they were **diverse and deceptive**.

The sense of isolation in this battle is reflected by the inclusion of being with *'wild animals'*, a detail only included by Mark, and the severity of this period understood by the need for '*ministering angels in attendance*'. These temptations were aimed at bringing down the Son of God and destroying the work His Father had given Him to do.

How glorious, in contrast, to read these words from **1 John 3:8** *'The reason the Son of God appeared was to destroy the devil's work.'* The blessed Lord Jesus triumphed over Satan – He did not yield to the temptations and in so doing set an example for all who would follow Him. In **1 Corinthians 10:13** the Scriptures state that *'No temptation has seized you except what is common to man. And God is faithful; he will not let you*

[13] Matthew 4:1-11. Luke 4:1-13.

be tempted beyond what you can bear. But when you are tempted, he will also provide a way out so that you can stand up under it.'

The beginning of Jesus' ministry. 1:14-15

> *'After John was put in prison, Jesus went into Galilee, proclaiming the good news of God. The time has come, he said. The kingdom of God is near, Repent and believe the good news!'*

Unlike Matthew and Luke, Mark gives no background regarding the circumstances that led John the Baptist into prison. He simply acknowledges the fact, and then takes up with Jesus. In one sentence he basically says 'John is in prison and Jesus has gone to Galilee.' However, later in **Ch 6** Mark returns to John's tragic death.

Mark now tells why Jesus went into Galilee,[14] '*proclaiming the good news of the kingdom of God'*. He now refers directly to the words of Jesus, giving a brief mention of Jesus' subject matter.

The Kingdom of God is near. This is not a geographical statement but a reference to the spiritual rule and reign of King Jesus within the human heart. Entrance to the Kingdom of God comes by believing in Jesus and receiving Him as Saviour and Lord, submitting to His will and purpose. Jesus made it clear that His Kingdom was not of this world, not an earthly but a spiritual Kingdom.[15] The Kingdom was also near because Jesus was present.

Repent. This was a challenge to completely turn around from the old life. To change direction from following one's own path and purpose, acknowledging the error of one's ways

---

[14] 'Galilee was the centre of a humming political and commercial life. It stood at the crossroads of the nations of the ancient world, through which the armies and the traders and the diplomats passed. It was the home of a thoroughly cosmopolitan population' S. Blanch, 'Encounters with Jesus' (Hodder & Stoughton) 1988) p31.

[15] See John 3:5 on entering the Kingdom and also 18:36 on the nature of the Kingdom.

and being totally willing to change. Repentance involves conviction, contrition and confession of sin.[16]

Believe the good news. This is to accept the truth in heart and mind that Jesus is the Son of God and is uniquely the only means of salvation for all who are unbelievers. This is a belief that actually involves commitment. In Jesus alone, fullness of life is to be experienced – this is good news! **Jn 10:10** *'I have come that they might have life, and have it to the full'.*

The calling of the first disciples. 1:16-20

> *'As Jesus walked beside the Sea of Galilee, he saw Simon and his brother Andrew casting a net into the lake, for they were fishermen. Come, follow me, Jesus said, and I will make you fishers of men. At once they left their nets and followed him. When he had gone a little farther, he saw James son of Zebedee and his brother John in a boat, preparing their nets. Without delay he called them, and they left their father in the boat with the hired men and followed him.'*

Jesus is now walking beside the Sea of Galilee; as He does so, He calls His first disciples. In this small group of men there was **Simon** (Peter), who was the impulsive and impetuous one, always eager to talk or act without hesitation. Then **James**, who was a faithful servant, and would become the first to wear the martyr's crown. **Andrew** the natural evangelist comes next; his main function was to bring others to Jesus. His brother **John** made up the four on this occasion and, like Mark in his gospel, he never mentions his own name, choosing to use phrases like

---

[16] 'In the present day we do not sufficiently realise the necessity for repentance. To some extent we have even forgotten what repentance means. We read the great classical outpourings of the contrite soul – the Psalms, or the confessions of St Augustine or the Imitation of A Kempis, or John Bunyan's Grace Abounding – and they appear almost hysterical'. The Great Texts of the Bible. T & T Clark. 1910. St Mark. James Hastings D.D. p81

'The disciple who Jesus loved **(Jn 20:2)**, and *'the disciple who outran Peter to the tomb* **(Jn 20:3)**.' Humility marked him out.

The choice of these men to be disciples and apostles is quite remarkable, for they were fishermen, unschooled with only basic education, not men who were outstanding in any way. Years later the apostle Paul wrote in **1 Corinthians 1:26** *'Brothers, think of what you were when you were called. Not many of you were wise by human standards; not many were influential; not many were of noble birth.'*

God did not call them because of what they were, but what He would make them. They understood what it meant to fish, so with this in mind Jesus said *'Come, follow me, and I will make you fishers of men'*. They were used to catching fish; from now on they would be catching men. The all important words are *'follow me* and *I will make you'*. They would discover, as is the case for all who seek to follow Christ, that it was not so much their **ability** or **inability** that concerned Jesus – but their **availability**, for Jesus said 'I WILL MAKE YOU'. Here is a truth that was not solely for these disciples but is for all who would follow Christ and thereby enter into a life changing relationship and experience with Jesus Christ.

Heeding the challenge, they left their nets and followed Jesus. We do well to note that this was no easy thing for them to do – this was their livelihood, their source of income to keep their families and provide stability for them in life. The voice of Jesus must have struck home to their hearts like nothing they had ever heard, for we read, *'at once they left their nets'*. In James' and John's case we read *'Without delay'*. Yet, in doing so, we may also note that they did not act recklessly or without thought for others, because in **v20,** we are told that *'they left their father Zebedee in the boat with the hired men and followed him.'*

And so, here are four men who, following their first encounter with Jesus, decided that in Him was One worth laying down their all to follow.

Jesus confronts evil in his first sermon. 1:21-28

> *'They went to Capernaum, and when the Sabbath came, Jesus went into the synagogue and began to teach. The people were amazed at his teaching, because he taught them as one who had authority, not as the teachers of the law. Just then a man in their synagogue who was possessed by an evil spirit cried out, 'What do you want with us, Jesus of Nazareth? Have you come to destroy us? I know who you are – the Holy One of God'. 'Be quiet!' said Jesus sternly. 'Come out of him!' The evil spirit shook the man violently and came out of him with a shriek. The people were all so amazed that they asked each other, 'What is this? A new teaching – and with authority! He gives orders to evil spirits and they obey him. News about him spread quickly over the whole region of Galilee'*

Just a few verses, yet in them, Mark introduces a new type of preaching, a confrontation between light and darkness and a demonstration of the power of God. As Jesus preached for the first time in the synagogue it became clear that there was an enormous contrast between what they were used to hearing and what Jesus was now saying – they had never heard or seen anything like this before!

A new age had begun as the Son of God taught the truth, and in so doing He pointed not to another, but to Himself. Although Mark does not inform us of what Jesus taught, it may be that Luke does, in **4:14ff**, though there is no absolute certainty. On that occasion the text declares that Jesus was teaching in the synagogue and after quoting Old Testament prophecy regarding the ministry of the coming Messiah,[17] He said, *'Today this scripture has been fulfilled in your hearing'*.

[17] See Isaiah 61:1-2.

He was the fulfilment! What a wonderful moment this was! If only His hearers had fully grasped the significance of His words!

Whether this is the same incident or not in Mark's gospel, the principle involved is established – that is, that Jesus pointed to Himself and no other as the means of Salvation. For those who consider this to be narrow-minded or arrogant, they do well to remember that Jesus Himself taught that he was '*the way and the truth and the life*' **(Jn 14:6)**. If this were not the case, it would make nonsense of the central doctrine of Scripture – that is, the Person of Christ and His mission of redemption.

Although the lifeless performances that so often took place in the synagogue might not have met with Jesus' approval, it was still His custom to be there on the Sabbath. In doing so, Christians have an example to follow. The first reason for Christians meeting together is that Jesus has promised to be there **(Mtt 18:20)**.

According to **v29** Jesus' new disciples must also have been with Him at this time. Whilst the synagogue was primarily the place for teaching, there were usually three components to the Jewish service. These were prayer, the reading of God's Word and the exposition of it; there was no music, singing or sacrifice. [18]

Following the teaching of Jesus, those who listened were astounded, thoroughly amazed, they couldn't believe their ears; they immediately drew a contrast between the teachers of the law and Jesus. One can only imagine the tone, tenderness and directness of Jesus' words, but Mark highlights one main distinction – *'he taught them as one who had authority'*. His words and demeanour conveyed the authority of God - for He was God incarnate!

The teachers of the law encountered by Jesus were legalists who cared more about dotting the I's and stroking the

---

[18] 'It may be said that the Temple was the place of worship and sacrifice; the synagogue was the place of teaching and instruction.' The Daily Study Bible. The Saint Andrew Press. 1979. W. Barclay p30

T's, dealing with minute details regarding rules and regulations, often adding their bits and pieces that were just a burden that the people could not carry. In contrast, Mark would show throughout his gospel that the ministry of Jesus breathed life, not dead dogma, and offered change, transformation and a hope previously unheard of.

During this Jewish Church service, something unusual happened, there was a public response to Jesus' teaching! There was a man in the congregation who was possessed by an evil spirit. Listening to Jesus and sensing His Holy presence, the evil spirit within him cried out, for he recognised that Jesus was the *'Holy One of God.'*[19] Previously, he could sit quite undisturbed and at home in this non-threatening 'Church' environment, there was nothing to expose his spiritual darkness and demon possession, but not on this occasion! Jesus challenged the evil spirit, commanding that he come out of this poor man.

With a shriek of resistance the evil spirit came out. *'Have you come to destroy us?* said the man **(v24)**. In fact, the opposite was true, for Jesus came to release this man from oppression and bondage, to bring light where there was darkness, and hope where there was none. Paul writes in **2 Cor 4:4** *'The god of this age has blinded the minds of unbelievers, so that they cannot see the light of the gospel of Christ'*.

In this incident there is a practical demonstration of the gospel of Christ. How incredible it is then, that in an age when men are trying to explain away and even deny the deity of Christ, in this passage, there is a startling recognition of His deity by the forces of evil.

What a day it must have been in that Jewish Church! The people could hardly believe what they had witnessed. They said **(v27)** *'What is this? A new teaching – and with authority!'* At

[19] 'Several times Jesus was confronted by men suffering from what we would be inclined to diagnose as some kind of mental or psychosomatic illness, and he cured them by a word. But demon possession differs from mental illness in that the possessed showed an uncanny insight into the true identity of Jesus'. I.H.Marshall. Scripture Union. Bible Study Books. St Mark 1967. p7

first hand they witnessed the power of God and a man with a testimony of transformation. It was no wonder that news about Jesus spread quickly over the whole region. This was just the beginning!

Jesus' healing ministry. 1:29-34.

> *'As soon as they left the synagogue, they went with James and John to the home of Simon and Andrew. Simon's mother-in-law was in bed with a fever, and they told Jesus about her. So he went to her, took her hand and helped her up. The fever left her and she began to wait on them. That evening after sunset the people brought to Jesus all the sick and demon possessed. The whole town gathered at the door, and Jesus healed many who had various diseases. He also drove out many demons, but he would not let the demons speak because they knew who he was.'*

The ministry of Jesus was wide in diversity and rich in quality. No sooner had Jesus taught in the synagogue than He moved with His disciples to Simon and Andrew's home where Simon's mother lay ill with a fever. Dr Luke tells us in **4:38** that it was a *'high fever'*.

From a public audience to the privacy of the home, it made no difference to Jesus, He must be about His Father's business,[20] carrying out His ministry that would bless human beings and bring glory to God. Jesus' heart of compassion opened up wherever there was need; on this occasion the brothers told Jesus about their mother and immediately Jesus *'went to her, took her hand and helped her up'*. In this short miracle, something of the tenderness and love of the Lord Jesus is witnessed. Notice the sequence:-

[20] Luke 2:49 Authorised Version.

- He **went** to her
- He **took** her hand
- He **helped** her up

In this miracle we have the simple and the sublime, deity and humanity coming together for the greater purpose of God and the restoration of this sick woman. She is completely healed and restored to normal health, no half measures, not a trace of her fever. And what was the outcome? Restoration that led to action; saved to serve, *'for she began to wait on them'*.

Following the miracles in the synagogue and the home, both taking place on the Sabbath,[21] the day is heading towards its close, when, the account continues, *'the people brought to Jesus all the sick and demon possessed'*.

Jesus must have already had a busy and tiring day; now before Him come what must have been a very large crowd of people – we can only imagine this! Men, women and children of all ages and varying dispositions, some struggling to walk, see, hear or think clearly. Illnesses that were physical, mental and the demon possessed were all represented. Mark, with just a few words sums it up – *'The whole town gathered at the door'* .

Full of compassion and love, we are told that *'Jesus healed many who had various diseases'*. Since Mark has already used the word *'all'* in **v32**, it would seem in order to assume that when he says *'many'* in **v33**, he is referring to volume rather than suggesting limitation. This further makes sense, since Jesus, the Son of God is entirely unlimited in power and healing ability.

Concluding this event, Mark reminds his readers that Jesus also drove out *'many demons'*. Why does Jesus not allow the demons to speak out? One would think that their recognition of

---

[21] 'The question of healing on the Sabbath does not seem to have yet arisen as a controversial question; presumably this was because the healing of the demoniac was well-nigh involuntary, and the healing of Peter's mother-in-law was inside a private house, and thus roused no stir of scandal among the orthodox.' R. Alan Cole. Tyndale New Testament Commentaries. Mark. P62

His deity would be a reinforcing factor, so why keep them quiet? Looking back at **v25**, it can be seen that in the synagogue, before Jesus commanded the evil spirit to come out, He said *'Be quiet.'*

For reasons that we cannot fully understand it seems that Jesus was reluctant to allow evil spirits to have their say, He wanted to give them no place other than to do what He commanded. It may be that demons and evil spirits are seen as 'controlling' a person for the purpose of Satan, and as such are, of course, antagonists of God and set against the purpose of God. Jesus' rebuke, therefore, may be seen as the natural and expected response. Since these forces of evil were hostile to God, the establishing of God's Kingdom clearly involved their overthrow as part of the Messiah's work.

Jesus sought the place of solitude for prayer. 1:35-39

> *'Very early in the morning, while it was still dark, Jesus got up, left the house and went off to a solitary place, where he prayed. Simon and his companions went to look for him, and when they found him, they exclaimed; 'Everyone is looking for you!' Jesus replied, 'Let us go somewhere else – to the nearby villages – so that I can preach there also. That is why I have come.' So he travelled throughout Galilee, preaching in their synagogues and driving out demons'.*

Having had a hectic day, ministering to others until late in the evening, what was Jesus' course of action the next morning? Taking His ease and slowly getting gathered - certainly not! Mark, not usually given to many words, paints a beautiful picture of the Lord's early morning activity.[22] Notice the detail.

[22] 'In Mark's gospel Jesus is seen in prayer only three times: on this occasion (Ch 1:35), after the feeding of the five thousand (Ch 6:6), and near the conclusion when Jesus is in Gethsemane (14:32-42). These three occasions have the character of a critical moment, the setting for Jesus' prayer in each instance is night and solitude' . William L Lane. The Gospel According to Mark. Marshall, Morgan & Scott. P81

'*Very early in the morning, while it was still dark'* - it wasn't just early, but very early, in fact, it was *still dark.* This was a time when the birds were echoing their first morning cries; a time of stillness, quietness, peace, an undisturbed location to engage in the sweet communion of prayer.

'Jesus got up, left the house and went off to a solitary place where He prayed.' Why did Mark mention that Jesus got up and left the house? Ordinary words, certainly, yet perhaps he is telling us that the **priority** of prayer in his Master's life was such that it mattered more than – even breakfast! One can almost sense a calculated urgency in Jesus' actions.

In this we have an example for all who would follow Jesus, for even the Son of God saw the need to come before His Father in heaven, to unburden His heart, to renew His strength for the day that lay ahead. Jesus knew that if He would meet with human beings, then He must first meet with God.

The disciples would learn much from the example of their Master, who chose the place and kept the appointment. He recognised the value of such a priority. Jesus could not live without prayer; neither should those who earnestly seek to be his disciples.

How long Jesus spent in prayer is not recorded. However, His disciples were soon hard on His heels, bringing before Him the promise of yet another hectic day. *'Everyone is looking for you!'*

Refreshed from being in the presence of His Father, Jesus suggested moving to other nearby villages where He may continue to preach the good news, saying *'That is why I have come'*. It must have seemed surprising to the disciples that Jesus' plan, rather than go to this crowd who were seeking Him out, was to move on to other places.

The needs around will always be greater than the resources to meet them (humanly speaking), yet the Church has the God-given mandate to be ever reaching out to the needy and unbelieving wherever and however He may lead by His Spirit. The direction Jesus was now taking was surely in keeping with the Father's purpose and revealed through prayerful communion. The next stage of His mission would now take place in Galilee where He would preach and drive out demons.

A man with leprosy. 1:40-45

> *'A man with leprosy came to him and begged him on his knees, 'If you are willing, you can make me clean.' Filled with compassion, Jesus reached out and touched the man. 'I am willing,' he said. 'Be clean!' Immediately the leprosy left him and he was cured. Jesus sent him away at once with a strong warning: 'See that you don't tell this to anyone. But go, show yourself to the priest and offer the sacrifices that Moses commanded for your cleansing, as a testimony to them.' Instead he went out and began to talk freely, spreading the news. As a result, Jesus could no longer enter a town openly but stayed outside in lonely places. Yet the people still came to him from everywhere'.*

There now occurs a most touching story where the weakness and sinfulness of humankind and the deity of Jesus Christ come together, and in so doing, bring blessing to this man and glory to God. *'A man with leprosy'*, that is how this poor outcast is described. Dr Luke says in his gospel **5:12** *'covered with leprosy'*. He was a marked man because of his condition. Whenever he came within range of others he had to cry out 'unclean' so that others could give him a wide berth. This loathsome and disfiguring disease involved ritual uncleanness and complete segregation from the community and the religious life of Israel.[23] In such a terminal and debilitating state he came to Jesus; hoping beyond hope that a miracle could take place.

With an expression of humility, faith and reverence, he fell to his knees declaring that if Jesus was willing He could heal him. In this scene there is in this man an image of **everyman**, in the sense that he was separated from others and had a disease that was incurable, as is evident from **Isaiah 59:2** *'But your iniquities have separated you from your God'* - **Ephesians 2:12** *'you were separate from Christ....without hope and without God in the world*'. In this man, there is an example: that is, he understood his need and sought to do something about it in the only way possible.

What glorious and telling words Mark uses, *'Filled with compassion Jesus reached out his hand and touched the man.'* Neither Matthew nor Luke used the word compassion - only Mark.

The Greek word for compassion is SPLANCHNIZOMAI, and means 'to be moved from within'. This indicates clearly that when Jesus saw this man He was deeply moved from within – He felt for this man and **did something that no-one else would do** – '*he reached out his hand and touched him'*.

There were others in the Bible who touched Jesus, but on this occasion it is Jesus who took the initiative. Declaring His willingness to heal the man Jesus said '*Be clean*!' and the account clearly states that '***immediately** the leprosy left him and he was cured*'. In just one fleeting moment, this mans life was transformed because of his encounter with Jesus. Not only was he physically cured by faith, but he also entered the Kingdom of God.[24] His life would never be the same again. Surely this epitomises the gospel of Christ!

Instructing him not to tell anyone about this, Jesus told him to go to the priest and offer sacrifices in accordance with the

---

[23] 'As this is the only cure of leprosy recorded by all the three first Evangelists, it is probably the first case of the kind; and if so, this leper's faith in the power of Christ must have been formed in him by what he had heard' David Brown. The Four Gospels. The Banner of Truth Trust. 1969. P51

[24] In Luke 5:12 and Matthew 8:2 we read that this man said 'Lord, if you are willing,' thus demonstrating his faith in Jesus as Saviour.

Law of Moses. Apart from this being the expected practice, there were TWO reasons for the man to do this:-

Firstly, to show his gratitude to God, for he was now reconciled to God. **Secondly**, to show that his body had now been healed and he was ready to be reconciled to humanity.

Although Jesus strongly warned this man not to tell others, there is a certain irony about it. Think for a moment! How could such a man go about unnoticed, especially having gone to the temple? The change was there for all to see. Who could blame him, for his joy knew no limit; **he just had to tell others**! This story concludes with the result of his zealous testimony.

Jesus was now inhibited in His movements and having to stay in remote places. However, we read that *'still the people came to him from everywhere'*

News about Jesus' life and ministry had certainly spread like wildfire; nothing like this had ever been witnessed by the people before. Among those who sought Jesus out would be those just like this leper, others with ailments and infirmities, together with the curious, but there may also have been some Jewish people who genuinely were looking for the Messiah. The testimony in **John 3:2** of Nicodemus, who was a teacher in Israel, affirms this – *'...no-one could perform the miraculous signs you are doing if God were not with him'*.

2

Faith in action. 2:1-12

> *'A few days later, when Jesus entered Capernaum, the people heard that he had come home. So many gathered that there was no room left, not even outside the door, and he preached the word to them. Some men came, bringing to him a paralytic carried by four of them. Since they could not get him to Jesus because of the crowd, they made an opening in the roof above Jesus and, after digging through it, lowered the mat the paralytic man was lying on. When Jesus saw their faith, he said to the paralytic, 'Son, your sins are forgiven.'*
> *Now some teachers of the law were sitting there, thinking to themselves, 'Why does this fellow talk like that? He's blaspheming! Who can forgive sins but God alone?' Immediately, Jesus knew what they were thinking in their hearts, and he said to them, 'Why are you thinking these things? Which is easier: to say to the paralytic, 'Your sins are forgiven,' or to say, 'Get*

up, take your mat and walk'? But that you may know that the Son of Man has authority on earth to forgive sins......' He said to the paralytic, 'I tell you, get up, take your mat and go home.' He got up, and walked out in full view of them all. This amazed everyone, and they praised God, saying, 'We have never seen anything like this!'

No sooner had Jesus arrived at Capernaum (which had become His home town) than word spread rapidly that He was there. Even at this early stage in His ministry the people recognised that this was no ordinary man and made every effort to get near Him.

Picture, if you will, this event, which Mark considers worthy to describe. Although certainty cannot be claimed, it is likely that this was Peter's home and no doubt his mother would be glad to welcome Jesus who had recently healed her. So many had gathered to listen to Jesus that the house was filled to capacity, with people crammed into every available corner, the entrance area and surroundings of the house were also packed; those who could not see were still desperate to listen.

Amidst this great throng of people there would be those who were seeking the truth, whose hearts were genuinely hungry for spiritual fulfilment; there would also be the curious and nosey, together with those who had diverse ailments and illnesses. From **v6** it can be noted that some of the teachers of the law were also there. Their motives were likely to be based on their judgemental attitude and not their own needs; they had come to see if the words and ways of Jesus measured up to the law, with all its minute details and additions which people like them had imposed.[1]

And so, in and around this house, there must have been a great spirit of expectation. It is in this environment that we are

---

[1] Speaking of the fulfilment of the law to such teachers, Jesus said in Matthew 5:20 'For I tell you that unless your righteousness surpasses that of the Pharisees and teachers of the law, you will certainly not enter the Kingdom of God.'

told what Jesus was doing – **v2** *'and he preached the word to them.'* The term 'preached the word' literally means 'spoke the gospel or good news to them.'

Time and time again in the ministry of Jesus, the preached word was central, whether in the synagogue or humble home, it was the great prerequisite to everything else. Amidst the many needs represented in this crowd, the hearing of the word was of first importance. The words of **Psalm 119:105** *'Your word is a lamp to my feet and a light to my path'* and **v133** *'Direct my footsteps according to your word; let no sin rule over me'* are pertinent to this assertion.

And so, as this very mixed crowd listened intently to His every word, something most unusual was taking place. Dust and dirt was falling on them from above. What was happening? Was the building starting to crumble due to the pressure of the crowd? The scene can scarcely be imagined! **Verses 3-4** tell about the adventures of four men taking part of the roof away so that they could lower their friend, who was paralyzed and could do nothing for himself. According to **v3** these men were only part of a larger group – *'Some men came, bringing to him a paralytic, carried by four of them'*

We might think this was a strange thing to do, asking how this could this be possible. However, it must be taken into account that this house, which would have been rather square in shape with a flat roof, would have had a stairway outside that led up to the roof. The construction of the roof made it a fairly simple task to remove part of it. A mixture of twigs, earth and matting would have been packed between the main beams that stretched across the width of the house, leaving ample space between through which to lower their friend.

Here were men who had carried their paralyzed friend (we don't know how far), for the purpose of being healed by Jesus. Having heard that Jesus had healed many others they saw this moment as their great opportunity, but when they arrived there was no room for them. However, they were men of faith and would not be stopped; their faith was persistent! Their love for their friend, and belief in what Jesus could do, meant that nothing would stop them bringing him to the feet of the great physician. This roof must be opened up, it was the only way. And so as the dust and dirt fall from above, and with the sunlight streaming in, together with some welcome fresh air, the man is lowered to the feet of Jesus.

What a beautiful picture this is; to bring others and lay them at Jesus' feet! Although these men did this physically, the opportunity is there for all who have faith in God to bring others before Jesus, through the power of prayer, laying them at His feet; for He is no less real and the way is ever open.

Notice that nothing is said about the disturbance, mess, or interruption. Mark tells us what Jesus saw in **v5** *'When Jesus saw their faith'*. Here was true faith in action, not just words. Regarding Abraham, James writes in **2:22** *'You see that his faith and actions were working together, and his faith was made complete by what he did.'* The evidence of their faith was seen by their actions.

When we read *'When Jesus saw their faith,'* is He referring to just the four men, or is He also including the paralyzed man? It would seem that Jesus is primarily thinking of the faith of the four; however, this by no means negates the faith of the man they brought to Jesus.[2] There is no need to judge in this matter, for the paralyzed man's faith may well be seen in his willingness to be brought to Jesus.

In this event we witness a spirit of perseverance and faith that ought to be an encouragement and example to all who follow Christ. These men went to a lot of trouble and expended great energy to bring their friend to Jesus. They did not simply pray about the matter, they put feet on their prayers and did not permit difficult circumstances to stop them. They did everything

---

[2] 'Their faith showed its reality by its very obstinacy and stubbornness in refusing to give up hope' R. Alan Cole. Tyndale New Testament Commentaries. Mark. P65

they could by bringing their friend to Jesus, and as a result their faith was rewarded.[3]

The question which must now be asked is, 'Why does Jesus say, *'Son, your sins are forgiven'* rather than refer to the physical healing of this man? Some may speculate that perhaps it was sin that led to this man's condition, or even that he himself sensed his need of forgiveness more than healing; there can be no certainty. There is yet another consideration. Which is the greater need, physical healing or the forgiveness of sins? The latter of course, for the blessings that come through forgiveness are eternal and also introduce the individual to blessings and benefits that will not cease this side of the grave.

The greatest miracle of all is undoubtedly that of salvation. **John 10:28** states *'I give unto them eternal life, and they shall never perish; no-one can snatch them out of my hand.'* **1 Peter 1:3-4** also proclaims '..... *In his great mercy he has given us new birth into a living hope through the resurrection of Jesus Christ from the dead, and into an inheritance that can never perish, spoil or fade – kept in heaven for you .....'* On the other hand, healing of the body, though a wonderful blessing, carries with it a limited duration.

That Jesus had just forgiven sins raised more than a few eyebrows for these teachers of the law who were present. The fact that Mark tells that Jesus knew what they were thinking, is once again a clear affirmation to the deity of Christ. In their hearts they were accusing Him of blasphemy, declaring, rightly so, that only God could forgive sins. With perfect and unlimited knowledge, Jesus confronted their thoughts, which must have staggered them. Jesus says in **v6** *'Why are you thinking these things?'* There is a sense in which their questions were answered by Jesus knowing their thoughts, for this was clear evidence that Jesus was no mere man – but the Son of God; this being the case,; of course He could forgive sins.

---

[3] For a further example in persistence, see Luke 18:1-8. 'The Parable of the Persistent widow'.

In **v9** it therefore seems a logical question to ask them – *'Which is easier to say to the paralytic, 'Your sins are forgiven, or to say, Get up, take your mat and walk?'* Both called for the supernatural power of God. Jesus could easily have said to them, 'If I can forgive sins then what is it to heal?

Because of their spiritual blindness they could not see Jesus as the Messiah, yet before their very eyes Jesus was fulfilling prophecy in such a way that bore witness to his deity.[4] It seems that the problem in understanding this theological issue is based simply on the fact that these teachers of the law had failed to discern in Jesus, the promised Messiah.

In **v10** Jesus refers to Himself as the Son of Man, this is a title used exclusively by the Lord of Himself, fulfilling the prophecy found in **Daniel 7:13**. This is the first of fourteen occasions where Mark used this title, in doing so he brings together the humanity and deity of Christ, demonstrating his compassion towards others, and also, as God, being able to alleviate suffering and need. (For further information on the Son of Man see **8:31ff**.)

The end product speaks for itself. Having forgiven this man his sins, Jesus says in **v11** *'I tell you, get up, take your mat and go home.'* Since it was Jesus' usual practice to respond with healing only on the basis of faith; this surely affirms the faith of this paralytic. **He was carried to Jesus – but he walked home**. Notice **v12** *'He ... walked out in full view of them all.'* What a glorious transformation! A manifestation of the power and mercy of God!

A blessing to this man it surely was – but notice please, that '*everyone praised God.'* We must also assume that this includes the teachers of the law. They may have questioned His words, but had to reconsider their views following what they had just seen. This miracle was for the glory of God! The people had never seen anything like this; God was at work in the person of His Son Jesus. There was nothing fraudulent about

[4] Isaiah 61:1-2

this – it was there for all to witness, not done in a corner but in public gaze.

The calling of Levi. 2:13-17

> *'Once again Jesus went out beside the lake. A large crowd came to him, and he began to teach them. As he walked along, he saw Levi the son of Alphaeus sitting at the tax collector's booth. 'Follow me,' Jesus told him, and Levi got up and followed him. While Jesus was having dinner at Levi's house, many tax collectors and 'sinners' were eating with him and his disciples, for there were many who followed him. When the teachers of the law who were Pharisees saw him eating with the 'sinners' and tax collector's, they asked his disciples: 'Why does he eat with tax collectors and 'sinners?' On hearing this, Jesus said to them, 'It is not the healthy who need a doctor, but the sick. I have not come to call the righteous, but sinners.'*

The next recorded occurrence is of Jesus strolling by the Sea of Galilee, as He often did. As soon as the people knew He was there they started to gather round Him again, and this process of gravitation towards Jesus continued for some time. It was common place for Jesus to preach in the open air, sometimes from a boat anchored just off shore. This seemed to provide an ideal platform, a kind of amphitheatre for good communication to the large crowds that flocked around him. Once again, it is found that a large crowd had sought him out, hungry and eager to listen to Him; never before had they heard such a preacher.

As was his practice, **v13** records that *'he began to teach them.'* Jesus did not seek popularity or try to impress others; His first priority was to address the needs of His audience through teaching the Word of God. Those who are responsible for preaching God's word do well to follow His example, for there seems to be an unhealthy attitude in Church life where the place given to the preaching of the Word has somewhat diminished.[5] In spite of all that Jesus did for the benefit and blessing of others, nothing was more important to Him than teaching the Word. It was always His first priority because it met humanity's greatest need.

Having preached to this open-air congregation, walking along He met a man referred to as Levi, son of Alphaeus, sitting at his tax collector's booth (house). Levi is known as Matthew, and, following his appointment as an apostle in chapter three, he was called Matthew. [6]

As a tax collector, he worked for Imperialist Rome under the cruel Herod Antipas. Tax collectors were notorious for many reasons; they were hated by the people, including the poor, because they extorted more tax than was due. The Jews also hated them because they did business with the 'ritually unclean' gentiles. Tax collectors were often defined as those who had lots of money – but few friends: it was common knowledge that they were extortionists.

It is probable that Levi came from very pious parents who were God fearing. He would have received godly teaching during his early years, and no doubt his parents had their hopes and dreams for him, which up until this time were not fulfilled! Levi's choice of profession would have been a disgrace to them; he could have been a priest but became a tax collector.

Jesus saw Levi sitting at his accustomed place of employment, with all its stigma and what it represented, and said to him *'follow me.'* Jesus met him where he was and just as he was.

He called Levi to follow him, not because of his spirituality or qualities at that time, but because of what he

[5] See Hebrews 4:12-13 with regards to the place, power and effectiveness of God's Word.

[6] 'The identity of Levi and Matthew can hardly be questioned, as a comparison of the three Synoptic accounts of this event proves'. William Hendriksen. NTC. Mark. Banner of Truth Trust. P93

would make him.[7] As the call of the Master registered in Levi's heart Mark states that *'Levi got up and followed him.'* Luke's account in **5:28** provides more information, he writes *'...and Levi got up, **left everything** and followed him.'* This is important, for it surely indicates that the Spirit of God had already been at work in his heart, preparing him for that special moment when Christ would issue His call.

No doubt Levi was already aware of the ministry of Jesus, everybody was talking about Him – nothing was done in private; Jesus would have been the subject of much discussion. Assuming that Levi had already given much thought about his life and the message of Jesus, then it can be understood why he *'left everything'* to follow Christ. Leaving everything behind would also be evidence that repentance had taken place. His heart was now ready to leave all behind and make a fresh start with Jesus.

Jesus was to find precious jewels amidst the darkest places; this was certainly true of Levi. How courageous and daring this man was, what must those who knew him be thinking? This was no easy thing to do, for it meant leaving behind a most lucrative business with all its security, and to trust that God would provide for his needs. Just like Elisha, the Old Testament prophet, he burned his bridges in obedience to the call of God and surrendered his all (see **1 Kings 19:21**).

The call of God upon men and women today is no less real. The challenge is ever there to forsake all and follow Christ. In Levi's case it is found that not everything in relation to his past occupation was a waste; for we find that the man with a pen in his hand would, in due course, be writing the Gospel of Matthew, instead of recording possible fraudulent figures for his personal gain! God took all the potential that belonged to Levi and turned it around for the glory of God.

What was the first thing Levi did as a new believer? He arranged a feast at his house with all his friends and fraudsters,

---

[7] See previous comments on the calling of the first disciples from Ch 1:16-20 re 'availability.'

he invited them because he had much to tell them. He wanted his friends to share in his great discovery; and surely hoped that his new Master would also have much to say.

According to **Luke 5:29** we can be sure that Levi not only personally arranged this event, but did so for Jesus. *'Then Levi held a great banquet for Jesus at his home.'* What an occasion this was! Many tax collectors and sinners were present, together with Jesus' disciples at that time, plus the teachers of the law who were Pharisees.

We may wonder why there is this dual description 'tax collectors and sinners.' Is there any distinction? Tax collectors we can understand but the Greek word used here for 'sinners' is 'HAMARTOLOS,' and has often more than one shade of meaning.[8] The vast majority of these people certainly didn't come from the high society of that day; they were like himself; outcasts, cut off from respectability and orthodoxy. Why these self-righteous Pharisees joined with this group we can only speculate. The likely reason is that it was yet another opportunity for self exaltation at the expense of others, pointing the finger at the irreligious and scoring points in favour of the law.

There is every reason to believe that Levi would have a wonderful spread, for it is described as a 'banquet.' Eating in such a way indicates that it was not just a casual snack being shared, but a gathering of friends. With this in mind, the Pharisees, rather than ask Jesus directly, rather timidly inquire from Jesus' disciples why Jesus is eating with such a group of people.

Time after time they miss the mark, they are so self-righteous that they cannot see need when it stares them in the face. In spiritual terms this house was more like an Accident and Emergency ward; it was full of people who were spiritually

[8] 'In this context the term probably denotes not simply all those who did not live according to Pharisaic principles but rather those who on account of their way of life were shunned not only by Pharisees but also by ordinary respectable people.' Cambridge Greek Testament Commentary. Cambridge University Press. St Mark. C.E.B. Cranfield. P103

sick and needed a doctor; on this occasion the Great Physician was in their midst. This is exactly the point that Jesus makes in **v17** *'On hearing this, Jesus said to them, 'It is not the healthy who need a doctor, but the sick. I have not come to call the righteous, but sinners'.*

What Jesus meant here was not that His love and salvation do not extend to the self-righteous, but that primarily He is seeking out those who recognise their need of forgiveness and salvation. Men like those gathered around him, who like Levi, were willing to repent of their sins, surrender all and follow Christ.

The Church has much to learn from this narrative, for it is amidst darkness that light finds its purpose. The purpose of the Church is not simply about believing certain things, singing the right songs, engaging in prayer with great piety and worshipping in sincerity; it is all this and more!

The Church, as seen in the book of Acts, was set in motion as a Missionary Church, sent out, moving towards men and women who needed a Saviour. Was it not this same Levi, called Matthew, who penned the words of his Lord in **Matthew 28:19** to *'go and make disciples of all nations'*?

Both then and now the true relevance of the Church can only be seen when it is 'going out' as the body of Christ, proving to be relevant as 'salt and light'; being where people are. Too often the Church is content with praying that those outside may come in; Jesus said 'go out.'

At times the Church can be rather judgemental towards Christians who mix with non-Christians, yet in our Lord Jesus we have a model example for all to follow, who, though He drew close to the sinner and social outcast, always did so with the right attitude and motives.

'When he saw the crowds, he had compassion on them, because they were harassed and helpless, like sheep without a shepherd' **(Matt 9:36)** - Though the apostle John writes in **1 John 2:15** that we are not to love the world, Jesus, as He prays

for His disciples in **John 17:15,** says *'My prayer is not that you take them out of the world but that you protect them from the evil one.'* The challenge is that of being in the world, just like the Lord, with compassion, grace and relevance, yet not of it.

A question about fasting. 2:18-22

> *'Now John's disciples and the Pharisees were fasting. Some people came and asked Jesus, 'How is it that John's disciples and the disciples of the Pharisees are fasting, but yours are not?' Jesus answered, 'How can the guests of the bridegroom fast while he is with them? They cannot, so long as they have him with them. But the time will come when the bridegroom will be taken from them, and on that day they will fast.' No-one sews a patch of un-shrunk cloth on an old garment. If he does the new piece will pull away from the old, making the tear worse. And no-one pours new wine into old wineskins. If he does, the wine will burst the skins, and both the wine and the wineskins will be ruined. No, he pours new wine into a new wineskin.'*

Looking back to John the Baptist, we remember one whose mission was fulfilled by pointing to Jesus as the Messiah, the Lamb of God who would take away the sin of the world. He directed others to look away from himself and to Jesus who would usher in the Kingdom of God.

John's life and worship were still under the Old Covenant, whilst in Jesus, and through His finished work on the cross there would be the beginning of the New Covenant, a way quite unlike that of the Old Covenant as found in the Old Testament. In contrast to the burdensome ritualism of rules and regulations which exposed the weakness of man, but could do nothing for it[9] – Jesus came with a message of grace, forgiveness and hope not based on human merit but on the acceptance of all that he had accomplished on others' behalf.

Already in the early ministry of Jesus it had become evident to all who observed, that in contrast to the religious people and their teaching of that day, Jesus was quite different, indeed, even radical. His message and attitude to others caused them to ask questions, it raised eyebrows.

Here was a man who acted with compassion, grace and love. He did not seek to exalt Himself or expose the sin and weakness of others with a judgemental spirit, but rather, sought to alleviate their troubles, improve their situation and forgive their sin. His ministry was one which addressed their social, health and spiritual needs; in every sense His ministry was holistic, caring for body and soul. In **John 7:46** there is the testimony of the temple guards who had gone to arrest Jesus on behalf of the Pharisees – *'No-one ever spoke the way this man does'*.

In **v18** the distinction is made, in that John's disciples were fasting but Jesus' disciples were not, and so they ask Jesus why! John's disciples were still, at this time, living with the old system in mind and it was their custom to fast once a year on the Day of Atonement **(Lev 16:29-34)**,[10] but with the passing of time they added many other fast days for varying purposes.

In response to their question Jesus pointed to Himself as the 'bridegroom' and said *'How can the guests of the bridegroom fast while he is with them?'* With Jesus in their midst the circumstances were entirely different. He was the focal person of their faith and was still with them. There was, therefore, greater reason to feast rather than fast because of His presence, as they did in Levi's home. Jesus then told them that

---

[9] ie Diagnosing the problem but offering no cure.

[10] 'In this context fasting is an act of repentance and in preparation for expiation. By the close of the prophetic period other occasions of fasting had become traditional, and these observances continued into the first century.' The New London Commentary on the New Testament. The Gospel of Mark. Marshal, Morgan and Scott. 1974. William L Lane p108

the time would come when, following His death and resurrection, it would be appropriate for His followers to fast. Fasting is of value and has its purpose in Christian life and worship, yet the right time, motives and purpose are important. Two examples may help an understanding.

Firstly, in **Matthew 6:16** Jesus warned his hearers not to make a great public show of fasting in order to impress others, this was the wrong reason – *' When you fast, do not look sombre as the hypocrites do, for they disfigure their faces to show men they are fasting'* .

Secondly, in **Acts 13:2** and in contrast, the Church was worshipping the Lord and fasting as they sought guidance in their missionary endeavours. *'While they were worshipping the Lord and fasting, the Holy Spirit said, 'Set apart for me Barnabas and Saul for the work to which I have called them. So after they had fasted and prayed, they placed their hands on them and sent them off.'* Here there is a good example where fasting was relevant and beneficial, it was not to impress others but to understand the mind of the Lord. In this way it was a form of abstinence that helped to focus the mind and heart.

The contrast in different motives for fasting is illustrated by two simple examples that the people of that day would fully understand.

The **first** was with regards to sewing a new piece of cloth into an old garment as a patch. Jesus suggested that no-one would do such a thing, it wouldn't make sense, for the new cloth would be far too strong for the old, so that when the garment is used and subsequently washed, it would cause a separation that would probably look worse than before it was patched – it just wouldn't work!

The **second** picture is that of pouring new wine into old wineskins. Old wineskins are no match for new wine that is still fermenting; they would just expand and burst! The end product would be a total loss of wine. In giving these illustrations, what is Jesus teaching?

This passage brings to the forefront a contrast between the old formal religious system and the new which came through Jesus Christ. In essence, Jesus' teaching was to show that the old was coming to an end and the new about to begin. The death of Jesus on the cross brought about that precise moment of change. This moment is recorded by **Mark** in **15:38**, and also in **Matthew 27:50-51** where Jesus breathed His last and gave up His spirit, *'At that moment the curtain of the temple was torn in two from top to bottom. The earth shook and the rocks split.'* This was without doubt one of the most wonderful moments in history.

The special place in the temple called the 'holy of holies' could only be entered once a year on the Day of Atonement, and that by the high priest, and was blocked from public view by this great elaborate curtain. So then, when Jesus had finished the work He came to do, all was now ready for the old way to finish and the new way, through His death on the cross, to begin.

No longer was continual animal sacrifice the way of forgiveness, now it was through one sacrifice for all time, Jesus! The curtain being torn from top to bottom signified the opening of the new way; men and women of faith could now draw near to God, without hindrance or barrier. The curtain being torn from the 'top' signifies that this was an act of God; He took the initiative! **Hebrews 7:18-19,** *'The former regulation is set aside because it was weak and useless (for the law made nothing perfect), and a better hope is introduced, by which we draw near to God.'*

The contrasts of fasting and the examples of the patch and the wine given by Jesus teach us that there cannot be compromise; there can be no mixing of old and new, the two must not and cannot co-exist. The old way was just a shadow of the real thing to come. The old, with all its imperfection, was temporary until the promised Messiah would come and usher in the new way.

What a glorious blessing this brings to all who put their faith in Jesus for salvation; no longer a barrier but intimacy and nearness; no longer the Spirit coming upon individuals at chosen times, but the Spirit of Christ personally inhabiting all believer's. **1 Corinthians 6:19** *'Do you not know that your body is a temple of the Holy Spirit, who is in you, whom you have received from God.'*

Lord of the Sabbath – in the cornfields. (Part 1) 2:23-28

> *'One Sabbath Jesus was going through the cornfields, and as his disciples walked along, they began to pick some ears of corn. The Pharisees said to him, 'Look, why are they doing what is unlawful on the Sabbath.' He answered, 'Have you never read what David did when he and his companions were hungry and in need? In the days of Abiathar the high priest, he entered the house of God and ate the consecrated bread, which is lawful only for priests to eat. And he also gave some to his companions.' Then he said to them, 'The Sabbath was made for man, not man for the Sabbath. So the Son of Man is Lord even of the Sabbath.'*

On the face of it, here is a simple and insignificant story about Jesus and His disciples out for a walk. As they walked along, their journey took them through a cornfield, and being hungry at that time, Jesus' disciples plucked some ears of corn to take the edge off their hunger. The nature of their hunger and the casual way of satisfying it would tell us that very little would have been eaten; it wasn't a meal, more of a nibble. **Luke** gives us more information in **6:1ff** *'and his disciples began to pick some ears of corn, rub them in their hands and eat the grain.'* So where was the big problem?

As was their practice, the Pharisees, who obviously were within sight of Jesus and His disciples at this time, were always trying to fix blame and find fault, in particular, in relation to their religious laws; any excuse would do! They considered that the disciples were breaking the law by plucking the ears of corn and rubbing them in their hands. So far as they were concerned, this constituted work on the Sabbath which was forbidden (**Exodus 20:8-11; 34:21**).

Notice that their question is addressed to Jesus, although He was the target. **Verse 24** *'Look, why are they doing what is unlawful on the Sabbath?'* In other words, 'doesn't it bother you that your disciples are breaking the law? The fact was; they were not breaking the law, **they were eating, not working!**

Once again these self-righteous Pharisees were on a point-scoring expedition, doing everything they could to catch Jesus out. Perhaps the real problem was that the purity and righteousness that emanated from Jesus' life in word and deed stood in stark contrast to their own religiosity. In response to their accusation, Jesus cited Scripture in His defence when He quoted what David and his friends did in **1 Samuel 21:4-6** by eating consecrated bread in the house of the Lord.

The Pharisees thought that they were head and shoulders above everybody else, especially common people such as the disciples. In their own eyes, they were men of knowledge and insight and sought to exploit the uninformed and irreligious.[11] What a great warning to all who consider themselves to be well informed; how easy it is to use knowledge as a means of self-exaltation, usually at the expense of others.

Knowledge is wonderful when used graciously for the benefit and blessing of others. Is it any wonder that Paul writes in **1 Corinthians 13:2** *'If I have ... all knowledge ... but have not love, I gain nothing.'* The Pharisees had knowledge, but love,

---

[11] 'It was, in the last resort, the professional jealousy of the Jewish theologians that hounded Christ to death. None were so blind as those who boasted themselves of their theological insight (Jn 9:41), a solemn warning to us today, if we pride ourselves on our 'enlightenment'. Tyndale New Testament Commentaries. Mark. 1983. R. Alan Cole. P73

grace and compassion were absent! It was therefore, just lifeless dogma; rules, regulations and rituals that laid burdens on people that they could not bear. Rather than build them up, it broke them down!

Not only did Jesus justify his disciples' actions from Scripture, but also pointed the Pharisees to a truth that would startle them, for they had lost sight of the purpose of the Sabbath. *'The Sabbath was made for man, not man for the Sabbath'* (**v27**). What does this mean?

Jesus pointed to a simple truth; which was, man was created before the elaborate and complex Sabbath laws ever existed. Human beings were not created to be the victim and slave of Sabbath rules and regulations. The Sabbath was intended to make life better for people, to be helpful and beneficial, not to enslave them.

The lesson that comes from Scripture quoted by Jesus is that 'human need' was more important than strict adherence to the letter of the law. Should David and his men not have eaten the consecrated bread, they would have starved for the sake of mere rules. The Sabbath was intended to be a blessing for people, and not a burden.

So then, what harm were the disciples doing in eating a few grains of corn? How could this possibly be an unlawful and unholy act? In what ways could their actions constitute breaching the law of God? The problem here was not the disciples' actions, but the overreaction of the Pharisees. Once again they failed in their attempt to catch Jesus.

In concluding this incident Mark brings before the reader once again the title 'Son of Man.'[12] It may be remembered that this title is one that only Jesus uses of himself (**2:10**). This is the second time that Jesus uses this title, and fittingly in connection with the Sabbath. What is the significance of its use?

---

[12] See 8:31 for further information on Son of Man.

Firstly, it demonstrates the human side of Jesus; evincing His love for humanity, caring even about food for their bodies. As the Son of Man He understood human need. He too was a man; He knew what it was to be hungry and experienced tiredness and all other symptoms that were common to man. Furthermore; and as already noted, the needs of mankind were a greater priority than adhering to ceremonial rules.

Secondly, the Son of Man was also the 'Son of God', therefore He was the Lord, even of the Sabbath. He has the absolute right to overrule the Sabbath if He will. Here is the Creator of the world and the Author of scripture, who laid down His principles for Sabbath observance. In every sense then, as the Son of Man He is the Lord of the Sabbath.[13]

[13] 'Was the Sabbath law framed for its own sake? Of course not! It was framed for the benefit of man, to give him time to worship God and to relax. One should always look for the purpose of the law not treat it mechanically.

3

Lord of the Sabbath – in the synagogue. (Part 2) 3:1-6

> *'Another time he went into the synagogue, and a man with a shrivelled hand was there. Some of them were looking for a reason to accuse Jesus, so they watched him closely to see if he would heal him on the Sabbath. Jesus said to the man with the shrivelled hand, 'Stand up in front of everyone.' Then Jesus asked them, 'Which is lawful on the Sabbath: to do good or to do evil, to save life or to kill?' But they remained silent. He looked round at them in anger and, deeply distressed at their stubborn hearts, said to the man, 'Stretch out your hand.' He stretched it out, and his hand was completely restored. Then the Pharisees went out and began to plot with the Herodians how they might kill Jesus'.*

Once again Jesus went into the synagogue; which one is not disclosed, but it was probably at Capernaum. The underlying issues are still those of breaking the Sabbath and the self-righteous Pharisees doing their utmost to ensnare Jesus. It would seem that on every possible occasion they were out to get Him, always looking, listening and scrutinizing Him, but not with any noble purpose.

With the passing of time their hatred only intensified towards Jesus. Failing in their attempts so far only served to exasperate and frustrate them. The conclusion of this story in **v6** demonstrates the depths to which they were willing to stoop. By linking up with the Herodians,[1] they plotted His assassination!

Sitting in the synagogue was a man with a shrivelled hand. Because of this man's deformity he would probably have been unable to work and provide for his family. Not only that, it would have had an impact on other areas of his life. Here was a man in need, but who was in the right place at the right time, for Jesus was there! The environment was just right for the Pharisees who were ready to pounce; the scene was set as they fixed their gaze on the Great Physician. What would He do? Would He take the bait?

In **verse 2** Mark tells us that they *'watched him closely to see if he would heal him on the Sabbath.'* The Greek word used for 'watched' is PARATEREO, and is helpful to the student of scripture, for it means 'to observe, especially with sinister intent.' This adequately sums up the minds of these Pharisees, for they cared little for this poor unfortunate deformed man. Catching Jesus was their goal! Jesus, knowing the intent of their hearts, addressed the situation and said to this man in **v3** *'Stand up in front of everyone.'*

Jesus, the all-knowing Son of God, then confronted these experts of the law in their own realm. He asked them a question relating to the law; for them it was a no-win question (**v4**), *'Which is lawful on the Sabbath: to do good or to do evil, to*

1 'The mention of the Herodians (also 12:13; cf. 8:15) with the Pharisees may have originated in the tradition. Perhaps the political groups linked with Herod co-operated with the Pharisees in the time of Jesus for political reasons, because they considered Jesus to be dangerous.' The Good News according to Mark. A Commentary of the Gospel. Eduard Schweizer. S.P.C.K. London 1971. p74

save life or to kill?' Not surprisingly, they (unusually so) were brought to silence.

With this poor man standing before them what were they to say? If they defended the O.T. law on finer points of detail they would appear to be hard hearted (which they were): on the other hand to show compassion towards this man and condone his healing was not in their nature and would be construed as breaking the Sabbath law. Silence was their chosen option.

Their hard, uncaring and insensitive hearts were a source of distress to the Lord, even causing Him to be angry **(v5)**. Anger itself is not wrong; it depends on what makes a person angry and what they do with it (**see Eph 4:26**). In this case our Lord's anger is 'righteous.' It wasn't an expression of sinful nature for He was the sinless Son of God: quite the opposite, it was a response to the unrighteous shameful attitude of the Pharisees.

The very fact that the Lord was deeply distressed tells us just how sensitive He was to sin and how it grieved Him; and yet, this same Jesus would become the great sin-bearer on the cross.[2] Picture the scene!

In the midst of this synagogue was the man with the shrivelled hand, around him the Pharisees, and Jesus having left them speechless, now stared into their faces as only the Son of God could – what a moment, as His all-seeing eyes penetrated their solid hearts! With a simple command Jesus told the man to stretch out his hand, he did so and was completely healed. Had these Pharisees embodied the true spirit of the law which they legalistically sought to defend tooth and nail, they would have rejoiced that God was at work.

They knew their Old Testament, with all its miraculous stories, including the healing of many individuals. However, to acknowledge that Jesus was the Messiah and that evidence of this had just taken place before their very eyes, was just too much for them! There was only one course of action, to take

---

2 1 Peter 2:24. 'He himself bore our sins in his body on the tree, so that we might die to sins and live for righteousness'.

sides with the Herodians, and with joint cunning, work out how they could eliminate Jesus. The fact that they began to 'plot' or 'work out' how they might kill Jesus (**v6**), tells us of how deliberate and calculated their intentions were; it was not simply a reaction! This was the deepest of scheming. The Pharisees and the Herodians had serious differences (see comments on **12:13-17**).

There are two lessons in this narrative.

Firstly, that living with a legalistic and judgemental spirit is insensitive and uncaring towards others, and is more concerned with being right than being helpful. Such an attitude does not match up with the spirit of the gospel.[3]

Secondly, whilst there is here the story of a man who has been gloriously healed in public view for all to see, and would prove to be a great blessing to him; this miracle has much wider ramifications, for it was primarily for the glory of God and a testimony to the deity of Christ. Likewise, in all the believer's endeavours for Christ, though proving beneficial to others, it must always be with the glory of God in mind. The Shorter Catechism reminds us that – *'Man's chief end is to glorify God and enjoy him forever.'* We read in **Colossians 3:23** *'Whatever you do, work at it with all your heart, as working for the Lord, not for men.'*

Large crowds flock to Jesus. 3:7-12

> *'Jesus withdrew with his disciples to the lake, and a large crowd from Galilee followed. When they heard all he was doing, many people came to him from Judea, Jerusalem, Idumea, and the regions across the Jordan and around Tyre and Sidon. Because of the crowds he told his disciples to have a small boat ready for him. For he had healed many, so that those with diseases were pushing forward to touch him.*

[3] Contrasting the spirit of legalism and the spirit of the gospel - see 2 Corinthians 3:1-6.

Whenever the evil spirits saw him, they fell down before him and cried out, 'You are the Son of God.' But he gave them strict orders not to tell who he was.'

Conflict with the Pharisees and the authorities would intensify with the passing of time, but it was not yet God's time for this to escalate; this would happen as the cross drew ever nearer.

And so, driven by the purpose of His Father, Jesus moved away with His disciples to another region without explanation or reason. The narrative tells that He withdrew with His disciples to the lake. As was expected, a large crowd from Galilee followed them. Mark informs us in **v8** that once word had got round that He was there, many more people travelled from every direction. Great crowds were now congregating along the lakeside to get near to Jesus.

There were in this vast crowd those who sought healing for many illnesses, the sceptics and curious, the antagonistic, legalistic and the genuinely spiritually hungry. Diversity in need and enormity in number marked them out. So many had gathered that Jesus told His disciples to get a small boat and prepare it as His floating pulpit. This was a very practical request and His disciples were more than able to meet His request since, for most of them, boats were part of their former livelihood.

In **v9** Jesus indicated that He was in danger of being crushed or overcrowded, so that He had to preach off-shore. It's difficult to imagine this event; the exact numbers are not divulged, but the places from which they had travelled suggest an extremely large audience.

Knowing that Jesus had healed many, it is stated that those with diseases were actually pushing to touch Him. Here is the simplicity and essence of faith; not springing from deep theological study or profound religious thought – just plain daring, believing that just to touch Jesus would bring healing and transform their lives. Men and women would be there, having tried countless other possible cures.

For such people this was a moment of great opportunity that could only have seemed like a dream before they heard of Jesus. They just had to touch Him! We read in **Matthew 14:35-36** *'And when the men of that place recognized Jesus, they sent word to all the surrounding country. People brought all their sick to him and begged him to let the sick just touch the edge of his cloak, and all who touched him were healed.'*

Among this great crowd were those possessed with evil spirits. Twenty nine times throughout Mark's gospel mention is made of evil spirits or demon possessed. It should be noted in this connection that our Lord steadfastly refused to let the evil spirits bear testimony to His deity, why should this be? In **v11,** for example, the evil spirit *'fell down and cried out, 'You are the Son of God.'* So then, why, when evil spirits recognised Jesus' deity, should He not welcome it? Surely this was a positive factor!

At that time, the people were under the tyrannical burden of Roman authority and looking for someone to deliver them; in fact they were ready to welcome anyone who could stand against Rome and bring liberty and freedom from oppression. However, they had misinterpreted the Old Testament concept of the Messiah, for they were looking for someone to sit on an earthly throne and be their King. But the Kingdom which Jesus came to introduce was not such a Kingdom, it was an eternal Kingdom, a spiritual Kingdom, that was superior and more noble than all earthly Kingdoms stacked together.

This truth was not fully realized even by the disciples until after the cross. In **John 18:36** we read *'Jesus said, 'My Kingdom is not of this world. If it were my servants would fight to prevent my arrest by the Jews. But now my Kingdom is from another place.'*

So then, Jesus did not want men to get the wrong message regarding His Kingdom, and this was in danger of happening should He allow the evil spirits to identify Him as the Son of God. Jesus' Kingdom was one which would bring about the reign of God within the human heart, thereby introducing the purpose of God. The power of His Kingdom would be seen in overpowering sin, including these evil spirits that held men captive.

The evidence that Jesus was the Messiah, the Son of God, was to be seen through His words and deeds, they would be His witness. In **Luke 7:20ff** it is recorded that the disciples of John the Baptist came to enquire if Jesus was the true Messiah or should they look for another; Jesus response was *'Go back and report to John what you have seen and heard: The blind receive sight, the lame walk, those who have leprosy are cured, the deaf hear, the dead are raised, and the good news is preached.'* What they **saw and heard** was to be the witness that Jesus was the true Messiah.

In **v12,** Jesus, therefore, silenced these evil spirits; they would not be the ones to verify His deity, only submit to it – the verification would come from Him alone. This was also in keeping with Old Testament prophecy.[4]

Jesus appoints the twelve apostles. 3:13-19

> *'Jesus went on a mountainside and called to him those he wanted, and they came to him. He appointed twelve – designating them apostles – that they might be with him and that he might send them out to preach and to have authority to drive out demons. These are the twelve he appointed: Simon (to whom he gave the name Peter); James the son of Zebedee and his brother John (to them he gave the name Boanerges, which means Sons of Thunder); Andrew, Philip, Bartholomew, Matthew, Thomas, James son of Alphaeus, Thaddaeus, Simon the Zealot and Judas Iscariot, who betrayed him.'*

[4] Isaiah 61:1-2

This was now an important and pivotal time in the ministry of Jesus.[5] Having travelled throughout much of that Galilean region, preaching, teaching, healing and expressing the true nature of the Kingdom of God, Jesus then called and empowered others to be part of, and to continue with, His ministry. Furthermore, in due course it would be some of these men who would become the human authors (inspired by God's Spirit) of the gospels that would bear testimony to all they had seen and heard. They were eye witnesses. (See **Acts 1:1**)

This occasion would be special for them, so Jesus led them up on a mountainside, seeking some sort of peace and tranquillity suitable for the setting of these men apart as apostles.

According to **Luke 6:12-13,** it would seem that these men were chosen from a larger group present at that time, and the choice that lay before Jesus was no lightweight matter, for Mark tells that, in preparation, He spent the whole night in prayer. What an important lesson for all believers who seek the mind and will of God! There are two simple things to notice here; simple yet profound in principle.

Firstly, in **v13** Jesus *'called to him those he wanted.'* This was a specific call for a specific purpose to specific men. As previously pointed out in the calling of the first disciples, they were not called because of their worldly credentials or abilities but because of their availability, and what Jesus would do with such people who were willing to leave all and follow him (**see 1:16-20**).

Secondly, he called them *'and they came to him.'* They responded to the invitation in acknowledgement of their Master, not only to be a supporting team around Him, but also to be the group who would be responsible for establishing the New Testament Church, following His death, resurrection and ascension. These verses also show that there are two constituent

---

[5] 'The appointment of the Twelve marks the formation of the messianic fellowship and anticipates the extension of Jesus' mission through them.' The Gospel According to Mark. Marshal, Moragn & Scott. 1974. William L. Lane. p132

elements of salvation – God's sovereignty in calling men and women to faith; for it is personal, specific and initiated by God, and also the human responsibility to respond.

Verse 14 tells that He appointed twelve – designating them apostles.[6] What a lovely thought that Mark brings to us- *'that they might be with him!'* Although Jesus was God incarnate, these words demonstrate something of the human need of Jesus, to have others around Him, supporting and helping in the daily duties of ministry and everyday life. These men were also called to be preachers and were given a special authority to drive out demons (**v15**).

Once again Mark separates the driving out of demons from other areas of Jesus' ministry; the expelling of demons is clearly something that the author wanted to highlight.

In today's world, these newly commissioned apostles would not have been recognised as preachers, not having attended any homiletics classes or studied theology. The seal of approval on their ministry would not come from any University or College, but from the lips of Jesus Christ. Their commissioning service would take place on this mountainside. The two basic credentials for being an apostle were:-

- they must have been eyewitnesses of the resurrected Christ.
- they must have been personally chosen by Christ.

What is known about these men?

Simon (= Peter). He was a son of Jonas or John and his occupation was a fisherman. Both he and his brother Andrew first lived in Bethsaida, later in Capernaum. According to John **1:42** it was Jesus who gave him the name Peter – *'Jesus looked at him and said, You are Simon son of John, You will be called*

[6] 'The very fact that Jesus appointed exactly twelve men, no more no less, indicated that he had in mind the new Israel, for ancient Israel had twelve tribes and twelve patriarchs.' New Testament Commentary. The Gospel of Mark. The Banner of Truth Trust. 1976. William Hendriksen. p124.

Cephas' (which, when translated, is Peter). This new name also means 'Rock', and was not an apt description of him at the time of his calling, but it was what he, by the grace of God, would later become. Peter was always quick with his tongue, always eager to speak and act on impulse, yet he had a big heart and took risks where others settled 'behind the safety barrier.'

Peter is always remembered for his thrice denial of the Lord. However, we do well not to forget that when Jesus restored him in **John 21:15-17**, he three times declared his loyalty. Following the Lord's ascension, Peter not only became a brave and courageous apostle, fearlessly declaring the gospel but he also wrote two New Testament letters – 1st and 2nd Peter.

He would end his life as a martyr, laying down his life for Jesus. Tradition tells that he refused normal crucifixion and was crucified upside down.

James (son of Zebedee). James was a Galilean fisherman, and was the brother of John, that's why Mark links the two together in **v17**. Both were given the surname 'Boanerges' by Christ. Mark, who is the only gospel writer to record this, tells that it means 'Sons of Thunder.'[7] James was known as one of the inner-circle; Peter and John being the other two. This means that James would have been closer to Jesus and shared some of His more intimate experiences. James was mentioned at the raising of Jairus' daughter **(5:37)**, at the transfiguration **(Matt 9:2)** and also in the garden of Gethsemane.

After requesting a place of honour in Christ's Kingdom, he was told that he would drink the cup His Master was to drink **(10:9)**. This prophecy was fulfilled when James became the first apostle martyred, by Herod Agrippa I in AD 44 who put James to the sword. **(Acts 12:2)**. He was also referred to as James the Great.

[7] 'If his translation is correct, the word either refers to their character ('sons of thunder' in Hebrew would mean 'person of a thundery kind') or, if Rendel Harris is right in saying that 'sons of thunder' is closely connected with the cult of twins, the name may have been given because James and John were twins.' The Pelican New Testament Commentaries. The Gospel of St Mark. 1063. D.E. Nineham. p116

John (son of Zebedee). Like James his brother, John was a fisherman and part of the family business. Details of James regarding the surname 'Boanerges' also apply to John, as do the three important occasions mentioned where the inner-circle were in attendance. John was the author of the fourth Gospel and the epistles known as 1st, 2nd and 3rd John. Human authorship of Revelation is also attributed to him (**Rev 1:12**).

He was obviously a humble man who was often found close to Jesus. His humility is seen in that he never mentions himself by name in his Gospel; he uses language such as *'One of them, the disciple whom Jesus loved, was reclining next to him'* **(John 13:23)** *'but the other disciple who outran Peter and reached the tomb first'* (**John 20:4**).

Unlike James, John lived to an old age, eventually being exiled and suffering on the isle of Patmos **(Rev 1:9)**.

As Jesus hung on the cross, although the other disciples had scattered, John was there, near to Jesus' mother. In those touching and heart wrenching moments, Jesus passed on the human responsibility to John to look after His mother (see **John 19:26-27**).

Andrew. (In Greek it means 'manly') Andrew was Peter's brother, and like Peter, he too was a fisherman. He was a disciple of John the Baptist (**John 1:35-42)** and accepted John's testimony about Jesus. Historically, Andrew has always stood out as the man who told others about Jesus; he was a personal evangelist. As soon as Andrew followed Jesus, the first thing he did was to tell his brother Peter, he says in **v41** *'We have found the Messiah.'*

In every sense he was a true Jew who found and followed the Messiah. In **John 12:21-22** Andrew is found being instrumental with Philip in directing Greeks to Jesus. Having become a disciple, this passage reveals that he was also called to be an apostle.

Philip. The leading similarity between Philip and Andrew are that both were good at pointing others to Jesus. **John 1:44** puts this in context; *'Philip found Nathanael and told him 'We have found the one Moses wrote about in the Law, and about whom the prophets also wrote – Jesus of Nazareth the son of Joseph.'* Clearly in Jesus he saw the fulfilment of Old Testament prophecy.

In **John 14:8-9** however, Jesus offered him a mild rebuke for being slow to understand certain things (how human he was) *'Philip said, 'Lord show us the Father and that will be enough for us.' Jesus answered, 'Don't you know me, Philip, even after I have been among you such a long time? Anyone who has seen me has seen the Father.'*

Philip stayed the course as an apostle of Christ, for he is found with the others in an upstairs room following our Lord's ascension; gathering to pray (**Acts 1:13-14**). He knew Jesus, followed Jesus, and pointed others to Jesus!

Bartholomew. It is generally accepted that this is the one also called Nathanael in John's Gospel (**1:45-49; 21:2**); however not all scholars agree.[8] Not too much is known of him out-with his appearances with the other disciples and apostles.

However, there is in **John 1:44-51** a wonderful narrative where Jesus converses with Nathanael. During their conversation, he is paid an unparalleled compliment by Jesus **(v47)** *'Here is a true Israelite, in whom there is nothing false.'* What was Jesus saying? Not that he was perfect, but that outwardly here was a man who was as straight as a die, nothing shady or false about him.

He was a true Israelite in that he sincerely looked for the Messiah and accepted what Philip told him about Jesus in **v45**. Having observed what Jesus said about Nathanael, what did Nathanael have to say about Jesus? **Verse 49** *'Rabbi, you are*

[8] 'Not infrequently Bartholomew is identified with Nathaniel (Jn 1:45), etc, but this suggestion of Swete, 60; Lagrange, 66; Westcoat, 26 is conjectural.' The Gospel According to Mark. The Macmillan Press Ltd. 1966. Vincent Taylor. p18-19

the Son of God; you are the King of Israel.' No man could have said more than that; from this statement it can be understood exactly where Nathanael stood with Jesus. Bartholomew/Nathanael was surely a man of sincere faith and great potential!

Matthew (also known as Levi). Matthew, like the other apostles, was a Jew and therefore familiar with Old Testament Scriptures. He came from a pious parentage and reared in true Jewish tradition. He was a tax-collector, which must have been an enormous disappointment to his parents. Tax-collectors were despised by all the people, both wealthy and the poor – for both were robbed by these taxmen.

As Matthew sat in his outdoor office Jesus said to him *'Follow me'...... and Levi got up, left everything and followed him'* (**Luke 5:27-28**). This was a courageous thing to do, for he left everything, he burned his bridges, turned his back on the past – and set out to follow Christ. What an example to all who want to follow Jesus! No half measures or compromise – complete commitment, turning from the old, and moving ahead into the new.

When Matthew walked out of his office to follow Christ he would continue to use his pen, but in a different way. Matthew would be God's chosen instrument for recording the first of the four Gospels – the Gospel that bears his name! He is an example of what Christ can do with those who are prepared to leave all and follow him.

Thomas[9] **(Greek version is 'Didymus'**) used three times by John in **19:16, 20:24, 21:2**). There are no personal references to Thomas in the 'Synoptics' at all, other than being listed as one of the apostles. Most of all he is remembered as 'doubting Thomas'.

[9] 'The name comes from Aram, meaning 'twin'. The question whose twin he was cannot be answered with certainty. Various traditions (Syriac and Egyptian) suggest that his personal name was Judas.' The New Bible Dictionary. The Inter-Vasity Fellowship. 1962. R. K. Harrison. p1273

In **John 21:20ff**, he was absent when our Lord appeared before the others. When they told him that they had seen the Lord, he said in **v25** *'Unless I see the nail marks in his hands and put my finger where the nails were, and put my hand into his side, I will not believe it.'*

These words would probably come back to haunt him many times over; yet thankfully they were not his last words. One week later, Jesus appeared again, and with tenderness and compassion invited Thomas to touch His wounds, saying *'Stop doubting and believe'* **(v27)**. *Thomas said to him, 'My Lord and my God'* **(v28)**. Jesus went on to point out that believing without seeing brings a greater blessing: surely an indication of the value of the way of faith. In Thomas there is an encouragement for all who have sensed their failure, lack of faith or are quick with words – failure or weakness need not have the final say!

James (son of Alphaeus). Often referred to as 'James the Less.' Some interpret this as meaning 'James the Younger', but the likelihood is that it refers to his stature, in contrast to James son of Zebedee (James the Great). Strange to say, but the distinguishing feature of James is that of his obscurity.

Among the apostles there was great diversity in character, gifting and ability. Some would make their name as prominent apostles such as Peter, John and Paul, who entered his apostleship at a different time following his conversion on the Damascus road **(Acts 9)**, but others, though equally called and just as important, had a lesser public role. Although no single incident is recorded about the ministry or activities of James, his name is preserved with the others as those whom Jesus called following a night of prayer. History and Heaven alone are his witnesses.

Thaddaeus (called Lebbaeus in certain manuscripts of Matt 10:3 and Mark 3:18). Another name is also attributed to him, for in **John 14:22** it is likely that he is called Judas (not Judas Iscariot). Regarding his previous occupation, parentage or background there is no information. Other than the question he asked Jesus in **v22**, which some suggest may imply a desire for self prominence, nothing more is known about him. Once again, obscurity may be his badge of honour among those called to apostleship.

Simon. (**the Zealot or Canaanite**). He probably has the addition of 'Zealot' because he may have belonged to a party known as 'the Zealots' who were revolutionary in their actions. No words or deeds of Simon find their record in Holy Scripture. It can only be assumed that, because of his early activities among the 'Zealots', he was an enthusiast and that such qualities, sanctified through faith in Jesus, were used for the Master and the expansion of His Kingdom. His calling by Jesus to be an apostle reminds us once again of the value of diversity and individuality among those called to faith in Christ.

Judas Iscariot. If some of the apostles are rather obscure in history, Judas certainly is not, for he is ever remembered as the one who betrayed Jesus. Jesus said in **Mark 14:21** *'But woe to the man who betrays the Son of Man! It would be better for him if he had never been born.'* The Gospels refer to him many times using different expressions.

This man, though entirely responsible for his wicked deeds, is referred to in **John 6:70-71**, by Jesus as 'a devil'. He was the one entrusted with the purse; he was the treasurer and held the funds for all the day to day needs and ministry of Jesus and the apostles. He was a deceiver and a thief. He opened his heart to Satan for the ultimate purpose of gain through betrayal.

In spite of all he had witnessed during three years with the Son of God, thirty pieces of silver, mere money, meant more to him than Jesus. *'Then one of twelve – the one called Judas*

Iscariot – went to the chief priests and asked, 'What are you willing to give me if I hand him over to you' **(Matt 26:14-15**). The details are there for all to consider; yet one can scarcely believe just how calculated, callous and stone hearted he was. Agreeing a betrayal figure, he led the soldiers into the garden; the words '*Greetings Rabbi*' are followed with a kiss.

Matthew 27 records his remorse and suicide. How telling are the words from **v5** *'So Judas threw the money into the temple and left. Then he went away and hanged himself.'* Judas realised all too late what a great mistake he had made. How sadly possible it is to be intimately near Jesus, as Judas was, who heard His gracious words, witnessed the miraculous first hand, listened to Him pray to the Father, looked into the eyes of one who loved as no other could; yet held back the allegiance of his heart, ultimately severing himself from the presence of Christ for all time.

From this brief glimpse of these apostles, it is evident that they were just ordinary men, typical of a cross-section of mankind, who became extraordinary because of Jesus Christ. In spite of their limited understanding and failures, they became powerful witnesses to the resurrection of Christ.

Through their transformed lives, and empowered by the Spirit of God, they committed their all to the Gospel of Jesus Christ. They would ultimately lay down their lives for His sake. Their story did not end with the Gospels, but continued in the book of Acts and other letters in the New Testament.

Through these men, who denied themselves, took up their cross and followed Jesus, it can be seen just what God can do with those who are prepared to leave all and follow Him. What made these men special was not what they were when they met Christ – but how they responded to Christ. Herein lies the same opportunity for all who will take up the mantle of discipleship and follow their example.

Jesus falsely accused of demon possession. 3:20-30

> *'Then Jesus entered a house, and again a crowd gathered, so that he and his disciples were not even able to eat. When his family heard about this, they went to take charge of him, for they said, 'He is out of his mind.' And the teachers of the law who came down from Jerusalem said, 'He is possessed by Beelzebub! By the prince of demons he is driving out demons.' So Jesus called them and spoke to them in parables: 'How can Satan drive out Satan? If a kingdom is divided against itself, that kingdom cannot stand. If a house is divided against itself, that house cannot stand. And if Satan opposes himself and is divided, he cannot stand; his end has come. In fact, no-one can enter a strong man's house and carry off his possessions unless he first ties up the strong man. Then he can rob his house.'*

Wherever Jesus went the people were sure to follow; such was the case as He entered yet another house. Whatever the views and opinions of the people, Jesus had an incredible drawing power; they pursued Him relentlessly to look, listen, and expect the miraculous.

On this occasion **v20** records that He and His disciples could not even get a moment to eat (that Mark makes the effort to record such a domestic detail gives us some idea of how frantic it was). It can only be imagined what it must have been like – pandemonium!

The noise, hustle and bustle; the expectations of many, but also the voice of satanic accusation from the teachers of the law; what a pressurised and volatile environment this was! This situation seemed so bad that His family, who were not present, heard about it and *'went to take charge of him, for they said, 'He is out of his mind'* **(v21)**. Why should they come to such a conclusion, after all, they were His own family? [10]

We must remember that during His earthly ministry Jesus was misunderstood by almost everybody, including His family and disciples. The first situation was introduced in the narrative when He was only twelve in **Luke 2:49-50**, *'Why are you searching for me?' he asked. 'Didn't you know that I had to be in my Father's house?' But they did not understand what he was saying to them.'*

It was only after His resurrection that much of what He had taught them and predicted about His death and resurrection fell into place. Yet, looking at it from a human standpoint, His family were already aware of the (seemingly disorganised) and hectic routine in the middle of which He existed.

From their perspective, they had seen a wonderful carpenter leave His profession to engage in this life style. They could also see Him on the way to a head-on collision with the religious leaders of that day; furthermore, they had witnessed others with successful businesses leave it all behind them and follow Jesus. Much of this left them puzzled and made no sense. Had He lost the plot? Perhaps in the nicest way and as best they could, they were extremely concerned and were trying to help to protect Him.

Thus, from **v22,** the teachers of the law, who '*came down from Jerusalem,'* seized their moment. Coming down from Jerusalem indicates how far Jesus' fame had spread. What they understood from Jesus' family (*'He is out of his mind'*), cannot be defined but it seemed to give them the cue to launch their own scathing and malicious attack.

Family and friends may have been puzzled or misunderstood Jesus, but it was left to these teachers of the law

---

[10] 'The initial reference to the family of Jesus (20-21) is not found in Luke or Matthew. Was it too daring? It certainly was true. The bringing together of unbelief, whether expressed in concern for Jesus' psychological state (21) or given a more sinister setting (22); whether from casual onlookers, or family or religious leaders, has the effect of identifying the battle lines in the epic struggle.' The Bible Speaks Today. The Message of Mark. Inter-Varsity Press. Donald English. p86-87

to completely misunderstand Him. Their accusations could not have been more cold, cutting or totally inaccurate. They accused Him of two things:-

Firstly, of being possessed by Beelzebub (Satan). **Secondly**, by the power of Beelzebub He was performing all the works that He was doing, including driving out demons.

The essence of **vv23-27** is as follows. Jesus called His accusers to Him and directed His remarks especially to them. He explained to them how thoroughly illogical their accusation was; going on to show this by means of a parable.

What is the point says Jesus, of Satan fighting against Satan? Why should Satan seek to expel his own demons? It doesn't make sense! When a king goes to war he does not fight against himself but his enemy. If Satan is actually making war with his own demons then he is finished as an effective power, because civil war has begun in the kingdom of Satan. So then, if Jesus was possessed by evil, why should He seek to cast out evil from others?

Jesus then illustrated this by an example of burglary. Once again, it is just plain logic. In ordinary life the burglar does not receive willing help from the home owner. Instead, in order to get what he wants, the intruder first ties up the owner; then he steals. The point is this, if Jesus is possessed by demons, then how could He cast out demons, who were just as powerful as Himself; only the more powerful one can expel the other!

The defeat of demons did not show that Jesus was on the same side (or in the same kingdom) as Satan; rather, it demonstrated that Satan's defences had been breached by a more powerful force; the power of God.

The Kingdom of Light was waging war against the forces of Satan and his hordes. Light was overpowering darkness through the ministry of Jesus; it was now visible for all to see, as in **Mark 8:27** *'Even the wind and the waves obey him'* and in **John 3:2** *'Rabbi, we know you are a teacher who has come* *from God. For no-one could perform the miraculous signs you are doing if God were not with him.'*

On the occasions when Jesus cast out evil spirits or demons it was always for the glory of God and evidence of His own personal deity: not forgetting the blessing and benefit to the person delivered. Those who had been delivered from the demons and spirits that had possessed them were set free, their lives were transformed. Later in **chapter 5** is found such a man who had been delivered. **Verse 15** ' *...they saw the man who had been possessed by the legions of demons, sitting there, dressed and in his right mind.'*

The unpardonable sin. 3:28-30

> *'I tell you the truth, all the sins and blasphemies of men will be forgiven them. But whoever blasphemes against the Holy Spirit will never be forgiven; he is guilty of an eternal sin. He said this because they were saying, 'He has an evil spirit.'*

'**What is the unpardonable sin?** This question has been the subject of much discussion over many years. In **vv28-30** lies the key to answering this, for any understanding can only be found within the context of the passage and the circumstances of Jesus' ministry on this occasion. By using the words *'I tell you the truth,'* Jesus was affirming the importance of what He is about to say.[11]

Firstly, it is important to examine what the word blasphemy means. It is normally associated with 'misusing the name of God and showing gross disrespect for God by uttering profanities.'[12] From this, it can be established that it is not the

[11] The words 'I tell you the truth' literally mean – 'Amen, I say to you.'

[12] 'blasphemies: This is not simply a matter of bad language. The word blaspheme meant in Greek to slander men or show irreverence towards gods, and in the Bible it is used of 'defiant hostility to God, His name, or Word, in speech which defies His power and majesty'. Pelican New Testament Commentaries. The Gospel of Mark. Penguin Books. D. E. Nineham. p125

sin of blasphemy itself that is unforgiveable, since **v28** tells us plainly that *'all sins and blasphemies of men will be forgiven them'* (i.e. all sins forgiven following repentance). If this were not true how could Peter's sin of denial in **Mark 14:71** be forgiven and his reinstatement take place in **John 21:15-17** Paul is yet another example; relating to his past we read from **1 Timothy 1:13** *'Even though I was once a blasphemer and a persecutor and a violent man, I was shown mercy.'*

According to **Matthew 12:32** Jesus made it clear that someone even speaking against His own person will be forgiven, but not against the Holy Spirit. In **Luke 12:10** we have the same thought - *'And anyone who speaks a word against the Son of Man will be forgiven, but anyone who blasphemes against the Holy Spirit will not be forgiven.'*

The distinction seems to be in relation to the Holy Spirit! All other sins, no matter their seriousness or gruesome nature, can be forgiven – yet not for blasphemous sins against the Holy Spirit.

The key to understanding is found in the **reason** given by Jesus Himself *'He said this because they were saying 'He has an evil spirit.'* In this company, among others, are these teachers of the law, who not only should have been well informed, but were also witnesses to the grace and mercy of God. Lives had been changed, demons cast out, miracles had taken place in full view for all to examine. Yet in spite of the visible manifestation of the power of God, testifying to the presence of the Messiah, rather than acknowledge Jesus, their hearts were so hardened and set against Him, that their only way out was NOT to try and deny what everyone had seen, but to attribute it to the powers of Satan.

This was and is the worst sin anyone can commit. To accredit Satan with the work of God declares just how far these men had stooped in distancing themselves from God.

Their sin was unpardonable because they were unwilling to walk the path that leads to pardon. Put another way – their sin was unpardonable because they rejected the offer of pardon.

This is not simple blasphemy, serious as that is, but a total denial and rejection of the Holy Spirit who is the voice of God, and is the means of communication between God and man. This sin is sometimes referred to as the 'sin of unbelief,' for where there is the refusal to believe, salvation is impossible. Jesus says in **John 3:18** *'Whoever believes in him is not condemned, but whoever does not believe stands condemned already because he has not believed in the name of God's one and only Son.'*

No-one will ever be kept out of heaven because they were not loved by God or the Way of life was not open to them, but they will be kept out on the basis of their unbelief.

The unbelief of these teachers of the law reached the bottom of the pit by **1)** rejecting Jesus as the Messiah. **2)** attributing His work to Satan. The words in **v30** *'they were saying, 'He has an evil spirit'* sums up their callous and hardened unbelief. They were guilty of an eternal sin for which there was no forgiveness.[13]

A word of warning, however, for this sin was not unique to these teachers of the law; Satan is no less active today than he was at that time and the activity of Satan is just as real.

His goal both then and today is summed up in **2 Corinthians 4:4** *'The god of this age has blinded the minds of unbelievers, so that they cannot see the light of the glory of the gospel of the glory of Christ, who is the image of God.'* Also **2 Corinthians 2:11** *' .....in order that Satan might not outwit us. For we are not ignorant of his schemes.'*

---

[13] 'It is clear from the context, that Mark has interpreted this as a deliberate refusal to acknowledge the activity of God's Spirit inJesus' ministry: it is the attitude which makes a man attribute the work of God to Satan and confuse goodness and evil, truth and falsehood.' Blacks New Testament Commentaries. The Gospel According to St Mark. A & C Black. Morna D Hooker. p117.

Who are the family of Jesus? 3:31-35

> *'Then Jesus' mother and brothers arrived. Standing outside, they sent someone in to call him. A crowd was sitting around him and they told him, 'Your mother and brothers are outside looking for you.' Who are my mother and my brothers?' he asked. Then he looked at those seated in a circle around and said, 'Here are my mother and my brothers! Whoever does God's will is my brother and sister and mother.'*

The final section in this chapter raises a question; who are in the true family of Jesus? That Jesus had real earthly parents and brothers is indisputable; and that He cared for them we cannot doubt, as any son and brother would do, let alone the perfect man.

Earlier, in **v21,** there is evidence of their concern for Him, though, in their ignorance they misunderstood Him. It now seems as though they are still outside this house, but because of the pressing crowd they ask someone to call on Him (**v31**). **Verse 32** tells that *'A crowd were sitting around him.'* Had the teachers of the law disappeared or were they just left without words? That is undisclosed. With Jesus in the midst of them we may assume that He now addresses them in the teacher/pupil mode.

During this time, word reached Him that His mother and brothers were outside looking for Him. What was Jesus teaching at this time? Was it about the nature of the Kingdom of God? That, too, is uncertain! However, because of His words that follow, Jesus certainly was introducing a new family concept to them which would have been in keeping with Kingdom teaching.

Jesus responded to the request of His earthly family with a question. **Verse 33** *'Who are my mother and my brothers?' he asked.'* Jesus was not socially disorientated, nor had he written off His earthly family, but He was about to teach them a new family concept. We have here a contrast of families: both mattered, both were important: one was physical, the other spiritual. The physical would be limited to life on earth; the spiritual would be eternal and without end.

That Jesus cared for ordinary family life was clearly seen in His teaching: there can be no occasion more caring or touching than when Jesus hung on the cross and looked at His mother, knowing that she would soon miss His physical presence. And so in **John 19:26-27** He linked John (though unnamed) to His mother for her continual care. *'And when Jesus saw his mother there, and the disciple whom he loved standing nearby, he said to his mother, 'Dear woman, here is your son,' and to the disciple, 'Here is your mother.' From that time on, this disciple took her into his home.'* [14]

Looking at them, Jesus said '*Here are my mother and my brothers! Whoever does God's will is my brother and sister and mother.'* Jesus now spoke of His true eternal family as those who do God's will. That is, those who will believe in Him, take up their cross and follow Him, would become children of God.

John 1:12-13 reads '*Yet to all who received him, to those who believed in his name, he gave the right to become children of God – children born not of natural descent, nor of human decision or a husband's will, but born of God.'* **John 3** gives an understanding of the nature of this new Kingdom and how entrance into it is gained. The apostle John also takes up the subject of being 'children of God' in relation to being 'born of God' in **1 John 3**.

And so, in this brief story Jesus introduced new thinking to His hearers. He pointed ahead to a new way, a new Kingdom, a new family, where there could be intimacy between God and mankind, as never before experienced. It was a way based on faith in Himself as the Saviour of all who would follow Him.

---

[14] It is likely that at this time Jesus' father Joseph was not alive. Hence John 19:26-27.

This was to be a way that stood in total contrast to the old religious system which did more to bind men than to free them. We may also notice from Jesus' words in **v35** that barriers between Jew and Gentile would be broken, for this new way was for all – no matter colour, creed or background - *'Whoever does my will'*.

4

The parable of the sower. 4:1-20

'Again Jesus began to teach by the lake. The crowd that gathered round him was so large that he got into a boat and sat in it out on the lake, while all the people were along the shore at the water's edge. He taught them many things by parables, and in his teaching said: Listen! A farmer went out to sow his seed. As he was scattering the seed, some fell along the path, and the birds came and ate it up. Some fell on rocky places, where it did not have much soil. It sprang up quickly, because the soil was shallow. But when the sun came up, the plants were scorched, and they withered because they had no root. Other seed fell among thorns, which grew up and choked the plants, so that they did not bear grain. Still other seed fell on good soil. It came up, grew and produced a crop, multiplying thirty, sixty, or even a hundred times.

Then Jesus said, 'He who hath ears to hear, let him hear.' When he was alone, the Twelve and the others around him asked about the parables. He told them, 'The secret of the kingdom of God has been given to you. But to those on the outside everything is said in parables so that, 'they may be seeing but never perceiving, and ever hearing but never understanding; otherwise they might turn and be forgiven!'
Then Jesus said to them, 'Don't you understand this parable? How then will you understand any parable? The farmer sows the word. Some people are like seed along the path, where the word is sown. As soon as they hear it, Satan comes and takes away the word that was sown in them. Others, like seed sown on rocky places, hear the word and at once receive it with joy. But since they have no root, they last only a short time. When trouble or persecution comes because of the word, they quickly fall away. Still others, like seed sown among the thorns, hear the word; but the worries of this life, the deceitfulness of wealth and the desires for other things come in and choke the word, making it unfruitful. Others, like seed sown on good soil, hear the word, accept it, and produce a crop-thirty, sixty or even a hundred times what was sown.'

What is a parable?[1] A parable is often defined rather simplistically, yet helpfully, as 'an earthly story with a heavenly meaning.' It is a form of pictorial language that uses practical everyday concepts from nature or human circumstances to teach a spiritual truth. The Greek word for parable is 'PARABOLE,' and means 'putting things side by side.' Therefore, a parable is

[1] 'A metaphor or a story connected with the affairs of daily life is used as an illustration of moral and spiritual truths, on the assumption that what applies in the one sphere is relevant in the other.' The Gospel According to St Mark. The MacMillan Press Ltd. Vincent Taylor. 1966. p249

an illustration placed alongside a truth to make it easier to understand. Care must be taken however, not to confuse a parable with a myth or fable, because a parable is a means of illustrating truth.

Christ's parables most frequently, though not exclusively, present truths related to the subject of the Kingdom of God, as is the case in this chapter. It is generally accepted that a parable is aimed at teaching **one main or leading truth**; although this does not exclude the value of subsidiary lessons. Having made this point, there is great danger that some preachers may try to squeeze a parable dry in their attempts to see things and make points that do not exist, and are found more in the imagination than the parable.[2]

Why did Jesus use parables in his teaching?

1) Jesus chose this method to make people listen and help them understand.

The preacher gets no prizes for confusing his audience and losing them. His goal was not to starve or choke them, but to feed them. On this occasion (by the lakeside) He was not in a synagogue or house where He had a captive audience; He had to keep their attention and used a language and method that helped them stay focussed. **Verse 2** '*He taught them many things by parables.'* Surely this indicates a greater use of parables than those actually recorded.

2) Jesus used a method with which his hearers would have been familiar.

Parables are not only to be found in the New Testament; they were used sometimes in the Old Testament. An example of this

[2] 'Over-elaboration and over-simplification are to be avoided in the interpretation of the parables, for in few spheres of Gospel exegesis is it easier to be tedious.' New Bible Dictionary. The Inter-Varsity Fellowship. 1962. p933

is found in **2 Samuel 12:1-7** where the story of the ewe lamb is told by the prophet Nathan as a means of revealing to King David the severity of his sinful actions and need of repentance. So then, Jewish people would understand Jesus' teaching, because they were familiar with this method.

3) Jesus knew that this method would cause men to think for themselves.

He wanted them to work things out in their own minds. This form of picture language would help His hearers take on board what He was saying – to analyze and apply the truth He was teaching. They had to come to their own conclusions and they could not do this unless they understood. At this time Jesus was introducing them to a new spiritual concept – the true nature of the Kingdom of God, and this had to be done in a way they could understand. This was radical new teaching and called for the most suitable method.

The parable of the sower.

Once again Jesus was teaching, and quite unrestricted by His environment. In fact, He made the most of it! It made no difference whether it was in a synagogue, a house, on the hill-side or by the lake as on this occasion: the crowds gathered in vast numbers to listen to His teaching. Wherever He went, 'He taught, and they listened,' spellbound and captivated by His every word. His motives were pure and honest, always with the best interest of His hearers at heart, for He loved them all deeply, as no other preacher could. His message was truly as a shaft of light from heaven that shone into their needy souls. They drank from His lips as He poured out the word of truth.

In **v1** Mark begins to construct a picture of this scene. He tells that the crowd that had (already) gathered round Jesus was so large that He got into a boat, sat down, then rowed out a little and anchored just off shore; far enough out to face His congregation without being crushed.

We are told that this sizeable crowd, (probably much larger than previous crowds) gathered along the water's edge, no doubt their numbers would stretch back up the slopes giving them good sight and sound of the Master as He unfolded His message before them. Jesus' first word of the parable is *'Listen!'* or 'pay close attention.'

To aid the understanding of this parable, analysis of the appropriate verses from nature with their counterparts for spiritual application is included.

The hard path and hard heart - v4 and 15

John 2:25 states that *'He did not need man's testimony about man, for he knew what was in a man.'* Jesus knew the hearts of all men, and through this farming illustration He pointed to FOUR different kinds of soil and hearts. In this story the seed is the Word of God – the soil is the human heart - and the sower is the preacher.

From **v4,** picture the farmer sowing his seed; his seed pouch is tied round his waist and as he walks he takes handfuls of seed and scatters it from left to right in a systematic manner. Although an expert in sowing, some of his seed falls on to a path that is hard packed and well trodden. Because it is solid ground, the seed just sits on the surface, and so it is a waiting target for the birds to come and gobble it up.

Jesus said in **v15** *'Some people are like seed along the path.'* He likens the seed to the Word of God that settles in the heart, but just rests on the surface because the heart is hard - spiritually hard that is - and not very receptive. Satan sees this and just like the bird plucking the seed, so he plucks the Word before it has any chance of taking root.

As Jesus preached, some of those sitting by the lake had hearts like this – not welcoming or prepared for the Word. They needed to heed the words of the prophet in **Jeremiah 4:3** when he said, *'Break up your unploughed ground'***.** The concept of the hard heart also typifies a heart that has become insensitive to the Spirit of God.

The shallow soil and shallow heart – vv5-6 and 16-17

Some of the seed also fell on soil that was rocky (**vv5-6**). There was little soil, no depth or quality to it and not ideal for sowing seed; the soil was too shallow. The result was that it shot up very quickly and for a short time looked good, but it had no root system, no means of food supply or stability in bad weather. It was quite unlike the picture of the tree planted by streams of water in **Psalm 1** '*He is like a tree planted by streams of water, which yields its fruit in season and whose leaf does not wither.....'* **Verse 6** tells that when the sun came up it scorched this new grain and it died because it had no roots.

According to **vv16-17** this shallow kind of heart welcomes the word, and does so even with joy, but there's no depth to it; only a quick, impulsive response that has not counted the cost and engaged rapidly without much thought. At the first sign of trouble, difficulty or persecution, this kind of person falls away. They may look like the real thing for a short time – but are not!

Here is a person who may take pleasure in sermons, even be moved to tears and emotionally stirred; but it's all on the surface, no spiritual depth. How often has this picture been seen? Here is yet another kind of heart, not ready for the Word. Among those listening to this lake-side sermon, there were just such hearts – stirred emotionally, recognising the truth in the message – but not ready!

The crowded soil and crowded heart – v7 and 18-19

There is now a third type of soil; it is a soil that is full of weeds and thorns which draws all the moisture and sustenance, depriving any plant or grain of its required nourishment. Some of the seed spread by the farmer falls on this kind of ground; it's not hard or rocky, just full of thorns and weeds. Jesus tells in **v7** that the seed which grew up didn't stand a chance – it was choked, there was not enough room for it to feed and expand. From general experience it is known that, before planting shrubs, flowers and herbs, anything that ought not to be there must be weeded out. It is a laborious task which is not an option, but a necessity, before planting or sowing.

The picture in **vv18-19** is one who receives the Word. He wants it. This heart recognises the truth of the Gospel and the need for forgiveness and the blessing of eternal life; he wants it all! But there is so much baggage and external things that are still important.

Here is a heart that wants Jesus plus many other things! This heart wants to hold on to much of what is there. A heart not ready to change! A heart not able to leave the worries and cares of life to Jesus! This heart still viewed wealth and materialism as a great priority and resisted the need to get rid of it. A heart with no room for Jesus! In **Luke 10:40-42** when Martha asked Jesus *'Lord don't you care that my sister has left me to do the work by myself'*. Jesus replied, *'Martha, Martha, you are worried and upset about many things, but only one thing is needed.'* Here is given the principle of prioritising!

A prepared soil and prepared heart – v8 and 20

This last soil was so different from the others; it was good soil because it was prepared and ready to receive the seed. It was free from rocks, weeds and thorns and was soft and welcoming to the seed. Hence we are told in **v8**; *'It came up, grew and produced a crop.'* And what a wonderful crop it was, it multiplied many times over. This, said Jesus, is a heart that is prepared to receive.

This is the picture of a person who has searched his heart, recognised his need, examined his life and priorities and welcomes the Word with joy. Amidst this vast crowd there would have been such people. In **v20** Jesus referred to this person as one who Hears, Accepts and Produces.

In this parable there was nothing wrong with the Farmer or the Seed; likewise there was nothing wrong with the Preacher or the Word. The main lesson from this parable has to do with the condition of the human heart. Though it may result in the asking of certain questions, it answers others. It helps an understanding as to why so many hear the Word but never make much of it; and why some start but never continue.

As Jesus preached to this great crowd He knew that it was the condition of the heart that would determine any response. Jesus offered a word of warning in **v9** *'He who has ears to hear, let him hear.'* In other words; 'listen very carefully to what I have to say!' Why? Because He knew that although many would hear, it would be the minority who would listen carefully with a heart ready to receive.

Jesus made this point in another way from **Matthew 7:13-14**; *'Enter through the narrow gate. For wide is the gate and broad is the road that leads to destruction, and many enter through it. But small is the gate and narrow the road that leads to life, and only a few find it.'*

The challenge of discipleship is woven throughout this parable; the words of Jesus can almost be heard as He lays down the challenge to leave all and follow Him. *'If anyone would come after me, he must deny himself and take up his cross and follow me. For whoever wants to save his life will lose it, but whoever loses his life for me and for the gospel will save it'* **(8:34)**.

In this Kingdom parable, the King is looking for the place of enthronement within the human heart. The challenge for all is to make way for the King of Kings and Lord of Lords; that He might live and reign within the realm of mere humanity. Such is the miracle of God's grace!

Before leaving this parable, mention must be made of **vv10-12** which is lodged at the centre of the parable, and has proved to be difficult to fully understand.[3] Most of the crowd had now departed and Jesus was alone with His chosen Twelve plus a few others around Him. With a greater sense of privacy they enquire further about the meaning of parables. No doubt they feel more at ease to pursue their enquiries in the absence of the larger gathering. Jesus' first response to their questions tells them that they were, in fact, privileged (**v11**). *'The secret of the Kingdom of God has been given to you.'* The Greek word for secret is MUSTERION, and means 'mystery'.

This word does not mean something which is complicated or beyond understanding, ie mysterious. It means something which is quite unintelligible to the person who has not been initiated into its meaning, but is quite clear to the person who has been so initiated.

To those then, who have given their heart to Jesus, and who have forsaken self and followed Him as Saviour and Lord: to such people, understanding is given. In spite of this, according to **v13** *'Then Jesus said to them, 'Don't you understand this parable?'* They were still slow to understand!

In contrast to those who understood, Jesus then referred in **v11** to *'those on the outside.'* Those who are 'outside' the Kingdom and whose attitude and response are represented in the first three soils and hearts. What Jesus said next is not easy to understand! The first impression would seem to be rather contradictory; for on the one hand parables were used to aid understanding; yet at face value the suggestion here is that those who are outside, and hear, are not really meant to understand, otherwise they might believe. This leaves the question; 'Is this not the ultimate purpose of a parable, to help men come to faith? How, then, can there be understanding of this passage, in particular **v12**?

[3] 'This section 4:10-12 is amongst the most difficult passages in the New Testament, first to understand with any degree of certainty, and secondly to accept if we get near to an understanding.' The Bible Speaks Today. The Message of Mark. Inter-Varsity Press. 1992. Donald English. p153

Among various interpretations on offer; [4] the most likely is the following. The words *'so that'* point towards a 'chosen response' by those who heard. Although parables were a method used to bring clearer understanding, many who listened with their ears and heard physically chose to block their minds to the truth of the message; and the reason; *'otherwise they might turn and be forgiven.'* This theory is neither complicated nor cluttered and makes sense for **three** reasons.

Firstly, in **v12** Jesus is quoting from the prophet **Isaiah 6:9-10** where Isaiah encountered callous hearts in his ministry. At that time many refused to believe by deliberately closing their ears to the truth. Their choice was rejection. Jesus, therefore, quotes from the historical experience of Isaiah, showing that such a position was also relevant at this present time.

Secondly, within the context of the parable there are three kinds of soil pointing towards three kinds of hearts: which, for the reasons stated in the parable, made no room for the truth. This was a question of choice! Why did some of the hearers not understand? Because they didn't want to!

So then, in spite of parables aimed at bringing clearer understanding of the message; there could still be human hardness of heart that would resist the temptation to believe. Put simply, such people had made their minds up not to believe! Parabolic teaching to those whose hearts were open was a great help, while those with closed hearts would remain in spiritual darkness.

Thirdly, the sovereignty of God must be taken into account. Though it does not make a definitive understanding any clearer, **two truths** must be borne in mind and must not be confused, but stand on their own right. For example; oil and water have their place in a car engine, but they must not be mixed together; in their proper place they complement each other. So it is with these truths.

---

[4] For other possible interpretations, see New Testament Commentary. Banner of Truth Trust. 1975. William Hendriksen. p153

1) God is sovereign in His electing purpose. *'In him we were also chosen, having been predestined according to the plan of him who works out everything in conformity with the purpose of his will'* **(Eph 1:11)**. C. H. Spurgeon views this wonderful doctrine of election, as one not to be easily understood, but wholly believed and embraced.

2) The individual responsibility of men and women to respond to the grace and calling of God cannot be ignored (this, however, does not suggest that they contribute to their salvation – **see Ephesians 2:8-9**), and in **2 Peter 3:9** *'The Lord is not slow in keeping his promise, as some understand slowness. He is patient with you, not wanting anyone to perish, but everyone to come to repentance.'*

Although human understanding will always be limited on this matter; one thing is for sure – God will work out His purpose and one day all will understand! For further consideration on God's sovereignty and human responsibility, see J I Packer.[5] See also **1 Peter 2:8.**

Don't hide your light! 4:21-25.

> *'He said to them, 'Do you bring in a lamp to put it under a bowl or a bed? Instead, don't you put it on its stand? For whatever is hidden is meant to be disclosed, and whatever is concealed is meant to be brought out into the open. If anyone has ears to hear, let him hear. Consider carefully what you hear,' he continued. 'With the measure you use, it will be measured to you – and even more. Whoever has will be given more; whoever does not have, even what he has will be taken from him.'*

In these few verses, FOUR distinct sayings which Jesus utters occur one after another without amplifying or expanding their

[5] Evangelism and the Sovereignty of God. Inter-Varisity Press. J. I. Packer. 1977. In particular, read Chapter Two in relation to an 'antinomy.' p18f

meaning. He simply makes the statements and leaves the hearer to consider. Elsewhere in the gospels similar thoughts are repeated but not tied together as Mark does here. For example, Matthew introduces them on separate occasions in **5:15, 10:26, 7:2, and 13:12.**

Firstly, v 21 *'Do you bring in a lamp to put it under a bowl or a bed? Instead, don't you put it on a stand?'* Common sense answers the question. Why light a lamp only to cover it up? If that were the case it would not fulfil its purpose. In the previous parable it was seen that there was an expectation from the good heart that received the word; it was expected to bear fruit in abundance. And so the blessing, benefits and spiritual fruit that develop as a result of receiving the word must become visible, for all to see. There is nothing secretive about it, quite the opposite.

Jesus not only declared Himself to be the *'light of the world'* (**Jn 8:12**), He also said to His disciples in **Mtt 5:14-16**. *'You are the light of the world ...... let your light shine before men, that they may see your good deeds and praise your Father in heaven.'* Having received this light, the believer has the responsibility to let that light be seen – not to hide it! Christianity is meant to be seen!

Secondly, v22 *'For whatever is hidden is meant to be disclosed, and whatever is concealed is meant to be brought out into the open.'* There is something very special about truth. Truth may be denied, refuted, suppressed, rejected or ignored, yet it is indestructible. With the arrival of Jesus Christ in this Galilean area and His unique ministry in word and deed, the truth had found expression in ways never seen or heard before.

In Himself, He was the truth, and His words were the embodiment of His character. His life and ministry had in a sense been hidden in ages past, but were now being revealed. **Romans 16:25-26** declares *'Now to him who is able to establish you by my gospel and the proclamation of Jesus Christ, according to the revelation of the mystery hidden for long ages* *past, but now revealed and made known ...'* It was time for truth to be revealed not concealed. It was now time for Christ and His gospel to come into full view; to be seen, heard, understood and received. This gospel was new (at least to those who were now hearing it); radical and life changing to all who would receive it.

As Jesus said in **1:15** *'The time has come,' he said, 'The Kingdom of God is near, repent and believe the good news.'* It would not be stretching the text to also suggest that a personal application is relevant – for the truth within the believers heart must be opened out into full view. It is not meant to be hidden away for personal gratification alone, but shared with all who will look and listen. *'If anyone has ears to hear, let him hear.'*

Thirdly, v24 *'Consider carefully what you hear,' he continued. With the measure you use, it will be measured to you – and even more.'* We have here a word of warning! To listen with care, giving what is heard our full attention. Like many of the Pharisees it can be so easy to 'listen conditionally,' that is, to listen only to what it is desired to hear and block the mind to everything else. Such a position is weak and unhealthy and is likely to restrict genuine sanctifying growth in Christ Jesus.

The second part of this verse is saying 'whatever you put in is what you'll get out.' Sad to say that Christians are often heard, following a Church service to say *'I didn't get anything out of that service, worship, message or singing etc.'* These people don't go to give, they go to get, and such an attitude tends to lead to spiritual narrowness and poverty. The words *'and even more'* indicate that those who have a giving spirit are likely to receive more than they give.

Fourthly, v25 *'Whoever has will be given more; whoever does not have, even what he has will be taken from him.'* In spiritual terms a believer cannot stand still, he must ever be progressing and growing. **1 Peter 2:2** commands *'Like newborn babies, crave pure spiritual milk, so that by it you may grow up in your salvation.'* To those who are making progress, more will be added. Genuine spiritual endeavour will have a compound effect; every blessing is a guarantee of further blessings to come.

John 1:16 states that *'From the fullness of his grace we have all received one blessing after another.'* On the other hand those who are rather static and not growing will lose the value and benefit of what they have, and this will have the effect of moving backwards: it is regression in contrast to progression.

Parable of the growing seed. 4:26-29

> *'He also said, 'This is what the kingdom of God is like. A man scatters seed on the ground. Night and day, whether he sleeps or gets up, the seed sprouts and grows, though he does not know how. All by itself the soil produces corn – first the stalk, then the ear, then the full grain in the ear. As soon as the grain is ripe, he puts the sickle to it, because the harvest has come.'*

This parable is about the kingdom of God, and is closely linked to the parable of the sower, it is recorded only in Mark's gospel. Why it finds no place in Matthew and Luke cannot be known. The gist of this parable is that the word of God will do its own work in the human heart so long as the heart is in the right condition. It describes the farmer with his field prepared and ready to sow: his responsibility is twofold, he sows and he harvests. He may prepare the earth diligently, weed and feed, but that's about all he can do. He then has to rely on a power source out-with himself and technology to produce a harvest.

Jesus made it clear that His kingdom was not of this world,[6] not an earthly, but spiritual kingdom where the seed of God's word would settle on the fertile heart and take root, thus bringing about a spiritual harvest. A preacher may preach

---

[6] John 18:36 'Jesus said, 'My kingdom is not of this world. If it were, my servants would fight to prevent my arrest by the Jews.'

faithfully, diligently, and with great sincerity, yet never see his hearers come to faith in Christ – for this is something only God can do. This point is made clear from **1 Corinthians 3:5-7** *'What, after all, is Apollos? And what is Paul? Only servants, through whom you came to believe – as the Lord has assigned to each his task. I planted the seed, Apollos watered it, but God made it grow. So neither he who plants nor he who waters is anything, but only God, who makes things grow.'*

What a lesson this is for all who seek to serve God! Just as human beings cannot be saved through good works alone, so the kingdom of God cannot expand and grow through mere physical commitment; it rests upon the power of God.

God's children must play their part as servants of God, but true spiritual life can only come from the hand of God. The kingdom of God can only be expressed through the power of God.

The parable of the mustard seed. 4:30-34

> *'Again he said, 'What shall we say the kingdom of God is like, or what parable shall we use to describe it? It is like a mustard seed, the smallest seed you plant in the ground. Yet when planted, it grows and becomes the largest of all garden plants, with such big branches that the birds of the air can perch in its shade.' With many similar parables Jesus spoke the word to them, as much as they could understand. He did not say anything to them without using a parable. But when he was alone with his own disciples, he explained everything.'*

Jesus begins this parable with an oratorical question, aimed at arousing the interest of His hearers in relation to understanding the nature of the kingdom of God. In this parable He seeks to show how from very small beginnings the Kingdom would expand into something truly great. The mustard seed points to the progress that Christianity would make throughout the world from that time on.

In Palestine a grain of mustard seed was recognised as the smallest possible seed, yet when fully grown it was probably the largest of all garden shrubs, often described as a tree, and could reach as high as five metres. This made its use in this parable significant, for Jesus likens the Kingdom of God to this small seed.

Twice in the gospels, in **Matthew 17:20** and **Luke 17:6,** Jesus used the smallness of this seed to illustrate the value of faith. The Kingdom of God found its beginnings in smallness and weakness; for in those disciples chosen by Jesus there was none with a reputation of greatness. Most were untaught and very ordinary men.

In the eyes of men, the beginning of the visible church was contemptible, insignificant, powerless and small; yet following the death and resurrection of Christ and the pouring out of the Holy Spirit at Pentecost, the Kingdom of God would expand rapidly, transforming thousands of men and women.

When started, it was something tiny, but with the passing of time it would reach every part of the world and continue to multiply to this present day. Billions have entered the Kingdom of God. Today, God's kingdom is still growing, still expanding, and will continue to do so until the personal return of Jesus Christ.

This parable also teaches us that in the eyes of God 'small is big' when placed in the hands of God. It is possible to be too big for God to use, but never too small.

In **v32** Jesus tells us that it has large branches and leaves where birds were able to perch under its shade – it was a place of refuge for them. Many have speculated over the years regarding the spiritual significance, if any, of these branches. Without adding further speculation, it is safe to say that the Kingdom of God, from its moment of inception, has become the shelter and refuge of countless men and women from all cultures, creeds and backgrounds, worldwide.

It is clear that Jesus was mindful of the disciples's difficulty in understanding what He had to say, for **v33** states that *'he spoke the word to them, as much as they could understand.'* Although Jesus used parables continually as a teaching method to help them understand; when the disciples were alone with Him, Jesus explained everything to them. The value and depth of what He taught them would not be fully appreciated until after His resurrection, when their eyes were opened in a new way to understand truth. (Regarding **vv33-34,** see earlier comments on **4:2** for the definition of a parable and why Jesus used parables in His teaching.)

Jesus calms the storm. 4:35-41

> *'That day when evening came, he said to his disciples, 'Let us go to the other side.' Leaving the crowd behind, they took him along, just as he was, in the boat. There were also other boats with him. A furious squall came up, and the waves broke over the boat, so that it was nearly swamped. Jesus was in the stern, sleeping on a cushion. The disciples woke him and said to him, 'Teacher, don't you care if we drown?' He got up, rebuked the wind and said to the waves, 'Quiet! Be still!' Then the wind died down and it was completely calm. He said this to his disciples, 'Why are you so afraid? Do you still have no faith?' They were terrified and asked each other, 'Who is this? Even the wind and the waves obey him.'*

Time after time in Mark's gospel there is a beautiful intertwining of the deity and humanity of Jesus. This perfect human being, the Son of God incarnate is seen to be totally involved in the day to day activities of human life; spending much of His time with ordinary everyday people. Not only did he rub shoulders with others; eating and socialising with them; He also got involved in their lives as one who loved and cared.

Just like everyone else, Jesus got weary and tired with the events of life. On this occasion He must have been exhausted following His ministry to a great multitude, as He taught them in parables from just off shore. As the day was nearing its end, He suggested leaving the crowd behind, getting back into the boat and crossing over to the eastern side of the lake.[7]

Not long after His departure, the power of God would soon be in evidence, as Jesus, the Son of God, exercised His authority by altering the very course of nature.

This introduced a new dimension in His ministry, and is the first 'nature miracle' recorded by Mark. It may also be noted that only Mark tells us that *'There were also other boats with him'* (**v36**). Why Mark wants us to know this is uncertain, for they play no further part in the story, yet for him it completes his record of the event as he recalls it. Mark's inclusion of this does however, make sense when it is taken into account that in this short event he provides other details; such as, the precise time, the vivid detail of the boat filling, the position of Jesus and the mention of such a simple thing as the cushion.

Bearing in mind that it was Jesus who said in **v35** *'Let us go over to the other* side', it is said in the following verse (**v36)** that *'they took him along, just as he was.'* Taking Him along is just another way of referring to the fact that they were the boatmen and they would do the rowing; in this sense 'they' take Him across. The phrase *'just as he was'* could mean 'without getting out of the boat' or perhaps 'not taking time to get belongings (no matter how meagre) or make other preparations.'

Verse 37 introduces us to a sudden storm, so furious that the waves came over the boat and threatened to sink it. In the

---

[7] According to Matthew 13:36 there is the possibility that Jesus left the boat and went into a house for a time before leaving again to cross over to the other side of the lake. 'Then he left the crowd and went into the house.'

eyes of the disciples this was a life or death situation, for they said in **v38** *'Teacher, don't you care if we drown?'* This was a serious problem; for these men, some of whom used to be fishermen, knew the seas. Things were bad! Sudden storms were not uncommon on the Sea of Galilee, the surrounding terrain and nature of the winds made this kind of storm all too frequent; they were dangerous and particularly so in the evening. And what was Jesus doing? He was sleeping in the rear of the boat with His head on a cushion.

Panicking and in fear for their lives we read in **v38** '*The disciples woke him and said to him, 'Teacher, don't you care that we drown?'*

How fickle faith is; here were men who left all to follow Jesus and who had witnessed healings and evil spirits being cast out, yet in the heat of the crisis, panic sets in and they say *'Don't you care?*

How often has the believer known and experienced special moments of grace and blessing, times they will never forget, times when God's presence was almost tangible, wonderful answers to prayer and they think; 'how could I ever doubt my Saviour again?'

Yet, just like these disciples, there are times when they have short memories and faith seems to fly out the window when adverse intrusions appear. It is well not to condemn these men without giving thought to the fickleness of all human hearts.

What initially bothered the disciples was the fact that Jesus was asleep, but the fact that He was asleep did not mean that He didn't care; He was still with them! Today, Jesus is in heaven, we do not see Him physically, but it does not lessen His care for us.

We read in **v39** *'He got up, rebuked the wind and said to the waves, 'Quiet! Be still!' Then the wind died down and it was completely calm.'* Both the wind and the waves obey Him. The words that Jesus used to address the wind and waves are exactly the same as those used to speak to the demon-possessed man in **1:25**.

Here is the voice of the one who only uttered a few words and all creation sprang into being. The Son of God now alters the course of nature with mere words. Here is the one who holds all things together by the word of His power (See **Colossians 1:15-17**). Notice the result of His command! Complete calm! (**v39**). There could have been no greater contrast.

An individual or a people may not always be responsible for the circumstances in which they find themselves, but they are responsible how they respond to them. Jesus is able to come alongside the believer and bring peace to the troubled heart, rest to the weary and to transform the darkest night.

Though this event took the disciples by surprise, Jesus knew exactly what would happen and would use this situation to challenge their faith. In doing so, the disciples would see their Master in a new light. Seeing men healed and demons cast out was one thing, but this was different, they were terrified! *'Why are you so afraid? Do you still have no faith?'* said Jesus **(v40)**.

The fact that Jesus was with them should have been enough, but it was not! They had still to grow in their faith and this event highlighted the shallowness of their faith.

The way Jesus phrased this question, using the word *'still,'* indicates an expectation of their faith that was not yet realised. Fear and lack of faith form a partnership here, for it was the fear of this awful storm that exposed the weakness of their faith. The Christian will never grow, deepen or develop in a truly sanctifying way, unless the storms of life are faced head on with eyes fixed on Jesus. We read in **Hebrews 12:2** *'Let us fix our eyes on Jesus, the author and perfecter of our faith.....'* The disciples had still to grow in their faith and learn to set their gaze upon Christ; to focus on Him; to be controlled by Him, so that adverse circumstances were not allowed to dictate. Paul confidently states in **Phil 4:11***'......for I have learned to be content whatever the circumstances.'*

This event had startled them to the extent that they were terrified **(v41)**. Whatever their understanding of Christ up until this time, it had now gone beyond what they had previously imagined, so that they say *'Who is this?'* Of course they knew that it was Jesus, but this was the first time they had seen such awesome power. With astonishment and reverence they said, '*Even the wind and the waves obey him.*'

Now that they had witnessed His authority over nature itself there should have been no further reason ever to doubt Him again, for their Lord would always be in control of every situation. Yet, as is the case for all who follow Christ, they learn, but never stop learning; they grow, but never stop growing; they get stronger, but are never strong enough; they follow closely, but never closely enough. And so the believer ever strives to reach that place of perfect trust.

How wonderful and reassuring it is to know that whilst striving towards this goal of perfect trust, there is in Jesus a Lord and Saviour who understands the times of weakness throughout the journey of faith, and is always there, just as He was for these disciples.

5

Transformed by the power of God. 5:1-20

'They went across the lake to the region of the Gerasenes. When Jesus got out of the boat, a man with an evil spirit came from the tombs to meet him. This man lived in the tombs and no-one could bind him any more, not even with a chain. For he had often been chained hand and foot, but he tore the chains apart and broke the irons on his feet. No-one was strong enough to subdue him. Night and day among the tombs and in the hills he would cry out and cut himself with stones.

When he saw Jesus from a distance, he ran and fell on his knees in front of him. He shouted at the top of his voice, 'What do you want with me, Jesus, Son of the Most High God? Swear to God that you won't torture me!' For Jesus had said to him, 'Come out of this man, you evil spirit!' Then Jesus asked him, 'What is your name?' 'My name is Legion,' he replied, 'for we are many.' And he begged Jesus again and again not to send them out of the area.

> *A large herd of pigs was feeding on the nearby hillside. The demons begged Jesus, 'Send us among the pigs, allow us to go to them.' He gave them permission, and the evil spirits came out and went into the pigs. The herd, about two thousand in number, rushed down the steep bank into the lake and were drowned. Those tending the pigs ran off and reported this in the town and countryside, and the people went out to see what had happened. When they came to Jesus they saw the man who had been possessed by the legion of demons, sitting there, clothed and in his right mind; and they were afraid. Those who had seen it told the people what had happened to the demon-possessed man – and told about the pigs as well. Then the people began to plead with Jesus to leave their region. As he was getting into the boat, the man who had been demon-possessed begged to go with him. Jesus did not let him, but said, 'Go home to your family and tell them how much the Lord has done for you.' So the man went away and began to tell in the Decapolis how much Jesus had done for him. And all the people were amazed.'*

Having just demonstrated His power over the wind and waves, Jesus now carries out an exorcism with a man so possessed by evil spirits that his name was Legion. In doing so, He demonstrated His power over an apparently untameable force. Exactly how many evil spirits possessed the man we do not know, but the word Legion was used at that time for a group of Roman soldiers numbering 6,000 men. Earlier in **1:23-27** Jesus had already cast out an evil spirit from a man in the synagogue, but this was a far more serious situation.

It would seem that this story follows immediately after the previous miracles over nature. This being the case, it makes for an eerie picture indeed, for it would have taken place in the evening; one can only imagine it! In this narrative we witness the wonderful power of God triumphing over evil; light dispelling darkness and a transformation that epitomises the very core and purpose of the Gospel of Christ.

Amidst the glory of this incident and the clear evidence of the manifestation of God's power, there are also questions to be asked that are difficult or perhaps impossible to answer. We may also note that, although Mark's gospel is the shortest, his record of this incident is longer and more detailed than either Matthew's or Luke's.

Verse 1 tells us that they arrived at a region of the '*Gerasenes.*'[1] Although the other disciples were with Jesus when they arrived at this location, it simply says that '*Jesus got out of the boat'* **(v2)**. Whether or not the disciples also got out of the boat at that moment is irrelevant for they play no part in the event itself.

This region was well known for its caves and tombs and it was from one of these tombs that this possessed man made his way towards Jesus as He left the boat. What is known about this man? The fact that his residence was in a tomb tells us much about his state of heart and mind. He is a poor man and to be pitied! He lived in isolation and seclusion, well away from society and people in general.

There is here a sad sorrowful picture of a person out of control. Night and day he would roam through the hills and tombs like a wild animal. He was both an enemy to himself and others, yet he is gripped by an uncontrollable power.

Undoubtedly, he would have been feared by many and classed as an embarrassment and someone unsuitable to mix in society. According to the account given in **Matthew 8:28**

---

[1] 'The original as represented by Grk NT. (A-B-M-W) has Gaderenes in Matt 8:28; Gerasenes here in Mark 5:1; and Gegresenes in Luke 8:26. In each case variant readings are recognised in the footnotes. In order to locate the place where Jesus landed, a description as given in the Gospels (Matt 8:28, 32; Mark 5:2, 13; and Luke 8:27, 33) is helpful. We learn that it was a region of caves used as tombs, and that a steep hill descended sharply to the very edge of the water. N.T.C. The Gospel of Mark. The Banner of Truth Trust. 1976. William Hendriksen. p151

(where he refers to two men) he makes the point that he was a violent man – *'They were so violent that no-one could pass that way.'* This being so, it helps understanding as to why people tried to bind him, even with chains, but with little or no effect! In fact in **vv3-4** it is claimed that he had often been chained, but such was his demoniac strength that he broke the chains.

What a frightening person he must have been! A wild man, who not only scared and threatened others, but also engaged in self harm **(v5)** *'he would cry out and cut himself with stones.'* Who could blame him for attempting to take his own life, for his existence was surely unbearable! Here was a man feared by many, perhaps even hated by most, yet loved by God. In his present state, he was all that God did not intend him to be: God's creatorial image had been distorted, he was separated from man and God; he was under the influence and direction of Satan.

The people of the town certainly believed this man to be out of his mind and insane, for his appearance and behaviour warranted such an opinion. They had tried to help him, but were unable; he was beyond human help – but not God's! He was not beyond the love, compassion and care of Jesus.

Verse 6 tells us that he saw Jesus from a distance. This would change everything! Jesus was now within sight and was this man's only hope. The people thought they were helping by trying to bind him; but it was Jesus who would provide the ultimate help by bringing about his release.

Many people see Jesus from a distance and remain there, but not him! For *'he ran and fell on his knees in front of him.'* No-one who runs to Jesus will ever be disappointed. This man was not! It is possible that by acting in this way, and saying what he did, he was taking up a position of defence.[2] However, both his attitude and physical prostration at Jesus' feet would seem to indicate submission to the deity of Christ.

---

[2] 'Its purpose is entirely defensive; seeing the identity of a dangerous opponent, the unclean spirit raises its voice to defend itself against him.' The New London Commentary on the New Testament. The Gospel of Mark. Marshall, Morgan and Scott. William L. Lane p182-183.

What a contrast between the religious leaders at that time, with all their 'knowledge' and pseudo spirituality, who could stare Jesus in the face, listen to His gracious words, and yet remain firm in unbelief. But this man runs to Jesus, falls on his knees, **v7** *'He shouted at the top of his voice, 'What do you want with me, Jesus, Son of the Most High God.'*

What is the significance of these words?

'*What do you want with me'* may be paraphrased - 'what do you and I have in common?' The distinction could not be greater and points to the fact that they had nothing in common. By using the title *'Jesus, Son of the Most High God'* the demoniac demonstrates once again that evil spirits are aware of Jesus' true identity (cf **1:24: 3:11**). In this case, Legion affirms that Jesus is the Son of God; he has already fallen at Jesus' feet in full knowledge of what he was doing. In doing so he submits to the superior power of God. Note also from **v7**, the element of fear; for he seeks assurance that Jesus will not torture him because he is possessed by those spirits who stand in opposition to God.

Verse 8 informs that Jesus had already commanded the evil spirits to come out - but seemingly without effect at that moment! It is clear that this man is in a state of turmoil, there is a war raging in his soul; he longs to be free, but is held by the forces of evil. **Ephesians 6:12** makes it clear that *' our struggle is not against flesh and blood, but against the rulers, against the authorities, against the powers of this dark world and against the spiritual forces of evil....'*

Jesus asked a question – *'What is your name?'* The man answered – *'My name is Legion, he replied, for we are many.'* He begged Jesus on behalf of the evil spirits not to send them out of the area, which is firstly, a concession of defeat, and secondly, reflects a belief that demons are related to a particular area. In this case, an area associated with skeletons, death, desolation and destruction: in such a place they would feel at home.

Notice the intensity of Legion's request, for he begged Jesus *'again and again'* **(v11)**. Why he makes such a persistent plea cannot be certain; perhaps it is because he is under such demonic influence that it is 'their will' that comes through his voice; they do not want to be homeless!

At this point in the story we have the appearance of a large herd of pigs feeding nearby. As the evil spirits make their plea through this poor distraught man, they beg Jesus to send them into these grazing pigs **(v12)**. We must notice that to the Jewish mind this would not be a great problem, for pigs were classed as 'unclean animals' and their meat was forbidden to Jews. This was a gentile situation and would have had no effect or loss upon Jewish life.

Jesus gave permission, and the evil spirits came out of the man and possessed these 2,000 pigs. There was, however, a sting in the tail for these evil spirits, they were looking for relocation, but hadn't bargained on their destruction. Rushing down the steep bank they were drowned in the lake **(v13)**. Two things happened!

Firstly, this man was released from demonic possession; he had been set free and rescued from the tyranny of Satan with all his destructive and degrading influence.

Secondly, not only had he been delivered from these evil spirits, but they had been destroyed. Their new home in the pigs was extremely short lived, for their end was swift and complete. In this there is evidence of the absolute supremacy of the power of God over that of Satan. Here is a picture of Satan's kingdom being plundered and his kingdom crumbling.

This was a battle with only one victor in mind; it was never in doubt, for the promise is given in **1 John 4:4** *'.....the one who is in you is greater than the one who is in the world.'* In response to the command of Jesus these evil spirits had no option but obey – even though it meant their end. Back in **1:27** when Jesus exorcised the man in the synagogue, the people said in response, *'A new teaching – and with authority! He even gives orders to evil spirits and they obey him.'*

In **v14** the events that have taken place are now conveyed to the town and countryside by the men who were looking after the pigs (and who could now be out of a job!). As a result, the people came to see for themselves all that had happened. Two things would immediately capture their attention.

Firstly, the absence of the pigs! Was Jesus being insensitive to innocent animals? What about the owner of the pigs, would he be recompensed? Were his actions ethical? Good and relevant as these questions are, yet to find any acceptable answer is almost impossible. Mark tells the story as it is, he makes sure that the relevant details are recorded about what actually happened; the lessons are clear in relation to the kingdom and power of God, but he makes no attempt to provide information with regards to the consequences.

It is not beyond reasonable expectation that some form of compensation had taken place, in spite of it not being recorded. Mark obviously viewed this as unnecessary information.[3]

If the absence of the pigs was the first thing to notice, then the **Second** was this 'Transformed man.' We are told in **v15** that this man who had been violent, wild and scary beyond belief, was now *'sitting there, dressed and in his right mind.'* What a transformation! What a glorious miracle! What an exhibition and demonstration of the purpose of God! No greater change could take place in any living person; this man had been 'transformed.' He is now in his right mind, in control of himself, rational and sensible – no madness or insanity; he had received a miracle of grace because of his encounter with Jesus Christ. He was now in a fit state for fellowship with humanity

[3] 'The ethical implications of Jesus' action in regard to the swine (11-13) has given rise to much discussion. Was it not wanton destruction of property with consequent heavy loss to the owners, and did Jesus anticipate the result, or did he not? Those who accept a psychological explanation of the demon possession are obliged to account for the panic of the swine by saying that in the paroxysm which accompanied his deliverance the man struck terror into the herd and drove them down the cliff. The more satisfactory view, however, is that the destruction of the swine was permitted by the Lord as an ocular demonstration to the demoniac that the demons had in fact departed from him, and to confirm his faith. The sacrifice of brutes and property is justifiable where the sanity and lives of persons are at stake.' The New Bible Commentary. Inter-Varsity Fellowship. 1961. C. E. Graham Swift. p816

and also entered into fellowship with God. In this, there is a picture of salvation.

Men and women may not be as this man was, yet the need for transformation and reconciliation to God are just as necessary for 'everyman.' *'For all have sinned and fall short of the glory of God, and are justified freely by his grace through the redemption that came by Christ Jesus'* (**Rom 3:23-24**).

How did the townspeople respond to this powerful and life-changing event? **Verses 15** and **17** state that they were afraid, and even pleaded with Jesus to leave that region. Evidence that God had been at work stared them in the face, something wonderful had happened that had changed this man, yet they had to get rid of the cause – Jesus! They are filled with alarm because of the presence of the supernatural. Perhaps their own inner needs and the darkness of their own souls were now surfacing! Reflective on the people's response, the words of **Luke 19:14** seem fitting **-** *'We don't want this man to be our King.'*

Back in **v6** the possessed man shouted *'What do you want with me, Jesus, Son of the Most high God?'* Now, in **v18** as Jesus was getting into the boat, he begged Jesus to let him go with Him –*'the man who had been demon-possessed begged to go with him.'* He was now a believer and wanted to (literally) follow Jesus. What a lovely and telling picture this is; yet Jesus had other plans for him.

In **v19** Jesus tells him to go home to his family and friends - *'tell them how much the Lord has done for you, and how he has had mercy on you.'* We can only picture this man walking into his village and presenting himself before his family and friends. He was totally transformed in mind, body and soul.

What a contrast! Once among the tombs - now at Jesus feet, once bound by chains – now enjoying complete liberty, once wild and out of control – now in his right mind, – once unclothed – now he is dressed, once at a distance from man and God – now he is near to both. This man was no more deserving of the grace of God than anyone else – but Jesus said to him *'Go and tell ......how he has had MERCY on you.'* He was a recipient of the mercy of God. What a merciful and gracious Saviour there is in Jesus! As the writer discerned in **Psalm 103:10** *'He does not treat us as our sins deserve or repay us according to our iniquities.'*

In obedience to the command of Jesus, and full of the joy of the Lord, this man went home and began to witness to all that Jesus had done for him. In **v20** Mark says that he *'began to tell in the Decapolis how much Jesus had done for him.'* The word Decapolis refers to a region which actually consisted of ten cities; he had become a true missionary, spreading his testimony of the grace of God. Is it any wonder that *'all the people were amazed at him?'* Among the lessons of this story, it is impossible for the believer to avoid the challenge to go and tell all that Jesus has done for them.

Raising a dead girl and healing a sick woman. 5:21-43

> *'When Jesus had again crossed over by boat to the other side of the lake, a large crowd gathered round him while he was by the lake. Then one of the synagogue rulers, named Jairus, came there. Seeing Jesus, he fell at his feet and pleaded earnestly with him, 'My little daughter is dying. Please come and put your hands on her so that she will be healed and live.' So Jesus went with him.*
>
> *A large crowd followed and pressed around him. And a woman was there who had been subject to bleeding for twelve years. She had suffered a great deal under the care of many doctors and had spent all she had, yet instead of getting better she grew worse. When she heard about Jesus, she came up behind him in the crowd and touched his cloak, because she thought, 'If I just touch his clothes, I will be healed.' Immediately*

her bleeding stopped and she felt in her body that she was freed from her suffering. At once Jesus realised that power had gone out from him. He turned around in the crowd and asked, 'Who touched my clothes?' 'You see the people crowding against you, his disciples answered, and yet you ask, 'Who touched you?' But Jesus kept looking around to see who had done it. Then the woman, knowing what had happened to her, came and fell at his feet and, trembling with fear, told him the whole truth. He said to her, 'Daughter, your faith has healed you. Go in peace and be freed from your suffering.'
While Jesus was still speaking, some men came from the house of Jairus, the synagogue ruler. 'Your daughter is dead,' they said. 'Why bother the teacher any more.' Ignoring what they said, Jesus told the synagogue ruler, 'Don't be afraid; just believe.' He did not let anyone follow him except Peter, James and John the brother of James. When they came to the home of the synagogue ruler, Jesus saw a commotion, with people crying and wailing loudly. He went in and said to them, 'Why all this commotion and wailing? The child is not dead but asleep.' But they laughed at him. After he put them all out, he took the child's father and mother and the disciples who were with him, and went in where the child was. He took her by the hand and said to her, 'Talitha koum' (which means, 'Little girl, I say to you, get up!'). Immediately the girl stood up and walked around (she was twelve years old). At this they were completely astonished. He gave strict orders not to let anyone know about this, and told them to give her something to eat.'

This passage brings into focus two miracles, linked by the theme of faith. Firstly by the child's father and secondly by the woman herself. The second of the miracles may be referred to as a 'miracle of interruption' since it takes place in the middle of the first. For the purpose of clarity in understanding both events, it is better to deal with the first miracle in its entirety and then return to the second.

Raising the dead girl. vv21-24 and 35-43

In **v21** it is found that Jesus had yet again crossed the lake by boat, landing on the Capernaum side; as usual there was a large crowd waiting for Him. News about Him had spread so far and wide that the people almost anticipated His every move.

According to **Matthew 9:18** the disciples of John the Baptist were part of this large crowd and were asking Him questions about fasting. It was while He was answering them that a man named Jairus arrived. What is known about this man?

Being a ruler of the synagogue means that he was a man of considerable importance. He would have been responsible for the management of the synagogue, including the conduct of the public services. Though not taking part in the services himself he would have overseen the duties of others. The synagogue ruler was usually a well respected person and of a high standing. Although Jairus was a Jew, and as such, may not have been a supporter of Jesus, it is amazing just how his circumstances dissipated his prejudice against Jesus. Strong views and opinions often take a lesser place when faced with a desperate situation, as is found here.

Having regarded Jesus as an outsider and possibly a heretic, Jairus is now found to have made his way to join with this large crowd, and as soon as he caught sight of Jesus *'he fell at his feet.'* What a change in attitude! No longer is he concerned for his status and dignity, he is a broken and distraught man, his world is collapsing around him. There is no other option open to him but to pocket his pride, which he does.

Verse 22 tells us that he *'pleaded earnestly with him.'* With submission and humility, he pleads his case - why? Because his twelve year old daughter was dying! According to Dr **Luke** in **8:42** it was his 'only daughter' and probably his only child. What a sad, sad situation! He would surely do anything if only his daughter could be healed; there was no price too great to pay – yet his only chance was to cast himself upon Jesus. Could this miracle worker heal his daughter?

Jairus had obviously heard much about Jesus and possibly seen Him in action, because in **v23** he invited Jesus to lay His hand upon her; *'Please come and put your hands on her so that she will be healed and live.'* What clear faith is exhibited by this man, if only Jesus would come and touch her, all would be well, things would be normal, and he would have his little girl back again!

In response to his heartfelt pleading, Jesus' heart opened up to his need and He left with Jairus, followed by the crowd, to go to the child **(v24)**. How gracious Jesus was! He did not rebuke this man for previous views or prejudice; but sought to alleviate his situation, and in doing so, revealed the mercy and glory of God.

In **v35** we find Jesus still speaking; having just performed the miracle of the interruption He now began His journey to the little girl. No sooner had Jesus set out than men arrived from Jairus' house to inform him that his daughter was now dead and there was no need to trouble Jesus any more.

There is no way of knowing how much time was used up with the healing of the sick woman, but it would seem reasonable to assume that Jairus must have been anxious, because his daughter was dying and time was slipping fast; the situation was critical! For Jairus, it was now too late; all hope of healing had gone.

With Jairus full of anxiety and devastation, we have Jesus at work, but He had not forgotten the little girl. The worsening of this situation would open the door for a far greater miracle than healing, though Jairus would not have realised this at that time.

Jesus had already proved His power and authority over nature **(4:35-41)**, now He would prove His divinity by raising the dead! The seeming delay in responding to Jairus' request was not accidental or unfortunate, but all part of the purpose of the great Physician and for the ultimate well-being of all concerned.

Jesus 'ignored' or 'paid no attention' **(v36)** to the sad news from the family home. Knowing that Jairus had just witnessed a very sick woman being healed, Jesus is able to say to him *'Don't be afraid, just believe.'* In other words, 'trust in me, just believe in me and you too will witness the miraculous for your little girl.' All is not lost! Jairus was obviously a man of faith, otherwise why come to Jesus in the first place? But Jesus wanted him to continue in his faith, and not to let this news stop him from believing what He, Jesus, could do. True faith will never be proved in the sunlight and cool breeze of the day, but often in the darkest moments when the winds of adversity are at their worst. Such was the case here, for this man's faith was being tested!

On their way to Jairus' home, Jesus dismissed the crowd and most of the disciples taking with Him just Peter, James and John **(v37).** These three formed a group known as 'his inner circle' and they were on a number of occasions privy to special times alone with Jesus.[4] Why these three were chosen we cannot be certain, but there were, in them, qualities that would have been supportive to Jesus during His earthly ministry. Though Jesus was the Son of God He was also human and needed fellowship and friendship and at a certain level – confidants.

---

[4] 'The limitation to three disciples may have been necessitated (as in 1:29-30) by the size of the room in which the girl's body lay, but in any case consistent with Jesus' tendency to allow the three 'nicknamed' disciples (see on 3:17) to be with him at moments of special revelatory significance; cf, 9:2 (the transfiguration); 13:3 (the final discourse with Andrew); 14:33(Gethsemane). The supreme miracle of raising the dead is also for their eyes only.' The Gospel of Mark. A Commentary on the Greek Text. W. B. Eerdmans Publishing Company. 2002. R.T. France. p239

In Peter is seen a man of strength, who in spite of his failures had a warm and zealous heart for his Master. John was always recognised as a disciple who loved Jesus and stayed close to him. It was to him that Jesus handed over the care of His mother as he offered up His life on the cross. James was faithful and reliable and would become the first apostolic martyr – as stated earlier.

Arriving at the home of the synagogue ruler they were faced with a group of people expressing their grief at the death of this child. **(v38)** Death is always sad, but especially so when it is a child. There was crying and loud wailing, emotions were high and grief was deep. And so in **v39**, into this sad, yet highly charged arena Jesus came, and going into the room, said *'Why all this commotion and wailing? The child is not dead but asleep.'* **(v40)**

Such remarks must have seemed absurd, ignorant and devoid of any real sensitivity; it is not surprising that we read *'But they laughed at him.'*[5] However, from the emotions of sadness, grief and laughing, they would soon experience a joy that knew no limit.

What did Jesus mean by saying that the child was not dead, but asleep? Did Jesus mean that she was in a coma and that He was about to waken her? This would not make sense, for the reason the people were laughing was because they knew she was dead. Furthermore, in **Luke 8:53** it is claimed that *'They laughed at him, knowing she was dead.'* Then in **v55** we read that *'Her spirit returned.'* There would have been no need for this had she only been in a coma!

In **John 11:11** Jesus also referred to Lazarus as having fallen asleep, yet in **v14** affirms that he was actually dead. So then, Jesus used this metaphor as a means of showing that death will not have the final say and that where true faith is present,

---

[5] 'The reference is probably to repeated bursts of derisive laughter aimed at humiliating Jesus. It seems that these mourners were endowed with the dubious gift of shifting in one sudden moment from dismal moaning to uproarious mirth. Does it not therefore also bear witness to the genuine nature of the child's restoration from death.' N.T.C. The Gospel of Mark. Banner of Truth Trust. 1975. William Hendriksen. p213-214

death will simply be like sleep. In **1 Corinthians 15:18** the apostle Paul refers to believers who had previously died and were awaiting the resurrection of the body, as those *'who have fallen asleep.'*

Jesus now put everyone out of the room except the parents and the three disciples. Earlier in **v23** we have the little girl's father pleading with Jesus to come and put His hand upon her so that she would be healed; he was however, about to get more than he asked for. **Verse 41** *'He took her by the hand and said to her, 'Talitha koum!' (which means, 'Little girl get up!').* Here we have Jesus, the Son of God, the one who merely uttered a few words and the whole of creation sprang into being, with a tone of endearment commanding life to enter this child's body. Death had to submit to Him. Behind this glorious miracle lies all the authority and power of the Almighty, demonstrating His concern and the fullness of his love for – yes, just a little girl!

Jesus addressed the child in her own native Aramaic tongue but Mark provides the translation for the sake of his non-Jewish readers. Notice **(v42)** that she *'immediately'* stood up and even walked around. This was no sleep-walk but a living resurrection; the dead had been raised! Who dares doubt what God can do in a person's life? Who can doubt the miracle of salvation and new birth? With God all things are possible!

Regarding those who witnessed this event, the account states that *'they were completely astonished.'* They were dumbstruck! Were they dreaming? Did they really see this happen? Yes they did! Oh what unbelievable joy must have flooded the hearts of these parents, how can we ever understand their joy?

In **v43** Jesus gave *'strict orders'* to those present not to tell anyone about this. There is a sense in which, although this was part of His ministry, Jesus did not want this to be sensationalised so that He was looked on just as some super magician. The miracle would speak for itself in the days to come and this family would no doubt continue to grow in faith and have a wonderful testimony. How lovely is the concluding thought! The humanity and sensitivity of Jesus is demonstrated in His telling them to give the girl something to eat. What a beautiful thought! It is also further evidence that she had been raised to full life again.

Healing a sick woman. vv25-34

The circumstances of this woman were desperate! In **25** it is asserted that for twelve long years she had some form of bleeding that caused her great distress and weakness; it sapped every ounce of energy and strained her emotions to the limit. It is a miracle of grace that she survived to find her place in Holy Scripture. The likelihood is that her chronic illness was associated with women.[6]

As the story unfolds, **v26** reveals that, having spent all that she had on doctors' fees, she got worse instead of getting better. During these years her quality of life must have been very poor and her financial position ever declining as she paid doctor after doctor. Indeed, having expended all her resources, she may have been in a state of abject poverty.

Furthermore, because of the nature of her condition she would have been classed as 'unclean' and therefore unable to attend the synagogue and worship with others. In short, her illness would have affected her physically, financially, socially and spiritually. She had searched for a cure but was just getting worse! All this was about to change because of her encounter with Jesus!

Bereft of all hope, the feelings of this woman can only be imagined when she heard about Jesus (**v27**). At long last she might be cured! She wasted no time and *'came up behind him in the crowd and touched his cloak.'* In humility and in her attempt to remain anonymous she reached out to Jesus from

---

[6] Her affliction is not simply physical, however; her complaint was presumably vaginal bleeding (a fact that male commentators assume, but which most coyly omit to state!) and she is therefore unclean.' Black's New Testament Commentaries. The Gospel According to Mark. A & C Black. London. Morna D. Hooker. p148

behind. Note that Jesus is surrounded by a large crowd, all pressing against Him. What wonderful simplistic faith this woman had! She did not seek the Saviour's voice, touch or even His gaze; she says in **v28** *'If I just touch his clothes, I will be healed.'*

Twelve years of failure and frustration changed instantly, and all because she reached out and touched Jesus. A simple act which produced a miraculous result – this was the touch of faith! **Verse 29** *'Immediately her bleeding stopped, and she felt in her body that she was freed from her suffering.*

It is important to note that the initiative is taken by the woman; Jesus neither saw her, spoke to her, or touched her; yet in response to her faith Jesus knew that power had gone out from Him **(v30)**, and asked *'Who touched my clothes?* Notice how specific Jesus is; not who touched me, but my clothes! It may have seemed a foolish question to ask because of the physical pressure of those around Him – but this is what his disciples were undoubtedly thinking.

In **v31** they mildly rebuked Him, suggesting that He could not possibly identify one individual amidst this great number. The reason that Jesus asked such a question was because it was a 'touch of faith.' It would normally have been Jesus who reached out and did the touching – but not in this case. According to **v32** Jesus wanted to find this woman; *'Jesus kept looking around to see who had done it.'* He wanted to reward such faith with more than just physical healing (great as this was); He had other blessings in mind. Identifying her would also be good for her because it meant a public confession of faith, which would strengthen her in days to come.

Jesus found the woman; she could no longer maintain anonymity and came and fell at His feet **(v33)**, *'trembling with fear, told him the whole truth.'* She is trembling and in awe of Jesus as she pours out her soul to Him; the love and compassion that would emanate from His being is almost tangible in the text of Mark's account.

Her physical healing had already taken place (**v29**); then from being just one of this needy crowd, she entered into a relationship with Jesus. Jesus said to her *'Daughter, your faith has healed you.'* The fact that Jesus called her, 'daughter' indicates that she had come to faith.

This woman had entered into wholeness of body and soul, she received the blessing of healing her body, but by far the greater blessing was the gift of eternal life as she became a child of God. *'But now in Christ Jesus you who once were far away have been brought near .....'* (**Eph 2:13b**). Free from all her debilitating illness with all its implications, Jesus now said *'Go in peace and be freed from your suffering.'*

- After his encounter with Jesus, the demoniac was to be found sitting, clothed and in his right mind.
- As a result of the father's faith in Jesus, he witnessed his little girl being raised from the dead.
- Finally this chapter concludes with the picture of a woman being gloriously restored.
- In all cases the power of God is seen interacting through the simplicity of faith, leaving all these people with a testimony of the transforming power of God. Jesus was their only hope and they were not disappointed!

6

Jesus – a prophet without honour in His home town. 6:1-6a

> *'Jesus left there and went to his home town, accompanied by his disciples. When the Sabbath came, he began to teach in the synagogue, and many who heard him were amazed. 'Where did this man get these things?' they asked. 'What's this wisdom that has been given him, that he even does miracles! Isn't this the carpenter? Isn't this Mary's son and the brother of James, Joseph, Judas and Simon? Aren't his sisters here with us?' And they took offence at him. Jesus said to them, 'Only in his home town, and among his relatives and in his own house is a prophet without honour.' He could not do any miracles there, except lay his hands on a few sick people and heal them. And he was amazed at their lack of faith.'*

Nothing is so blind as the heart that cannot see! For thirty years Jesus, the Son of God had lived in this area of Nazareth. During that time the people were blissfully unaware of His true identity. Had they reflected on the purity and perfection of His life, surely they would have recognized something very special about Him – but not so! All that He was in character and conduct was lost to them. It is a plain fact of life that 'familiarity breeds contempt'. True greatness is rarely discernable by one's peers, family or friends: it was so with Jesus!

In **v1** Mark tells us that Jesus and His disciples moved on from where they were (Capernaum) and arrived at Nazareth, Jesus' home town. Entering the synagogue on the Sabbath Jesus began to teach. This would have been at the invitation of the synagogue ruler and therefore meant some form of recognition **(v2)**. It is worth noting that this would be the last time that Jesus would be depicted as welcome in a synagogue.

The response to His teaching was amazement! Many recognised His wisdom and charisma. This was not the usual repetition of Old Testament passages with predictable explanations. His words would have been relevant, informative and inspired. They could not understand where, or how, He acquired such knowledge and ability; they said *'Where did this man get these things? ... What's this wisdom that's been given him, that he even does miracles?'*

They are puzzled for at least two reasons.

Firstly, in **v3** they said *'Isn't this the carpenter?'* The Greek word used for 'carpenter' is TEKTON, and means more than just a joiner; it refers to a 'craftsman' - a person whose skills were wide-ranging in working with wood and possibly, even metal. As a craftsman Jesus would have been a man of the people, a man who was well liked and recognised for His contribution within the community.

Secondly, *'Isn't this Mary's son and the brother of James, Joseph, Judas and Simon?'* They knew His family, and in so doing considered Jesus to be no-one special, not distinct from His brothers or sisters. The fact that only His mother is referred to, with no mention of Joseph, tells us that Joseph was probably dead at this time. This being the case, it meant that Jesus would have spent His first thirty years with His own family and taken on the responsibilities as the head of the home, in accordance with Jewish custom.

And so the passage relates, for these two reasons, *'... they took offence at him.'* The people of Nazareth despised Him because they knew His family and background. Why should they commit themselves to a 'commoner? Who did He think He was?

According to **v4** it was Jesus Himself who recognised that He did not get the respect or honour that was due Him because He was known by them, and so He states a general truth, *'Only in his home town, among his relatives and in his own house is a prophet without honour.'* Rather than embrace the wonderful truth that Jesus taught, they could not get past their own prejudice.

Mark tells us in **vv5-6** that Jesus was limited in what He could do because of their lack of faith. He healed only a few sick people. What a contrast to the previous faith of the sick woman and the father with a dead child who was raised! Why should this be? Why should Jesus be limited in what He could do because of the low spiritual state of others?[1]

Since Jesus was the Son of God, and as such was omnipotent, there was indeed nothing that He could not do; He was all-powerful in every sense and His power could never diminish. When Mark says *'He could not do any miracles there'* he is not saying that Jesus was 'incapable,' but rather that He would not force His healing power where unbelief was prevalent.[2]

Jesus could say to the sick woman of **5:34** *'Daughter, your faith has healed you.'* It is not surprising, then, that **v6** records, *'And he was amazed at their lack of faith.'* There is a principle

---

[1] See Matthew 13:58.

[2] 'As the word will not produce spiritual growth where the capacity for response is barren, choked or scorched (4:1-20), so the presence of Jesus will not produce miracles in the atmosphere of total unbelief and resistance.' BST The Message of Mark. I.V.P. 1992. Donald English. p119.

here that also manifests itself in salvation, for Jesus will not force a person into a state of belief, but offers the gift of salvation to all who will come by faith. This is made clear in **Romans 1:16** *'I am not ashamed of the gospel, because it is the power of God for the salvation of everyone who believes'*, in **John 3:36** *'Whoever believes in the Son has eternal life, but whoever rejects the Son will not see life ...'*, in **John 3:15** *'that whoever believes in him may have eternal life'*, and in **Romans 1:17** *'For in the gospel a righteousness from God is revealed, a righteousness that is by faith from first to last.'*

This synagogue incident presents us with a strong reminder of the importance of faith; for it is faith in Jesus, the Son of God, which unlocks the vaults of heaven, so that His grace and mercy may fall upon all who are willing to receive it in accordance with His sovereign purpose.

The Twelve sent out on mission. 6:6b -13

> *'Then Jesus went round teaching from village to village. Calling the twelve to him, he sent them out two by two and gave them authority over evil spirits. These were his instructions: 'Take nothing for the journey except a staff – no bread, no bag, no money in your belts. Wear sandals but not an extra tunic. Whenever you enter a house, stay there until you leave that town. And if any place will not welcome you or listen to you, shake the dust off your feet when you leave, as a testimony against them.' They went out and preached that people should repent. They drove out many demons and anointed many sick people with oil and healed them.'*

Having moved from His home town of Nazareth where He was discredited, it was now time for Jesus and His disciples to teach in the local villages. For some time now the disciples had been with Jesus, listening, learning, and indeed being called to apostleship **(3:13-19)**, now it was time for their own ministry to begin. In **v7** Jesus called them to Him; no doubt with endearment and love, for He knew what lay ahead of them; not just in the days to come but in the years ahead. This was their mini launching out! Mark says *'he sent them out two by two and gave them authority over evil spirits.'* Two things to notice.

Firstly, He sent them out two by two. Why two by two?

Practically it made sense as a source of encouragement and mutual help.

To validate their ministry.

In both Old and New Testaments in certain circumstances two witnesses were called for.[3] In missionary enterprise, especially in the book of Acts, we find God's servants often working together – ie in **Acts 12:4** Paul and Barnabas, *'The two of them, sent on their way by the Holy Spirit.'*

Secondly, He *'gave them authority over evil spirits.'* Mark mentions this in distinction from other areas of ministry. Why does He specifically refer to *'authority over evil spirits'*? Because in all areas of ministry, the ministry of Jesus was seen as ushering in the Kingdom or reign of God; in so doing, the power of God would dispel and overcome the power of evil and kingdom of darkness. These kingdoms could not co-exist, and so He gave His disciples authority over all dark and demon powers, to cast them out as a demonstration that God's Kingdom had arrived in Jesus. A new Kingdom of love, power and righteousness had come!

In **vv8-11** they were given practical instructions for their ministry. **Verse 8** says that they are to take 'nothing' for their journey, *'no bread, no bag, no money...'* The only exception was a staff,[4] perhaps to protect themselves against any wild animals or snakes. Sandals are allowed and only one tunic, no more (**v9**).

---

[3] See Numbers 35:30. Deut 19:15. Matt 18:16. John 8:17. 2 Cor 13:1.

[4] According to Matt 10:10 and Luke 9:3 they are told NOT to take a staff.

From the details given by Mark, the meaning is clear; the resources, both spiritual and material for their future ministry would come from God, He would provide for them – they were called to a new way of living that meant absolute faith and dependence upon God. Their ministry was to be an expression of the ministry of Christ.

From **vv10-11** Jesus has two things to say about their accommodation and hosts.

Firstly, whatever house you enter, stay there until you leave. They had to exercise common courtesy to their host.

Secondly, where you are not made welcome or will not be listened to, show your disapproval when you leave by shaking the dust from your feet. In the East, hospitality was viewed as a sacred duty. It was not the responsibility of a stranger entering a village to seek accommodation, but the duty of the locals to offer it. Furthermore, to listen to their guests was good manners and to be expected. Hosts who were unwelcoming and impolite were actually rejecting both messenger and message.

To such people, shaking the dust off the feet was a testimony against them; a form of judgement or symbolic gesture of divine displeasure. Paul and Barnabas did this (see **Acts 13:50-51**).

Verses 12-13 summarise the ministry of the disciples at this time. Following in their Master's footsteps their first priority was to preach the word and challenge the people to repent, as Jesus did in **1:15.** A new message was being heard, for there was a new Kingdom to enter.

Not only did they preach the word but performed the miraculous through driving out demons, anointing the sick with oil and healing them. Apart from **James 5:14**, this is the only other reference to anointing with oil in relation to healing in the New Testament. The Greek word used in **James** is the verb ALEIPHOO, and means 'to grease or massage', it conveys the idea of the oil being used medically together with the prayer of faith.[5]

Though oil is often used when sick people are being prayed for, the value of the anointing is more symbolic as an act of fellowship than anything special about the oil itself. The ministry of the disciples must have been very successful, for in **v14** it is stated that it came to King Herod's attention.

King Herod's party and John the Baptist's death. 6:14-29

> *'King Herod heard about this, for Jesus' name had become well known. Some were saying, 'John the Baptist has been raised from the dead, and that is why miraculous powers are at work in him.' Others said, 'He is Elijah.' And still others claimed, 'He is a prophet, like one of the prophets of long ago.' But when Herod heard this, he said, 'John, the man I beheaded, has been raised from the dead.' For Herod himself had given orders to have John arrested, and he had him bound and put in prison. He did this because of Herodias, his brother Philip's wife, whom he had married. For John had been saying to Herod, 'It is not lawful for you to have your brother's wife.' So Herodias nursed a grudge against John and wanted to kill him. But she was not able to, because Herod feared John and wanted to protect him, knowing him to be a righteous and holy man. When Herod heard John, he was greatly puzzled; yet he liked to listen to him. Finally the opportune time came. On his birthday Herod gave a banquet for his high officials and military commanders and the leading men of Galilee. When the daughter of Herodias came in and danced, she pleased Herod and*

---

[5] For a wider understanding of 'anointing with oil' in relation to faith and healing, see The Patience of Hope (An exposition of James). AMG Publishers Chattanooga. Spiros Zodhiates. p121-124

> *his dinner guests. The King said to the girl, 'Ask me for anything you want and I'll give it to you.' And he promised her with an oath, 'Whatever you ask I will give you, up to half my kingdom.' She went out and said to her mother, 'What shall I ask for? 'The head of John the Baptist,' she answered. At once the girl hurried into the King with the request: 'I want you to give to me right now the head of John the Baptist on a platter.' The King was greatly distressed, but because of his oaths and his dinner guests, he did not want to refuse her. So he immediately sent an executioner with orders to bring John's head. The man went, beheaded John in the prison, and brought back his head on a platter. He presented it to the girl, and she gave it to her mother. On hearing this, John's disciples came and took his body and laid it in a tomb.*

Verses 14-16 bring before us three verdicts on Jesus. Due to the ministry of the disciples, news about Jesus had spread far and wide; now reaching King Herod.[6] There is no way of knowing the content of what Herod had heard about Jesus.

The fact that Mark records it this way, *'for Jesus' name had become well known'*, is synonymous with 'all He said and did.' The words *'some were saying'* introduce us to what was being said.

Some said John the Baptist had been raised. Although John had not performed any miracles, he still had a powerful and anointed ministry that led many to repent and seek God's Kingdom. The influence and effect of John's life caused some to think that he had been raised from the dead. John was

[6] 'Herod Antipas (son of Herod the Great) was not in fact king, but tetrarch (as Matthew and Luke both correctly record) of Galilee and Peraea from 4 BC to AD 39. A tetrarch exercised limited authority, being himself subject to, and dependent on Rome. It was Herod's request to Rome for the title of king which led to his deposition and banishment.' The Gospel According to St Mark. Black's New Testament Commentaries. A & C Black. 1991. Morna D Hooker. p159

regarded by many as a holy and righteous man and his life had made an enormous impact on people's lives as he paved the way for Jesus.

Some said that he was Elijah. True Jews waited for the coming Messiah and they believed that before His coming, Elijah, the greatest of all prophets in their eyes, would be raised to be his forerunner (predicted in **Malachi 4:5**). Rather than see Jesus as the Messiah, their clouded view only allowed them to consider Jesus as the resurrected Elijah.

Others said he is a prophet. Not too much can be said about this, but this third group considered Jesus as being a prophet like that of the Old Testament. (These opinions are also found in **8:28**).

Herod was quite emphatic in sharing his view, *'John, the man I beheaded, has been raised from the dead.'* Herod had mixed emotions, for although some time had passed since John's execution he was riddled with anxiety and had a deep sense of guilt, he could have stopped John's death but pride and loyalty to his oath prevented it. Perhaps Herod's opinion was more wishful thinking than a genuine belief, for this in some way would make him feel better about himself and the past. It must have pained Herod greatly to say *'John I beheaded.'* What follows is a retrospective view of John's execution.

Verses 17-20. How sad it is that Herod had John arrested, bound and put in prison just to please someone else - his unlawful wife, who in marrying him entered into an incestuous and adulterous relationship, for she was his brother Philip's wife. It is also possible that Herod had John put in prison for his own protection (**v20**). This is a sad story which confronts the reader with human nature, with all its deceit, treachery and hard heartedness exposed for all to see.

In Herod is seen something of a weak, unwise man who let his celebratory emotions run ahead of him, making spur-of-the-moment decisions that he would live to regret all his life. We see in this the great danger of acting on impulse. The source and irritation behind all this was the fact that John, as a preacher of the truth, had made it clear to Herod that he had broken the law by marrying Herodias. This in turn caused Herodias to nurse a grudge against John (**vv18-19**). She hated him and wished him dead.

Herod was in an unenviable position. On the one hand he was drawn to John; *'Herod feared John'*[7] and admired his *'righteous and holy'* character and teaching; *'he liked to listen to him'* even although it caused him distress **(v20).** On the other hand, he was committed to his wife, Herodias. It was difficult for Herod, he was in a no-win situation, yet with John in prison it enabled him to cope with them both, at least for a time.

Verses 21-23. It was Herod's birthday and a lavish banquet was arranged. All the high officials and important people were there, including the leading men of Galilee. This was not just a birthday party but an opportunity for Herod to impress the influential! Of all people to make their entrance, it had to be the daughter of Herodias (Salome) who would provide the entertainment by dancing. Her dancing pleased all who were present to such an extent that Herod, probably intoxicated, acted on impulse and with exaggerated emotions, committed himself to a course of action that he would live to regret.

As a way of showing his gratitude, Herod promised the girl anything she wanted up to half the value of his kingdom. What a mistake! Immediately the girl confides in her mother, who has no hesitation in asking for the head of John the Baptist (**v24**). Herodias' wildest dream had come true! (No doubt Herodias had already given thought to the possibility of reward following the dancing display!) Notice the sense of urgency – *'at once the girl hurried in to the king with the request: 'I want you to give me right now the head of John the Baptist on a platter'* (**v25**). How tragic and sad! Not just an execution, but John's head displayed on a 'platter' for all to see.

No time was to be wasted in case Herod changed his mind. Herodias had no sense of shame and this macabre request tells

[7] The Greek word used here for feared is PHOBEO and means 'to show reverential fear.'

us just how deep her hatred was. Sin had blinded her eyes and captured her evil and hardened heart. The voice of the preacher could be silenced. There would be no more stress because of John's ministry which exposed her unlawful relationship with Herod. The end of John would rid her of the inconvenience of facing the truth!

Verses 26-28. From the delight of dancing and pleasure of the occasion, Herod's emotions are suddenly reversed – *'The king was greatly distressed!* He made his promise on oath in the presence of his friends and dignitaries. He could not back down! And so reluctantly, he sanctioned the request for John's head on a platter. What a grotesque picture is generated in the mind! Yet perhaps it only endorses the condition of the heart that made such a request. Herein lie's the potential of the human heart.

According to **v29** John's disciples came to take his body and give him a proper burial. According to **Matthew 11:2ff** his disciples were allowed to visit him during his imprisonment. It therefore makes sense for their return to take away the decapitated body of John. It would seem that following John's death his disciples would have become followers of Jesus, as some did even while John was alive (see **John 1:35-37**).

Feeding the five thousand. 6:30-44

> *'The apostles gathered round Jesus and reported to him all they had done and taught. Then, because so many people were coming and going that they did not even have a chance to eat, he said to them, 'Come with me by yourselves to a quiet place and get some rest.' So they went away by themselves in a boat to a solitary place. But many who saw them leaving recognised them and ran on foot from all the towns and got there ahead of them. When Jesus landed and saw a large crowd, he had compassion on them, because they were like sheep without a shepherd. So*

> *he began teaching them many things. By this time it was late in the day, so his disciples came to him. 'This is a remote place', they said, 'and it's already very late. Send the people away so that they can go to the surrounding countryside and villages and buy themselves something to eat. But he answered, 'You give them something to eat.' They said to him, 'That would take eight months of a man's wages! Are we to go and spend that much on bread and give it to them to eat?' 'How many loaves do you have?' he asked. 'Go and see.' When they found out, they said, 'Five – and two fish.' Then Jesus directed them to have all the people sit down in groups on the green grass. So they sat down in groups of hundreds and fifties. Taking the five loaves and two fish and looking up to heaven, he gave thanks and broke the loaves. Then he gave them to his disciples to set before the people. He also divided the fish among them all. They all ate and were satisfied, and the disciples picked up twelve basketfuls of broken pieces of bread and fish. The number of men who had eaten was five thousand.'*

The miracle of 'feeding the five thousand' is the only miracle recorded in all four gospels, apart from the resurrection of Jesus. It is a simple yet profound story considered worthy by all gospel writers of inclusion in the Word of God. It was not done in secret or in a small room with only a few present, but before at least five thousand people.

The story begins in **v30** with the apostles meeting with Jesus and reporting back on their recent mission. They told Jesus both what they had done and taught. This had been their first tour of duty and no doubt they were eager to share all the detail of their mission. There would be (for Mark gives no detail) their excitement as they tell of demons cast out, healings and the power of the preached word drawing people to faith in Christ.

Faith in Christ at that time would have been somewhat primitive and based on limited knowledge and experience. There would have been much scope for the maturing of their faith. It was also an experience of faith in their commission, for their Master had not been with them! The response of Jesus in **vv31-32** is so in keeping with his character. People were coming and going, a hive of activity, all seeking the counsel and care of the great Physician.

Recognising how busy they had been and the energy that had gone forth from them, Jesus said *'Come with me by yourselves to a quiet place and get some rest.'* How touching and sensitive He is! They needed to regain their strength and be away from people for a time, and so they set out by boat for a solitary place.

How needy this is for all who seek to serve the Lord. There are times when giving out drains the human being, body and spirit, and it is essential to draw aside to the quiet place and enjoy the presence of the Father without feeling a failure or weak.

Verses 33-34. However, it was not possible for them to leave incognito – they were seen by many, who *'ran on foot from all the towns and got there ahead of them.'* It is not possible to gauge the excitement and anticipation of these large crowds. Mark is so explicit when he tells us they were running on foot. So eager were they that they arrived before Jesus and the apostles.

The planned rest would not happen! What would the response be? Instead of peace and tranquillity, there was a vast crowd clamouring for attention. Some would have said 'clear off, go home and give us peace, we are tired and need to rest.' But not Jesus. He would not turn them away.

Before the gaze of this vast crowd the Saviour opened up His heart. O what glorious words Mark brings before us! *'When*

Jesus....saw a large crowd, he had compassion on them because they were like sheep without a shepherd.' What did Jesus see? He saw their sickness, their sin, their stress, their emptiness, their spiritual hunger. Like straying sheep they were lost, hungry, harassed and helpless, without direction. The Greek word used for 'compassion' is SPLANCHNIZOMAI, and means 'to be moved from within.'

The Lord Jesus does not simply feel sorry for them – He is moved from His innermost being, and to such an extent that He wanted to help them. What He felt for them, no other human could feel – not even the apostles; it is the heart of God incarnate that is moved to reach out with tenderness and love to these people. And so the first priority is addressed – '... *he began teaching them many things.'* From the lips of the Saviour they receive precious manna from heaven that would satisfy their souls.

Verses 35-44. It's now getting late in the day and the apostles came to Jesus and reminded Him that this was a remote place and by now these people must be hungry. *'Send the people away'* they said, *'so that they can buy themselves some food.'* In **v37** Jesus' reply must have seemed strange to them; *'You give them something to eat.'*

What funds they had or had not we don't know, probably little or none, but they reckoned it would take the equivalent of eight months wages to buy them food. Why did Jesus say *'You give them something to eat?'* Here was an opportunity for them to trust their heavenly Father, and test their faith. So far the only options they came up with were either to 'send them away or find eight months wages.'

In **v38** Jesus teases them in the right direction by asking what resources they have – *'How many loaves do you have?'* They replied *'Five – and two fish.'* [8] The Lord was about to strengthen their faith by witnessing a quite unbelievable miracle. Jesus was really saying 'all that you have is all that you

8 According to John 6:9 the loaves and fish came from a boy. This being the case they must have been very small loaves and fish indeed.

need, when placed in the Master's hands.' Jesus asked no more from them than what they had! Yet when laid before the Lord, the ordinary became the extraordinary, the mundane became the miraculous and the natural became the supernatural. What a lesson we have here for all who follow Christ! Little is much in Jesus' hands!

From **vv39-44** we have the miracle itself. The time of year was obviously right for there to be green grass and the beauty of the location can only be imagined as the vast crowds are seated on the grass and have as their window the magnificent view over the Sea of Galilee. Jesus then instructed the disciples to have all the people sit down in a very organized and structured way **(v40)**. Acting in obedience was their initial commitment to faith, for they were preparing the people for something they had never seen before; unless these people were fed, the disciples were going to look foolish.

Taking just five loaves and two fish our Lord turns towards heaven with gratitude and also expectancy as He seeks the Father's approval and blessing **(v41)**. Though Jesus was moving in compassion to meet the hunger of these people, the overriding purpose of this miracle was that of glorifying God and authenticating the deity of Jesus.

John writes in **20:30-31** *'Jesus did many other miraculous signs in the presence of the disciples, which are not recorded in this book. But these are written that you may believe that Jesus is the Christ, the Son of God, and that by believing you may have life in his name.'* In **v41** Jesus passed the meagre resources to His disciples to distribute among the people – in doing so they would witness the miracle of abundance and become part of the miracle itself as they act in faith.

Then they all ate and were satisfied **(v42)**; every single one of them, no-one was left hungry. This was not a snack but a meal! This is an important lesson! No-one who comes to Jesus will ever be dissatisfied. Whether it be in mind, body or soul, ultimate satisfaction and fulfilment can only be experienced through faith in Jesus Christ.

This miracle provides us with a simple, yet profound example of just what God can do with so little when presented to Him. At times there may be a sense of smallness and insignificance, yet placed in the Master's hands it gives Him the opportunity to do something great and God glorifying.

Not only were all satisfied **(v43)**, but each disciple picked up a full basket of bread and fish. No matter how much God gives it never lessens His supplies.The apostle Paul writes in **Philippians 4:19** *'And my God will meet all your needs according to his riches in Christ Jesus.'* Nothing was left or wasted; it would be used in the days ahead. Notice also that there was more food left over than that with which they started! 'Our God is a great big God.' The final phrase reminding us of the numbers present in **v44** simply affirms the magnitude of the miracle.

Jesus walking on water. 6:45-52

> *'Immediately Jesus made his disciples get into the boat and go ahead of him to Bethsaida, while he dismissed the crowd. After leaving them, he went up on a mountainside to pray. When evening came, the boat was in the middle of the lake, and he was alone on land. He saw the disciples straining at the oars, because the wind was against them. About the fourth watch of the night he went out to them, walking on the lake. He was about to pass by them, but when they saw him walking on the lake, they thought he was a ghost. They cried out, because they all saw him and were terrified. Immediately he spoke to them and said, 'Take courage! It is I, don't be afraid.' Then he climbed into the boat with them, and the wind died down. They were completely amazed, for they had not understood about the loaves; their hearts were hardened.'*

The continued care of the Lord Jesus for His disciples is once again in evidence as Jesus *'made the disciples get into a boat and go on ahead of him to Bethsaida* (**v45**).' There were THREE possible reasons for this.

Firstly, the disciples were tired; they had been engaged in ministry on their own and also participating in the glorious miracle of abundance, they needed a break but were unlikely to get it while Jesus was in their company, so He sent them away for recuperation and rest. How sensitive He was to their needs!

Secondly, according to John's account of this in **6:14-15,** the crowds, after witnessing the feeding of the five thousand wanted to push things too far and install Jesus as a king by force. They were getting into a frenzy and Jesus did not want His disciples to get caught up in this contagious atmosphere. It would not be good for them!

Thirdly, He needed the communion of prayer with His Father **(v46)**. He had to unload His burden and replenish His strength; sense the smile of His Father and be affirmed in His mission. How difficult it must have been for Jesus, the perfect man, to walk on this earth, rub shoulders with sinful humanity; and all this on a journey that would lead Him to the cross. And so, having dismissed the crowd, *'he went up on a mountainside to pray.'* How Jesus managed to dismiss or disperse the crowd is not known, but we remember His unique authority.

In **v47** Mark tells that it was now evening. It is likely then, that Jesus had been in communion with His Father for several hours. At a time when the disciples were half-way across the lake and Jesus alone on the mountainside, '*he saw the disciples straining at the oars.'* He would have a good vantage point and the distance would have been about two miles. Rowing into a wind meant that they were '*straining at the oars.'* Jesus saw them in their struggle.

How true this is for every believer, the all-seeing eyes of deity capture every step and sense every struggle. As the

Psalmist records in **139:3** *....you are familiar with all my ways.'* So it is with these disciples, they come under the watchful eye of Jesus. **Verse 48** tells us that it was about the fourth watch of the night, possibly around 3am, that Jesus went out to them, walking on the lake.[9]

Amidst the various speculations as to why Jesus was about to pass by them, is the likelihood that He would catch their attention, which He did. Why did they think He was a ghost **(v49)**? Why did they not immediately recognise Him? Because at that time and under those circumstances they did not expect to see Him! They were startled and cried out; in fact they were terrified **(v50)**. The presence of someone walking on the water, and during the night would scare anyone. They had never seen Jesus do this before. Furthermore, their faith was still in its infancy.

Jesus intended to be noticed – that is why He left His place of communion, to come and join them. And what was the first thing He said to them **(v50)**? *'Take courage! It is I. Don't be afraid.'* Not a rebuke, but rather, words of encouragement and peace. They were far from perfect and their faith was weak – but He loved them and sought to alleviate their distress.

In this episode there is a lovely picture of the compassion of the Lord Jesus – recognising need and moving towards it (**see 6:34**). What a difference the presence of Jesus makes! They were now at peace. Back in **4:39** at His command the wind died down and the waves were made still, then as He entered the boat His very presence caused the wind once again to die down.

Verses 51-52 says that *'They were completely amazed, for they had not understood about the loaves; their hearts were hardened.'* At this point Mark refers to the miracle of the loaves and fish. In spite of participating in such a miracle they had still not understood what happened. It meant that up to this

---

[9] 'The Jewish night ran from 6pm -6am and was divided into four watches – 6 - 9pm. 9 – 12 midnight. 12 midnight - 3am and 3am – 6am.' The Daily Study Bible. The Gospel of Mark. The Saint Andrew Press – Edinburgh. 1979. William Barclay. p160-161

time they were unable to draw the necessary conclusions from all the miracles they had witnessed – they were still learning.

During our Lord's earthly ministry much of what they witnessed and had been part of would not be fully understood until after His death and resurrection. It is easy for believers today to question the disciples' inability and lack of perception, yet it is well to remember that every day with Jesus was a new experience for them, they had no Bible (although acquainted with the Old Testament) like we have as a basis for faith, no track record. History was in the making and they were part of it. In all this, both then and now, in Jesus, there is One who fully and graciously understands.

The demands of the people. 6:53-56.

> *'When they had crossed over, they landed at Gennesaret and anchored there. As soon as they got out of the boat, people recognised Jesus. They ran throughout the whole region and carried the sick on mats to wherever they heard he was. And wherever he went – into villages, towns or countryside – they placed the sick in the market-places. They begged him to let them touch even the edge of his cloak, and all who touched him were healed.'*

This little closing section addresses the popular continuation of Jesus' ministry. As soon as He stepped off the boat He was recognised and the people made towards Him. Such was their desire to be healed, restored and hear His words that *'They ran throughout the whole region.'* Nothing would stop them, they pressed upon Him and even *'begged him'* with a faith which was as yet in its infancy but which was full of expectation – if only they could just touch Him or even His clothes, they would be made whole.

Infancy of faith is suggested because the indication is that their desire was more for physical healing (what they could get out of it) than dealing with the condition of their spiritual needs – though no doubt, many were also restored spiritually. It is also clear from this event that the 'selfishness' of their desires (though understandable) did not stop Jesus blessing them. Irrespective as to their motives, these verses are a treasure trove, for they remind us of the Lord Jesus who can still restore, heal and bring wholeness. With Him, nothing was, and nothing is impossible!

7

The emptiness of external traditions. 7:1-23

'The Pharisees and some of the teachers of the law who had come from Jerusalem gathered round Jesus and saw some of his disciples eating food with hands that were 'unclean', that is, unwashed. The Pharisees and all the Jews do not eat unless they give their hands a ceremonial washing, holding to the tradition of the elders. When they come from the market- place they do not eat unless they wash. And they observe many other traditions, such as the washing of cups, pitchers and kettles. So the Pharisees and the teachers of the law asked Jesus, 'Why don't your disciples live according to the tradition of the elders instead of eating their food with 'unclean' hands?' He replied, 'Isaiah was right when he prophesied about you hypocrites; as it is written: 'These people honour me with their lips but their hearts are far from me. They worship me in vain; their teachings are but rules taught by men.' You have let go of the

> *commands of God and are holding on to the traditions of men.'*
> *And he said to them: 'You have a fine way of setting aside the commands of God in order to observe your own traditions! For Moses said, 'Honour your father and your mother, and, 'Anyone who curses his father or mother must be put to death.' But you say that if a man says to his father or mother: 'Whatever help you might otherwise have received from me is Corban' (that is, a gift devoted to God), then you no longer let him do anything for his father or mother. Thus you nullify the word of God by your tradition that you have handed down. And you do many things like that.'*
> *Again Jesus called the crowd to him and said, 'Listen to me, everyone, and understand this. Nothing outside a man can make him 'unclean' by going into him. Rather, it is what comes out of a man that makes him 'unclean'. After he had left the crowd and entered the house, his disciples asked him about this parable. 'Are you so dull?' he asked. 'Don't you see that nothing that enters a man from the outside can make him 'unclean'? For it doesn't go into his heart but into his stomach, and then out of his body.' (In saying this, Jesus declared all foods 'clean'.) He went on: 'What comes out of a man is what makes him 'unclean.' For from within, out of men's hearts, come evil thoughts, sexual immorality, theft, murder, adultery, greed, malice, deceit, lewdness, envy, slander, arrogance and folly. All these evils come from inside and make a man 'unclean'.*

In this passage Mark introduces the reader to the source of 'true religion,' which stood in contrast to the 'superficial religiosity'[1]

[1] 'Religiosity' derives from 'religiose' meaning 'Affectedly or extremely pious and sanctimoniously religious.' Collins Dictionary of the English Language. 1981.

of the Jewish hierarchy at that time. On every possible occasion the Pharisees and Scribes tried to discredit Jesus, always looking for opportunities to prove Him wrong. This section is about one such occasion when the religious leaders sent their investigators from their Jerusalem headquarters to deal with Jesus. Their mission was more to do with 'fault finding' than 'fact finding'.

The tradition of the Pharisees and Teachers. 7:1-5

The setting for this story finds the disciples of Jesus having something to eat. The Pharisees who were near Jesus and His disciples noticed (as only they would) that the disciples were eating with unclean hands, that is, unwashed. This gave them the opportunity to open up! '*Why don't your disciples live according to the tradition of the elders'* they asked?

On previous occasions they had already clashed with Jesus and His disciples. In **John 1:25** they questioned John the Baptist about his right to baptise. In **Mark 2:8** they wondered why the disciples were not fasting. Then in **2:24** they asked why the disciples were picking ears of corn on the Sabbath.

The Pharisees were very strict orthodox Jewish teachers and lawyers. Fundamentally, the law meant two things to them. The Ten Commandments and the first five books of the Old Testament are known as the Pentateuch. They also accepted the prophets. Their lives centred on rules and regulations, they were their religious safety barrier.

Apart from what they accepted from the Old Testament, they literally added thousands of rules and ordinances of their own. They went in for great detail and thrived on having knowledge of all the minute details of rules and clauses, sections and sub-sections, footnotes and references. Their own bits and pieces which they had added were known as 'the oral tradition of the elders', which Mark alludes to in **v13**, but in a different way, *'And you do many things like that'*.

The issue they addressed about the disciples eating with hands unwashed had nothing to do with their hands being dirty, hygiene, or even the law – only their tradition. The key is found in **vv3-4** and has to do with 'ceremonial washing of hands'. If these people had been anywhere near non-Jewish people, in particular at the market-place, they would engage in the 'ceremony of washing their hands' because they had been in contact with 'Gentiles'.

Their tradition taught that unless they washed in this way they were considered to be 'unclean'. They made a great show of all this – pride and self-exaltation! In all their rites and rituals they wanted others to think they were very righteous and holy.

Here we have a religion that seemed to be more about outward appearance than inner reality, just a shell, skin deep! So in **v5** they challenged Jesus, asking Him why His disciples had not 'decontaminated' themselves by 'ceremonial washing'.

The condemnation of Jesus. 7:6-13

The first thing Jesus did was to point to Scripture, in particular to the words of Isaiah the prophet (**29:13),** found here in **vv6-7** *'These people honour me with their lips, but their hearts are far from me. They worship me in vain; their teachings are but rules taught by men.'* Jesus is quite scathing, and leaves them in no doubt about their falsehood. He called them 'hypocrites'. The Greek word used here is HUPOKRITES, and means 'a play actor', pretending to be something they were not. This is the only occasion in Mark where Jesus used this word, but He uses it fifteen times in Matthew and four in Luke.

Jesus was always caring, loving and kind to the outcast, sick, poor and hungry, but for these hypocrites He had nothing but contempt, for their outward expression of religion was all that it should not have been. There was nothing spiritual about their religion, just an empty facade that exalted man, and not God. But they were left in no doubt about the reasons for Jesus' criticism. In **vv8-9** Jesus told them where they had gone wrong. He cites three areas.

- They had **substituted** their own word for God's - **v8** *'You have let go of the commands of God and are holding on to the traditions of men'.*
- They had also **rejected** God's word - **v9** *'You have a fine way of setting aside the commands of God in order to observe your own traditions'.*
- They had **robbed** God's word of its power - **v13** *'Thus you nullify the word of God'.*

The barrenness of their attitude towards God's word was almost unbelievable, yet in their own darkened spiritual state they were oblivious to the severity of their actions. To emphasise His point, Jesus quoted from Moses, regarding a child's attitude and responsibilities to his parents. What He said should have been understood by them, but it seemed to have made no difference.[2]

Jesus' rebuke of these Pharisees ought to be a solemn warning to all who are tempted to travel down the empty road of legalism and ritual, which may be considered to be a denial of the gospel of Christ, and the absence of love, light, grace and truth. Their legalistic position did more to break people, than to make them whole.

The heart of the matter. 7:14-23

Jesus now gathered the crowd around Him to explain the true source of spirituality. It has nothing to do with the external; it is all about the heart. No matter how clean a person is on the outside it will have no bearing on the condition of his heart, that is, his spirituality. **1 Samuel 16:7** declares that *' .....The Lord does not look at the things man looks at. Man looks on the outward appearance, but the Lord looks at the heart'.* Jesus is both logical and practical in His response for He says *'Nothing*

[2] It is not at all easy to understand the clear meaning of v10-12. However, William Hendriksen makes helpful suggestions in his New Testament Commentary. Banner of Truth Trust. 1975. p277-278

outside a man can make him unclean' **(v15)**. He is referring to the heart, for no amount of pampering or attention given to the body will produce the righteous and holy life.

What Jesus sought to impress upon the people was the true nature of salvation. This could not be found by adhering to rules and regulations, form and ritual pseudo holiness – it was not about 'outward pomp', it could not be obtained by works. **Ephesians 2:9** states of salvation *'It is the gift of God – not by works, so that no-one can boast'*. Therefore, no amount of 'self-effort' could make a person right in God's sight. The rich young man in **Matthew 19:16-30** was under the same delusion as this Pharisaic delegation. He said to Jesus in **v16** *'What good thing must I do to get eternal life?'* [3]

Some time later when Jesus was away from the crowd and the Pharisees, the disciples asked Him to expand on what He had been saying. He responded in **v18** with *'Are you so dull?'* Behind this rather terse response, Jesus is making the point that, unlike those blind traditionalists, He expected them, having spent so much time with Him, to have a better understanding.

Jesus explained to them, in plain logic, about the physical anatomy – that is, when food is eaten it goes into the stomach, it is processed and then the waste is ejected, it has nothing to do with the heart. So then, what a person eats has no direct bearing on his or her spiritual state or rightness before God; that is why Mark adds his own understanding of the words of Jesus in **v19** *'(In saying this, Jesus declared all foods clean')*.

In **vv20-23** Jesus made a final point; it is the state of the heart that will be the determining factor on what comes from a person's life (*For from within, out of men's hearts, come ....'* **v21***)*. He then goes on to list moral and spiritual defilements that come from the heart. Heading up this list, Jesus refers to *'evil thoughts'*. The springboard for all that is good or bad, righteous or evil, comes from our 'thinking'. All courses of action find their source in the mind; that is why the believer is

[3] Mark 7:16 in the Authorised Version reads 'If any man have ears to hear, let him hear'. Some manuscripts do not have this verse, including the N.I.V.

challenged to submit his mind to the things of Christ, so that his mind comes under the influence and power of God.

In **Romans 12:2** Paul writes *'be transformed by the renewing of your mind'*. It is from the renewed mind that right thoughts and actions come. Again in **Philippians 3:19**, referring to those who were set against Christ and the cross, Paul writes *'Their mind is on earthly things'*. Writing in **Colossians 3:2** Paul once again challenged his readers to *'Set your minds on things above'*. It is safe to suggest that when the Lord has a person's mind, then He will have their heart; hence the importance of what is allowed to enter the mind.

The catalogue of varying evils listed by Mark (**vv21-23**), is probably not with the intention of them being raised as subject matter for discussion. It was to make the all-important point – that all these evils and more - the list could be endless - do not find their source externally, in particular, linked to the ceremonial washing of hands.

The list provided was meant to be a sample or example of sinful actions that come from the heart. They point to evil that degrades God's human creation, commits offence against others, exalts self, and is the product of the sinful nature that is devoid of the life of Christ. Jesus draws no distinction between sins of the mind and sinful actions – all of them begin from within, hence **v21** *'For from within, out of men's hearts ....'*

Faith of the Syro-Phoenician woman rewarded. 7:24-30

> *'Jesus left that place and went to the vicinity of Tyre. He entered a house and did not want anyone to know it; yet he could not keep his presence secret. In fact, as soon as she heard about him, a woman whose little daughter was possessed by an evil spirit came and fell at his feet. The woman was a Greek, born in Syrian Phoenicia. She begged Jesus to drive the demon out of her daughter. 'First let the children eat*

> *all they want,' he told her, 'for it is not right to take the children's bread and toss it to their dogs.' 'Yes, Lord,' she replied, 'but even the dogs under the table eat the children's crumbs.' Then he told her, 'For such a reply, you may go; the demon has left your daughter.' She went home and found her child lying on the bed, and the demon gone.'*

Jesus now moves to the area of Tyre.[4] In doing so He moved away from a largely Jewish region into Gentile territory; a move that was not typically Jewish, yet it makes sense with the earlier incident in mind, where Jesus taught about clean and unclean foods. Could it be that, symbolically, there is an allusion of bridging the gap between clean and unclean people?

Mark tells us that Jesus entered a house, the exact house is uncertain. It is reasonable to suggest that rest and respite would have been most welcome, for He did not want anyone to know He was there. Mark states that, try as He might, it was impossible to get around completely incognito **(v24)**.

Throughout the gospels there is a continual dichotomy, where Jesus was engaged in public ministry that bore testimony to His deity, yet did not want to attract too much (or the wrong) attention before His entrance into Jerusalem, which eventually led to his crucifixion.

In **v25**, Mark introduces a woman who heard that Jesus was there and wasted no time in coming to Him, for she had a great need, and believed that her need could only be met by Jesus. How much information she had with regard to Jesus' previous activity is not clear, but one thing is obvious – whatever she had learned about Him and His ministry seems to have drawn her to true faith. And so arriving at this home and seeing Jesus, she fell at His feet – a mark of submission and deep humility.

---

[4] This is the Tyre whose kings in bygone days had formed an alliance with David and Solomon. It furnished timber and skilled artisans for Israel, while the latter shipped to Hiram and later rulers the grain needed by Trye's people (1 Kings 5. Acts 12:20). It was Tyre that had introduced Baal worship into Israel. William Hendrisen, New Testament Commentary. Banner of Truth Trust. 1975. p297

Two questions may be asked.

Who was this woman? Verse **26** tells that she was a Greek, born in Syrian Phoenicia. In religious terms this meant that she was pagan, not a Jew, and as such, was breaking the rules of tradition between Jew and Gentile by coming and falling at Jesus' feet, and also because she was a woman. However, her need was of greater importance than falling in line with protocol or tradition. Due to the fact that no mention is made of her husband it is probable that she was also a widow.

What was her need? Her daughter **(v25)** was possessed by an evil (or unclean) spirit and her mother saw in Jesus the only hope of deliverance. She loved her child and longed for normality in her little life, as any mother would, so she fell at Jesus' feet and begged (or pleaded with) Him to drive out the demon.

Jesus' response to this woman in **v27** is easier to comprehend if we think on the word '*children*' as a reference to the 'Jews' and the word '*dogs*' to the 'Gentiles'. Unless this is understood, the words of Jesus could seem harsh and insensitive, which of course He could never be. How then did Jesus' reply? He said that His ministry was firstly to the Jews, in spite of their unbelief and rejection **(Jn 1:11-12)**, but not exclusively so.

Though his commitment was firstly to the Jews, by the use of the word *'first'* in **v27**, Jesus surely indicates that the Gentiles were not without hope. In the book of Acts this principle was being worked out in the great missionary enterprise of the early Church as the word of God also reached the Gentiles.[5] The apostle Paul writes in **Romans 1:16** *'I am not ashamed of the gospel, because it is the power of God for the salvation of everyone who believes: first for the Jew, then for the Gentile.'*

This woman responded to Jesus with a wonderful expression of faith **(v28)** – *'Yes, Lord'* she said. Although the

[5] From Peter's vision in Acts 10 regarding the expansion and attitude of ministry to the gentiles, we read in v34 -35. 'I now realise how true it is that God does not show favouritism but accepts men from every nation who fear him and do what is right.'

word 'Lord' could mean 'Sir', Mark chooses to use 'Lord', for it suitably described the spiritual state of the woman. She suggested to Jesus that although food on the table was meant for those sitting at the table, yet there are still crumbs that fall off which dogs under the table may eat.

Here was a woman of faith, perhaps faith as small as a crumb, yet it was not the volume of her faith that mattered, but the direction of it, her faith was in Jesus the Son of God, her trust was in Him alone for the restoration of her little girl. What an important principle is taught by this woman; her faith finds only one direction – Jesus!

In **v29** her persistent faith is suitably rewarded, Jesus saying to her – *'For such a reply, you may go; the demon has left your daughter.'* Believing what Jesus said she returned home and found her daughter to be delivered of the evil spirit that had tormented her (**v30**). She is lying in bed at peace and resting, perhaps, for the first time in her short life. The mother must have been overwhelmed with joy and gratitude for all that her Lord had done.

Jesus heals a man who cannot speak or hear. 7:31-37

> *'Then Jesus left the vicinity of Tyre and went through Sidon, down to the Sea of Galilee and into the region of the Decapolis. There some people brought to him a man who was deaf and could hardly talk, and begged him to place his hand on the man. After he took him aside, away from the crowd, Jesus put his fingers into the man's ears. Then he spat and touched the man's tongue. He looked up to heaven and with a deep sigh said to him, 'Ephphatha!' (which means, 'Be opened!'). At this, the man's ears were opened, his tongue was loosened and he began to speak plainly. Jesus commanded them not to tell anyone. But the more he did so, the more they kept talking*

> *about it. People were overwhelmed with amazement. 'He has done everything well,' they said. 'He even makes the deaf hear and the mute speak.'*

Mark now tells that Jesus moved away from the region of Tyre and headed down to the Sea of Galilee into the region of the Decapolis.[6] That He travelled through Sidon, which is almost twenty miles to the north, indicates that He must have taken a circular route. Why He chose to go north before heading south is not vital to understanding the narrative; it is enough to know that Jesus had a reason.

On Jesus' previous visit to this area the people asked Him to leave them (**5:17**); on this occasion, however, they begged for His help. Perhaps with the passing of time and seeing the change in the demoniac's life (**5:15**), they too had changed in their attitude towards Jesus!

Verse 32 provides the reason why these people begged Jesus to help. They brought a man to Him, who had what seemed to be a twofold disability - hearing and speech impediments! He was obviously well known and cared for by them. Otherwise why should they be concerned about his difficulties? In bringing the man to Jesus it is safe to suggest the presence of faith in the people and the man. To have one of these disabilities is sad enough, but to have both, it must be almost impossible to understand, or enter into the daily implications of life.

Mark states that the man '*could hardly talk*'. Whether this means that his speech was impaired because he could not hear (which is not unknown), or had an actual problem with talking, is uncertain. Either way, the people brought a man who needed to be healed. Believing that Jesus could heal him, they begged Him to place His hand on the man (**v32**). The Greek word used for 'begged' is PARAKLEO, and means 'to call to one's aid', and is used for the kind of calling which is meant to produce a particular effect.

---

[6] See Mark 5:20 for more information on the word 'Decapolis'.

So then, these people begged Jesus, with the expectation of healing! The request for Jesus to place His hand on the man may have been based on something previously witnessed by them, for Mark records in **6:5** ' .... *except lay his hands on a few sick people and heal them'*. See also **5:23** and **8:23**.

In **v33** Mark says that Jesus took this man aside, away from the crowd. Jesus wanted this to be a private consultation, away from public glare. This was to be a time of intimacy and personal healing which would gloriously transform this man and also bring glory to God. By taking him aside, readers are reminded of the personal interest, love and compassion of Jesus. Then Jesus put His fingers into the man's ears and also touched his tongue. Why did He do this? Does this not seem rather crude (for He also spat on his fingers)? This man was deaf to Jesus' words – but was sensitive to his touch. Jesus made contact with him in a way that directed the man's attention to his impediments. The fact that Jesus 'spat' suggests no vulgarity, for in those days saliva was often associated with healing (see **John 9:6** for another example).

Having looked up to heaven **(v34)**, and with a deep sigh (or groan of sympathy) said to him *'Ephphatha',*[7] (which means, 'Be opened!') Notice that Jesus firstly looked to 'heaven' and then addressed the man. This was to show that His help came from above. Heaven was involved in this miracle of grace! This man and his needs mattered to the Father in heaven, who expressed His feelings through Jesus His Son.

Verse 35 leaves us in no doubt about the result! His *'ears were opened, his tongue was loosened and he began to speak plainly'*. The One who uttered a few words and the whole of Creation sprang into being (**Heb 1:2**), now commands the healing and restoration of this poor man. As a result of his encounter with Jesus, he would never be the same again – his life would bear testimony to the grace and power of God.

This was not the first occasion when Jesus gave orders not to tell anyone (**see 5:43**), yet it made no difference! It is

---

[7] The word 'EPHPHATHA' meaning 'Be Opened' is an Aramaic word which was Jesus` mother tongue.

understandable that silence must have been impossible; the joy and excitement of this man, and those who brought him to Jesus, can only be imagined. Not only was there great joy, but **v37** informs us that the *'people were overwhelmed with amazement'*. In spite of their initial faith, the end product seemed more wonderful to them than ever they anticipated.

This story fulfilled the intended purpose of the miraculous ministry of Jesus. Though such miracles were a great blessing to those who were on the receiving end of Jesus' words and touch, they were intended, primarily, to be a testimony to the deity of Jesus; affirming Him as the Son of God.[8] Mark leaves us in no doubt about this, for it is the first subject which he introduces to his readers in **1:1** *'The beginning of the gospel about Jesus Christ, the Son of God'*. How fitting were the words of the people in **v37** *'He has done everything well'*.

---

[8] John 3:2 '.......For no-one could perform the miraculous signs you are doing if God were not with him'.

8

Jesus feeds the four thousand. 8:1-10

'During those days another large crowd gathered. Since they had nothing to eat, Jesus called his disciples to him and said, 'I have compassion for these people; they have already been with me three days and have nothing to eat. If I send them home hungry, they will collapse on the way, because some of them have come a long distance.' His disciples answered, 'But where in this remote place can anyone get enough bread to feed them?' 'How many loaves do you have?' Jesus asked, 'Seven,' they replied. He told the crowd to sit down on the ground. When he had taken the seven loaves and given thanks, he broke them and gave them to his disciples to set before the people, and they did so. They had a few small fish as well; he gave thanks for them also and told the disciples to distribute them. The people ate and were satisfied. Afterwards the disciples picked up seven basketfuls of broken pieces that were left over. About four thousand men were present.'

It is difficult to read this narrative without thinking of the feeding of the five thousand in **6:30-44**. There are some scholars, who, because of the degree of similarity, consider viewing these events as one and the same.[1] However, in **v1** Mark writes, *'another large crowd.'* The Revised Standard Version uses the word *'again'* whilst the New English Bible records *'on another occasion'*.

Apart from these expressions, which indicate more than one event, there is no reason why there should not be two. After all, Mark records what he has personally witnessed and is bearing testimony to what he had seen. There was no need for him to duplicate and amend.

This second miracle was important for the continued development of the disciples **(vv17-21)** and also to meet the needs of the recipients. Furthermore, in the gospels, we only have a selection of all the miracles performed by Jesus (See **John 20:30-31: 21:2**). Guided by the Holy Spirit, the gospel writers had to be selective. Unless two events actually took place, it would make little sense for Mark to record the same event twice, thereby adding unnecessary narrative, possibly to the exclusion of other material. We may also note that Jesus Himself refers to both miracles **(vv19-20)**.

Gathering His disciples around Him **(vv1-3)**, Jesus now shares His feelings for those who had travelled, some a long distance, to listen to His teaching. They had listened for three days and had little or nothing to eat. Once again we read of the 'self-declared' compassion of Jesus. He said *'I have compassion for these people.'* He felt what they felt, and understood both their physical and spiritual needs. In every sense, He was compassionate. The Greek word used both in **6:34** and **8:2** for 'compassion' is SPLANCHNIZOMAI, and means 'To be moved from within'.

---

[1] 'The dominant critical opinion is that there was one event which was reported in various forms in the tradition and a highly divergent version provided the basis for the second feeding reported in Ch 8:1-9. The New London Commentary on the New Testament. The Gospel of Mark. Marshall, Morgan and Scott. 1974. William L. Lane. p271

The Lord Jesus did not simply feel sorry for them – He was moved from His innermost being; and to such an extent, that He wanted to help them. What He felt for them no other human could feel. Both the deity and humanity of Jesus are wonderfully displayed in events such as this.

Such was their physical weakness that Jesus believed they would collapse before they reached home. Never should a believer doubt for one fleeting moment that Jesus cares and understands for every detail and aspect of life. We read in **Matthew 10:29-31** *'Are not two sparrows sold for a penny? Yet not one of them will fall to the ground apart from the will of your Father. And even the very hairs of your head are numbered. So don't be afraid; you are worth more than many sparrows.'*

Jesus already knew what He intended to do, but He wanted to awaken the disciples to the need around them, so they would in some measure feel a sense of responsibility for this needy gathering. And so in **v4** they respond, *'Where in this remote place can anyone get enough bread to feed them?'* It seemed that the disciples had not retained the lesson from the past similar experience.

How easy it might be to criticise the disciples for their seeming lack of understanding, yet, those who seek to follow Jesus may be made only too aware of their own weakness of faith and understanding. But for the differing amounts of bread and fish, the narrative that follows in **vv5-8** is very similar to **6:38-44**. In both accounts there are **two** points of interest worthy of highlighting.

Firstly, in **6:42** and **8:8**, we may note that *'they all ate and were satisfied.'* Although this refers to their physical hunger, there is also the spiritual aspect of satisfaction. These people had feasted on the Master's teaching for three days; it therefore seems reasonable to suggest that they had also benefitted spiritually, indeed, more than that, they had been 'satisfied'. Their initial desire to make their way to Jesus was not their physical hunger (this was the result of coming), but spiritual.

Secondly, in **6:41** and **8:6** Mark writes *'When he had taken seven loaves and given thanks, he broke them and gave them to the disciples to set before the people.'* On each occasion it was the disciples who served and played a vital part in this miracle. They saw everything! They saw how much could be done with so little when God was involved. This was a lesson, though not fully appreciated at the time, on which they must surely have reflected at a later date.

The time would come, when, in all their spiritual infancy and inexperience as apostles, they would discover how much God could accomplish through them. These events proved to be a necessary training ground for their spiritual growth and development. It is not surprising then, that Mark records two very similar events.

In **v9** Mark finds it important to inform his readers that there were four thousand men present. The exact number, who were fed spiritually and physically, we cannot be certain, for there must also have been women and children present. Though numbers may not be the all important thing, they do help us understand the magnitude of the grace, love and power of God. In this miracle we see that Jesus is not only able to repeat these mighty works, but also perform them before Jew and Gentile. From that situation **(v10)**, Jesus and His disciples got into a boat and went to the region of Dalmanutha (probably located south of Gennesaret.)

The Pharisees look for a sign. 8:11-13

> *'And having sent them away, he got into the boat with his disciples and went to the region of Dalmanutha. The Pharisees came and began to question Jesus. To test him, they asked him for a sign from heaven. He sighed deeply and said, 'Why does this generation ask for a miraculous sign? I tell you the truth, no sign will be given to it.' Then he left them, got back into the boat and crossed to the other side'.*

Moving from the previous location, Jesus arrived at the western, more Jewish (although still ethnically mixed) side of the Sea of Galilee. The Pharisees wasted little time in approaching Jesus. They had already confronted Him on previous occasions (**2:6,16; 3:22; 7:1,2**). Verse **11** informs us of their purpose, *'The Pharisees came and began to ask him questions.'* Having previously heard Jesus' teaching, and having witnessed some of the miracles, they now pressed Jesus further, asking for a *'sign from heaven.'* The request for a sign was *'to test him.'* Their motive was not to learn, but to find fault. But why did they ask for a sign? Many false prophets appeared around that time, claiming to be the Messiah, and promised the people special signs.

The Pharisees wanted to discredit Jesus and were asking Jesus to do something supernatural and spectacular - not just the usual tricks employed by other false prophets, but by defying the laws of nature and astonishing people. The words *'from heaven'* indicate that they looked for a quite extraordinary sign! Any thought of Jesus being the Son of God was a great threat to them - if only Jesus would attempt something and fail in public view!

Underlying their test question lay a spirit of unbelief, for genuine faith does not insist on signs. The Pharisees looked for a reason to remain the way they were; for even a suitable sign or miracle would not convince them. **Matthew** writes in his gospel, **12:38-39** *'Then some of the Pharisees and teachers of the law said to him, 'Teacher, we want to see a miraculous sign from you.' He answered, 'A wicked and adulteress generation asks for a miraculous sign! But none will be given it except for the sign of Jonah.'*

Their request was met with Jesus' grief and disappointment! In **v12** Jesus refused to yield to their request. The words *'sighed deeply'* indicate that Jesus was grieved in His innermost being at their unbelief and hardness of heart. The Pharisees' attitude was the very antithesis of faith. The

Greek word used for 'sigh' is ANASTENAZO, and means a sigh that is *'deep drawn'* and is only used on this occasion in the New Testament.

Jesus often rewarded simple faith by the manifestation of His power, for the wellbeing of human beings and the glory of God. But on this occasion, He removed himself from this group without satisfying their devious and faithless demands **(v13)**. With His disciples, Jesus got into the boat and crossed to the other side of the Lake.

The yeast of the Pharisees. 8:14-21

> *'The disciples had forgotten to bring bread, except for one loaf they had with them in the boat. 'Be careful,' Jesus warned them. 'Watch out for the yeast of the Pharisees and that of Herod.' They discussed this with one another and said, 'It is because we have no bread.' Aware of their discussion, Jesus asked them, 'Why are you talking about having no bread? Do you still not understand? Are your hearts hardened? Do you have eyes but fail to see, and ears but fail to hear? And don't you remember? When I broke the loaves for the five thousand, how many basketfuls of pieces did you pick up?' 'Twelve,' they replied. 'And when I broke the seven loaves for the four thousand, how many basketfuls of pieces did you pick up?' They answered, 'Seven.' He said to them, 'Do you still not understand?'*

There is a sadness associated with this part of the narrative. Having recently fed more than ten thousand people from a very small quantity of bread and fish, the impact and lessons from those events seem to have made little impression on the disciples. How disappointed Jesus must have been!

In spite of the shortage of bread being the central issue, which brought about two glorious miracles, Mark, in **v14**, draws to the reader's attention the fact that the disciples had forgotten to bring bread for their own personal use, except just one loaf. With bread as the topic of conversation, Jesus presents them with a warning.

He used the word 'yeast' (or leaven), which was an essential ingredient in bread, to refer to the 'false teaching' of the Pharisees. Jesus said *'Watch out for the yeast of the Pharisees....* **(v15)**' [2] What did Jesus mean by 'watch out for the yeast (or teaching) of the Pharisees?' Simply this! Their teaching, at that time, involved a rejection of Jesus' teaching. They had hardened their hearts against what He taught and did.

In response to this warning, the disciples had a discussion **(v16)** and said '*It is because we have no bread.*' We read in **v17** that Jesus was aware of their discussion, and almost exasperated with them said, *'Why are you talking about having no bread?* In other words, 'Is that all you can think about - bread?' Clearly, they are at cross purposes, and do not understand what Jesus said.

Now, with four direct questions **(vv17-18)**, Jesus targets their own inaptitude to understand. Although Jesus is pointing to the hard heartedness of the Pharisees, He is faced, sadly, with His disciples, in some measure suffering from hard hearts also.

- *'Do you still not see or understand?'*
- *'Are your hearts hardened?'*
- *'Do you have eyes but fail to see, and ears but fail to hear?'*
- *'And don't you remember?'*

Then, referring to both miracles, with facts and figures, Jesus reminded them of what they had recently witnessed,

[2] 'Leaven' is a familiar metaphor in the New Testament and rabbinic literature, and usually stands for something evil (cf 1 Cor 5:6-8. Gal 5:9; contrast Matt 13:33 / Luke 13:20f). The Gospel according to St Mark. A & C Black (Publishers Ltd) 1991. Morna D Hooker. p194.

indeed, they had been part of it **(vv19-20)**. In both cases, to drive home His message, Jesus invited their response. Then in **v21** Jesus, almost reluctantly, had to say – *'Do you still not understand?'* One can sense the disappointment and sadness in Jesus' words. He had expected more from them.

Due to the period of time that the disciples had spent with Jesus, their lack of insight and understanding is surprising. Yet, Jesus was patient with them – they were still learning, still making mistakes, still slow to understand, still not what they should have been. But Jesus had plans for them; they mattered to Him – even in their weakness and smallness of faith His love remained constant, His care never lessoned, and His purpose never diminished. How encouraging this must be for all who seek to follow Jesus!

The healing of a blind man. 8:22-26

> *They came to Bethsaida, and some people brought a blind man and begged Jesus to touch him. He took the blind man by the hand and led him outside the village. When he had spat on the man's eyes and put his hands on him, Jesus asked, 'Do you see anything?' He looked up and said, 'I see people; they look like trees walking around.' Once more Jesus put his hands on the man's eyes. Then his eyes were opened, his sight was restored, and he saw everything clearly. Jesus sent him home, saying 'Don't go into the village.'*

Jesus and His disciples arrived at Bethsaida, which was situated on the north-eastern side of the Sea of Galilee. This was also the village where Peter lived **(Jn 1:44)**. Although Mark refers to Bethsaida as a 'village', Luke, in **9:10f**, (where the feeding of the five thousand took place), called it a 'town.' There is no discrepancy here since Bethsaida was a developing and expanding place. This narrative **(vv22-26)** is only found in Mark's gospel, and like all other miracles, is unique, for though there were many similarities with some miracles, no two are entirely identical.

Once again we discover people who cared for their friend that was blind (**see 2:2: 7:32**). They wanted him to be healed and, obviously, with Jesus' arrival came the opportunity for this to happen. The fact that Mark is saying they *'begged Jesus to touch him'*, helps us to understand how much they cared for him. The Greek word used for 'begged' is PARAKLEO, and means 'to call to one's aid', and is used for the kind of calling which is meant to produce a 'particular effect.' So then, these friends begged Jesus, with the expectation of healing!

As was often the case **(v23)**, Jesus took the blind man outside the village. Privacy in performing miracles seems to have been a feature in Mark's gospel, where faith was expressed away from public gaze (**5:40; 7:33**). It is worthy of note that Mark includes detail such as - Jesus took the man *'by the hand and led him outside.'* In this kindly and gentle act, the compassion, love and humility of Jesus are in evidence. Here we have the King of Kings and Lord of Lords, indeed, the Son of God, expressing physically how He felt from within, to just one man.

This is a most unusual miracle; sometimes referred to as a 'two stage' miracle. Jesus, having spat on, or touched the man's eyes with saliva, and put His hands on him, invited the man to tell what has happened. It seems right to assume that both the blind man and his friends had faith, that is why they came to Jesus – yet, complete healing does not take place immediately. Rather than complete restoration of sight, the man saw people walking around like trees, indicating only partial vision **(v24)**!

In **v25** Jesus repeated the procedure, only then did the man see with complete clarity *'he saw everything clearly.'* Exactly why this miracle comes in 'two stages' has not been revealed to us. We can be certain that it was not a lack of power on Jesus' part.

There is a somewhat recent view that the lack of faith was the problem. This view, however, carries little weight since Jesus Himself taught that even faith as small as a mustard seed could remove mountains **(Mtt 17:20)**.[3] Although Jesus encouraged growth and increase in faith, the all-important thing is the direction of faith – not in self – but in Him!

The story ends with Jesus sending the healed man home, but commanding him not to go into the village (or town). Why did Jesus warn him? A similar warning had been given to others **(1:44: 7:36)**. Perhaps this was to avoid any false expectation regarding the nature of His Kingdom, and to avoid unnecessary excitement and distraction, before his entrance into Jerusalem which would eventually lead to His crucifixion.

The difference in this man's journey home can only be imagined. No longer did he need to be led and guided by others, now he could see every step of the way and enjoy the beauty of the surrounding land, probably for the first time. What a difference Jesus made to his life!

Peter's confession of Christ. 8:27-30

> *Jesus and his disciples went on to the villages around Caesarea Philippi. On the way he asked them, 'Who do people say I am?' They replied, 'Some say John the Baptist; others say Elijah; and still others, one of the prophets.' 'But what about you?' he asked. 'Who do you say I am?' Peter answered, 'You are the Christ.' Jesus warned them not to tell anyone about him.*

Progressively throughout this gospel, the disciples have been taught by Jesus, and also witnessed miracles of power and

[3] 'The healing by stages is unusual. Surely it does not mean that healing can be performed only in proportion to the amount of faith which a person has at a particular time. Apparently, in this popular narrative, it is merely a means of presenting more graphically the difficulty of the healing and the magnitude of the miracle.' The Good News According to Mark. London S.P.C.K. 1971. Eduard Schweizer. p163

greatness, transforming men and women, thereby bringing glory to God. Although they were undoubtedly growing in their faith, they still had further to go, as was evident from **7:17-21**. This short passage brings before us a high-point so far in this gospel.

From this time on the focus is very much on Jesus' journey towards the cross.[4] Only two more miracles occur *en route;* one is the story of the epileptic boy, the other, an account of blind Bartimaeus. From the disciples' perspective, in particular Peter, the focus is now turning towards the 'Person of Christ.' It was as Jesus and His disciples travelled through the villages around Caesarea Philippi, that He began to stretch their minds regarding who He was.

Unusually, and for the first time, Jesus asked them *'Who do people say I am?* **(v27).** This was no ego trip or self exaltation. Jesus was not asking what others 'thought' of Him; this was a question regarding 'identity,' who was He? Had the people discerned that He was more than just a miracle-working teacher? Had they perceived from His life and teaching that He was the Messiah, this was the real question. In **v28** the disciples reply with options. The possibilities were – John the Baptist (back to life), Elijah (returned) or another prophet.

This question, however, was simply a precursor to the main question. From the opinions of the people, Jesus turned His attention to the disciples, and, in **v29**, asked the all-important question - *'But what about you? Who do you say that I am?'* Typically, Peter is quick with his response and it is likely, though not certain, that he also spoke on behalf of the others. He said *'You are the Christ.'* (The word 'Christ' may be translated 'the Anointed One, the promised Messiah.' Peter's confession is emphatic and uncompromising.

Although Peter said *'You are the Christ'*, we cannot be certain as to the depth or level of his understanding at this time. Peter's response was no doubt genuine and a sincere 'gut

[4] 'Traditionally, this story has been regarded not only as the watershed of Mark's gospel, but as an equally important event in the ministry of Jesus.' The Gospel According to Mark. A & C Black. 1991. Morna D Hooker. p200

reaction.' If so, how right he was, and to be admired for this momentous affirmation!

It may be noted that Jesus makes no attempt to counter or refute this confession, even in Mark's gospel, where the story is typically short, but accepts it. According to **Matthew** in **16:15-19**, Peter said *'You are the Christ, the Son of the living God.'* These words must have pleased Jesus greatly, for Jesus went on to encourage Peter, saying *'Blessed are you, Simon son of Jonah, for this was not revealed to you by man, but by my Father in heaven.'*

In these words of Jesus we have a truth that lies at the core of the gospel, that is, that all who echo the confession of Peter will be blessed, for such discernment (as Peter's surely was) can only be a work of the Spirit of God. Jesus, in **v30,** warned them not to tell anyone about Him. This seemed a strange request, since the overriding purpose of their calling was 'to proclaim the good news about Jesus.'

The time, however, was not yet right. Their understanding of the Messianic Mission (in particular His death on the cross) was limited. This is evident from the next part of the narrative.

Jesus predicts His own death. 8:31-33

> *He then began to teach them that the Son of Man must suffer many things and be rejected by the elders, chief priests and teachers of the law, and that he must be killed and after three days rise again. He spoke plainly about this, and Peter took him aside and began to rebuke him. But when Jesus turned and looked at his disciples, he rebuked Peter, 'Get behind me, Satan!' he said. 'You do not have in mind the things of God, but the things of men.'*

Now, for the first time in Mark's gospel, Jesus began to teach His disciples, in the most direct way, the ultimate purpose of His mission on earth. In just one verse **(v31)**, Jesus introduced them to His future suffering, rejection, death and resurrection. Bearing in mind their limited understanding at that time, this seemed to be an overwhelming bombardment of information for them to consider.

It must be assumed, however, that Jesus elaborated more on these subjects than Mark has chosen to record. The time following Peter's confession was the appropriate time for Jesus to expand on the nature of His messianic mission.

Jesus, once again, referred to himself as the 'Son of Man,' this is a title used exclusively by the Lord of Himself, fulfilling the prophecy found in **Daniel 7:13f.**[5] This is the third of fourteen occasions where Mark used this title; in doing so he brings together the humanity and deity of Christ, demonstrating His compassion towards others and also, as God, being able to alleviate suffering and need.

Theologically, the 'Son of Man' is one of the most important designations used in the Synoptic Gospels. In gospel tradition this title was Jesus' favourite way of referring to Himself (in the Synoptic Gospels), and, was the only title which He used of Himself. Within the Synoptic Gospels the Son of Man can be identified in three different categories.

1) **The earthly Son of Man.**
Mark 2:10. *Authority to forgive sins.* **2:27** *Lord of the Sabbath.*

2) **The suffering Man.**
Mark 8:31 *The Son of Man must suffer.* **9:12** *The Son of Man will suffer.* **9:9** *The Son of Man risen from the dead.* **9:31** *The Son of Man delivered into the hands of men.*

---

[5] 'The probable Old Testament background is the vision of Daniel, where he sees four fierce beasts arise successively out of the sea. These symbolize four successive world empires. 'Afterwards 'I saw ....and behold, with the clouds of heaven there came one like a son of man, and he came to the Ancient of Days and was presented before him. And to him was given dominion and glory and kingdom, that all peoples, nations, and languages should serve him; his dominion is an everlasting dominion, which shall not pass away, and his kingdom one that shall never be destroyed.' (RSV) 1971. A Theology of the New Testament. Erdmans Publishing Company 1974. George Eldon Ladd. p147

10:33 *The Son of Man delivered to chief priests, condemned to death, rises again.* **10:45** *The Son of Man came to serve and give His life.* **14:21** *The Son of Man goes as written, but woe to the betrayer.* **14:41** *The Son of Man is betrayed to sinners.*

3) **The apocalyptic Son of Man**.
Mark 8:38 *When He comes in His Father's glory.* **13:26** *They will see the Son of Man coming in clouds with power and glory.* **14:62** *You will see the Son of Man sitting at the right hand of the Mighty One and coming on the clouds of heaven.*

The thought of Jesus being rejected by the elders, chief priests and teachers of the law may not have surprised the disciples for they had already witnessed this (chapter 7). However, to hear Jesus speak of suffering and death must have come as a great shock to them. How could this be possible?

This was the man who cast out evil spirits, who healed, and even controlled, the forces of nature. Whatever their hopes of Him were, suffering and death did not form part of it. Even the mention of His resurrection did not cushion the blow, for they were still trying to absorb the thought of His suffering and death. From **v32**, *'He spoke plainly about this ..,'* informs us that He tried to explain these things in an understandable way.

Immediately, Peter once again steps right in! He dares to take Jesus aside and rebuke him. We are not privy to what Peter said, but Jesus wasted no time in turning on Peter and, in front of the other disciples, He rebuked him. Turning to them and looking straight at them, He said to Peter *'Get behind me, Satan!'* **(v33).**

Although not intentional by Peter, his attitude was seen as a hindrance to the purpose of God, and an instrument of Satan. The very last thing Satan wanted was for Jesus to die on the cross; for while the cross was a victory for Jesus, it was defeat for Satan. Neither Peter, nor the others, could fully appreciate that the purpose of God for His Son Jesus was to be fulfilled through His suffering, death and the resurrection. In **John 10:17-18** Jesus said '.....*I lay down my life – only to take it up again. No-one takes it from me, but I lay it down of my own accord. I have authority to lay it down and take it up again.'* The death of Jesus was part of God's will, this was what Jesus meant when He said to them *'You do not have in mind the things of God, but the things of men* **(v33)**.'

The challenge of discipleship. 8:34-9:1

> *'Then he called the crowd to him along with his disciples and said: 'If anyone would come after me, he must deny himself and take up his cross and follow me. For whoever wants to save his life will lose it, but whoever loses his life for me and for the gospel will save it. What good is it for a man to gain the whole world, yet forfeit his soul? Or what can a man give in exchange for his soul? If anyone is ashamed of me and my words in this adulterous and sinful generation, the Son of Man will be ashamed of him when he comes in his Father's glory with the holy angels.' And he said to them, 'I tell you the truth, some who are standing here will not taste death before they see the kingdom of God come with power.'*

Throughout this gospel, Mark, in fairly rapid form, has been affirming the truth about Jesus Christ, the Son of God. The deity and humanity of Jesus have been in evidence through miracles, casting out evil spirits, challenging Pharisaic legalism, teaching and showing love and compassion. Mark's account of the life of Jesus leaves the reader in no doubt as to Jesus' true identity: this was Mark's intended purpose.

From the unfolding of the life of Jesus, to the challenge of Peter's confession, followed by the self disclosure of Jesus' suffering and death, the tables now turn, and the focus is now on the disciples and the crowd. In the light of all they had seen and heard – how would they respond to the radical challenge of discipleship from Jesus himself? Jesus did not smudge the issue but made it abundantly clear, that the way ahead for all who wanted to follow Him would not be easy, but costly!

As Jesus called them to Himself **(v34)**, He was in no doubt that amidst this vast number there would be the inquisitive, the critics, and those who were sincerely seeking. To such, Jesus laid down the gauntlet of discipleship. The challenge was unrestricted - *'If anyone would come after me.'* There was no prejudice, the challenge was to all present. The words 'come after' mean 'to attach oneself'. The inference, at that time, meant more than just accepting Jesus' teaching, but to literally follow Him wherever He went. Jesus laid down two requirements for those who wanted to become His disciples.

Firstly, they should 'deny' themselves, *'he must deny himself'.*[6] Self denial is essentially saying no to self. Yet, it can also mean saying 'No' to much in life, that is not necessarily sinful – but a hindrance or disadvantage in the pursuit of true discipleship. In **Hebrews 12:1-2** the author affirms this point when he writes *'let us throw off everything that hinders and the sin that so easily entangles, and let us run with perseverance the race marked out for us.'* Garibaldi, the great Italian patriot, appealed for recruits with these words – *'I offer no pay, nor quarters, nor provisions; I offer hunger, thirst, forced marches, battles and death. Let him who loves his country in his heart, and not with lips only, follow me.'*

The **Second** requirement was to *'take up his cross and follow me'*. In this narrative there are two crosses, one that belonged to Jesus and the other which belonged to those who would follow Him. What did this mean? At that period in history, many were punished for their crimes by crucifixion, and

[6] 'To deny oneself is to disown, not just one's sins, but one's self, to turn away from the idolatry of self-centredness. So it is something much more radical than any mere ascetic or trivial 'self-denials.' The Gospel According to Mark. Cambridge University Press. 1959. Cranfield, C.E.B. p281-282

had to carry their own cross to the place of execution. It was a 'one way journey.' Self no longer mattered, future plans became obsolete – the cross meant the end for self.

Unlike the person being crucified and carrying his cross under duress, the follower of Jesus would carry his cross because he wants to, not because he must. It is an act of willing surrender and love for Jesus. It involves a life of trust (**Jn 14:1**), walking in Jesus' footsteps **(1 Pet 2:1)**, obeying Jesus commands **(Jn 15:14)**, and continuing **(Phil 2:12)**.

In **John 15:18** Jesus taught His disciples that just as the world hated Him so, likewise, those who followed Him could expect nothing less. Those who would follow Jesus should not expect an easy journey through life because they followed in the footsteps of the Master.

In **v35** we have a great paradox – *'For whoever wants to save his life will lose it, but whoever loses his life for me and for the gospel will save it.'* The challenge of discipleship now takes on board the concept of 'investment.' Saving one's life in this context, refers to living according to ones own passions, desire and will; in other words - living a life 'independent of the purpose of God.' When a person invests in such a way, it is viewed, according to Jesus, as a life lost; wasted, for its value is limited to their earthly life.

On the other hand, the life surrendered to Jesus, and His gospel, is a life invested in the eternal kingdom of God. This is an investment that will involve sacrifice and commitment, yet will be one of fulfilment and eternal reward.

In **John 12:24** Jesus said *'I tell you the truth, unless a grain of wheat falls into the ground and dies, it remains only a single seed. But if it dies, it produces many seeds.'* The picture is clear! The seed that is planted in the earth dies, but as a result, it produces many seeds. It has been a great investment! The ultimate and highest example is surely that of Jesus' own death on the cross. As a result of His death, countless men and women would come to faith.

From **Isaiah 53:10b**, the result of Christ's death is recorded prophetically[7] '*The plan was that He give Himself as an offering for sin so that He would see life come from it – life, life, and more life. And God's plan will deeply prosper through him.*'

The true value of discipleship is further stressed by Jesus in **vv36-37**, where He made it clear, that, even if a person possessed all this world's treasures, he would still be in spiritual poverty if that is all he has, because he has forfeited or neglected the priority of his soul.

The apostle Paul shares his testimony in **Philippians 3:7-8** – '*But whatever was to my profit I now consider loss for the sake of Christ. What is more, I consider everything a loss compared to the surpassing greatness of knowing Christ Jesus my Lord, for whose sake I have lost all things. I consider them rubbish, that I may gain Christ....*'

It must be noted, however, that Jesus did not condemn being wealthy, but was making the point that wealth, no matter how great, will always have limited value; it can never be a substitute for the spiritual inheritance that comes through faith in Jesus Christ **(see 1 Peter 1:3-5).**

This narrative recorded by Mark, though neither heavy in theology or academic input, was of vital importance to all would-be followers of Jesus. The challenge of Christian discipleship had to be clear and direct. And so, Jesus, in **vv37-38** had a final word of exhortation. He referred to a future occasion when He would personally return to earth with His holy angels. Following this event and because of their accountability to God the judgement of everyone would take place.

With this in mind, Jesus was saying that if anyone was too proud to confess Him openly in this life (if they are ashamed), then He too will be ashamed of them when He returns; He will not confess them before His Father in heaven. '*If anyone is*

[7] The Message. The Bible in Contemporary language. Eugene H Peterson. Navpress

ashamed of me and my words .....the Son of Man will be ashamed of him when he comes...'

The challenge brought before them was that of 'taking their stand for Jesus Christ' - to stand up and be counted, unashamed to follow Jesus, no matter the pressures or difficulties that may face them. These words of Jesus continue to this day, as 'a sharp two edged sword' to all who contemplate investing their lives in the pursuit of Jesus. History reveals that many have paid dearly, even with martyrdom, because they were *'not ashamed of the gospel of Christ.'***(Rom 1:17)**.

It is not easy to interpret **9:1**. Amidst the possibilities there are two worth considering.

Firstly, bearing in mind the context, it could be that reference is being made to the second coming of Christ (*the kingdom of God come with power).* This immediately, of course, presents the difficulty of how any of those present could possibly be alive when Jesus made His personal return. However, it may not be as far fetched as one might think.

In the days of the early Church, following Christ's death, resurrection and ascension, there was a growing belief among Christians that Christ would return during their own life time; indeed, they believed His personal return was imminent. Holding to this view caused many of them to refrain from work or even considering marriage; they thought, 'what is the point for such a short period? However plausible, this is not a commonly held view.

Secondly, it is more likely that Jesus was referring to the period immediately following his resurrection. During the beginnings of the early Church period, the kingdom of God expanded rapidly after the outpouring of the Holy Spirit at Pentecost (**Acts 2**). Thousands came to faith and the kingdom of God became visible through the work of the Spirit and the ministry of the apostles. The Church was born and the kingdom of God and the power of God were in evidence. This view makes sense according to Jesus' words - *'I tell you the truth, some who are standing here will not taste death before they see the kingdom of God come with power.'*

9

The transfiguration of Jesus. 9:2-13

After six days Jesus took Peter, James and John with him and led them up a high mountain, where they were all alone. There he was transfigured before them. His clothes became dazzling white, whiter than anyone in the world could bleach them. And there appeared before them Elijah and Moses, who were talking with Jesus. Peter said to Jesus, 'Rabbi, it is good for us to be here. Let us put up three shelters – one for you, one for Moses and one for Elijah.' (He did not know what to say, they were so frightened.) Then a cloud appeared and enveloped them, and a voice came from the cloud: 'This is my Son, whom I love. Listen to him!' Suddenly, when they looked around, they no longer saw anyone with them except Jesus.

As they were coming down the mountain, Jesus gave them orders not to tell anyone what they had seen until the Son of Man had risen from the dead. They

> *kept the matter to themselves, discussing what 'rising from the dead' meant. And they asked him, 'Why do the teachers of the law say that Elijah must come first?' Jesus replied, 'To be sure, Elijah does come first, and restores all things. Why then is it written the Son of Man must suffer much and be rejected? But I tell you, Elijah has come, and they have done to him everything they wished, just as it is written about him.'*

This story is known as the 'Transfiguration.' It was an actual event as recorded by Mark, and we have no reason to doubt its historicity; though other interpretations have been offered.[1] The other synoptists, Matthew (**17:1-13**), and Luke (**9:28-36**), also bear witness to the actuality of the event. All three, view it as something that transcended normal experience. It is a most mind-stretching passage, for though it is deeply thought provoking, it is also shrouded in mystery. It affirms the authenticity of past Biblical history, deals with the present and points to the future.

According to **v2** there would seem to be a six day gap since the previous event. The scene is set with a simple statement – *'Jesus took Peter, James and John with him and led them up a high mountain.'* From the time of Moses through the Prophets, and into the life of Christ; Mountains, it seems, were a geographical focal point for times of communication and communion with God.[2]

This particular mountain was probably Mt Hermon and was more than 9,000 feet high. It may be asked, why only Peter,

---

[1] 'Various views have been suggested as to the origin of this story. It has been said to have been a vision by which Peter became convinced of Jesus` Messiahship. Or it has been described as a post-resurrection experience, the six days afterwards referring to that event. A third explanation is that it is a piece of Christian symbolism, Moses and Elijah, representing the law and the prophets, being made to testify to Jesus` Messiahship.' The Gospel of Mark. Hodder and Stoughton Ltd. 1948. Branscomb, B. Harvie. p 160

[2] Moriah – the sacrifice of Isaac stopped, Gen 22. Sinai – the giving of the law, Ex 19. Horeb – reassurance for Elijah, 1 Kings 19.

James and John were to be privy to such an occasion. God's sovereign choice may be a mystery at times; mere men can only speculate. Previously in **(5:37)**, these same men were the only disciples allowed to be present when a young girl was raised from the dead. The reason for the inclusion of Peter, James and John on certain occasions, may simply be that they were growing in special aptitude and spiritual maturity.

From a human standpoint, it may also be that Jesus drew support and strength from their fellowship. Whatever the reasons, these were the men chosen to be with Jesus on that mountain. Mark's inclusion of *'where they were alone'* is helpful in picturing this event; it is suggestive of solitude and stillness in preparation for what was about to take place.

Once again, the disclosure of Jesus' identity takes place in private **(v7)**. At this time, the shadow of the cross was beginning to stretch across the path of Jesus. Among other things, the 'Transfiguration' was a means of strengthening Him for what lay ahead.

Mark writes in **v2** *'There he was transfigured before them.'* The Greek word for transfigured is METAMORPHOO, and means 'to change into another form.'[3] This is in keeping with Luke's account, where we read that *'the appearance of his face changed.'*

Any attempt to describe or define the change in form that took place, is not possible. Luke provides additional detail by informing us that Jesus was 'praying' at the moment of his transfiguration **(Lk 9:29)**.

Such was the impact and effect of Jesus' communion with His Father, that, not only did His face change, but also His clothes; **v3** *'His clothes became dazzling white, whiter than anyone in the world could bleach them.'* Mark is making the point that there was no known way, humanly speaking, to get

---

[3] 'The literal meaning is 'to be transformed,' or 'to change one's form,' and in the light of v3, the idea seems to be that Jesus temporarily exchanged the normal form that he bore during his earthly life for that glorious form he was believed to possess after his exaltation to heaven, and which believers also hoped to be clothed with after his second coming.' The Gospel of Mark. Pelican New Testament Commentaries. 1963 Nineham D.E. p234

clothes as white as this. A purity that found its source in the supernatural realm was in evidence on this occasion.

The example of prayerful communion with the Father and the effect that it had on the *persona* of Jesus, presents a powerful challenge to all who would follow Jesus. As is revealed in **2 Corinthians 3:18** *'And we, who with unveiled faces all reflect the Lord's glory, are being transformed into his likeness with ever increasing glory, which comes from the Lord, who is the Spirit.'*

Following Jesus' communication with His Father, there appeared Moses and Elijah, who were talking with Jesus (**v4**). The presence of these men was significant. Moses was the supreme law-giver of Israel and represented the law. He was also the man used to institute the sacrifice of the Passover Lamb **(Exodus 12)**, which directly pointed towards the cross.

Elijah was the first and considered the greatest of the prophets; no prophetic writing, however, was ever attributed to him.

Both these men represented the Old Covenant in the Old Testament period of history.

It is also of interest that both Moses and Elijah had unusual departures from this life (**Deut 34** and **2 Kgs 2**).

Although Mark records that *'they were talking with Jesus'*, he made no mention of what they talked about. Luke, however, provides us with more detail in **9:31** with **two** additional pieces of information.

Firstly, they *'appeared in glorious splendour.'* This can only be imagined! How they were transported from glory to this mountain is not for men to know! These things are beyond human understanding (see **Acts 1:7** *'It is not for you to know*).

Secondly, it is stated that the topic of their conversation was Jesus' death, *'they spoke about his departure.'*

There ought to be no surprise in this, for Jesus said in **Matthew 5:17** *'Do not think I have come to abolish the Law and the Prophets; I have not come to abolish them but to fulfil* *them.'* Jesus, in every sense, was the fulfilment of all that had gone before and no doubt was being confirmed in the rightness of the way of the cross.

Moses and Elijah saw in Jesus all that history had longed for, and hoped for, and looked forward to. It may also be assume that the presence of Moses and Elijah was a means of encouraging and strengthening Jesus for what lay ahead of Him. This was a momentous occasion indeed, a mountain of 'communion and confirmation.'

In this event, as is the case throughout all Scripture – the cross was central!

In **v5** Peter's response to all this is found. He addressed Jesus as 'Rabbi'; according to Matthew **(17:4)**, as 'Lord'; and in Luke **(9:3)**, it is the word 'Master.' There is no real problem here since these translations may be viewed as 'synonyms' for the Aramaic word used by Peter. All are apt descriptions for Jesus.

How right Peter was when he said *'it is good for us to be here.'* Peter, James and John were truly privileged to be part of this glorious occasion. Moses and Elijah would have been two of their great historical heroes, yet how they recognized them, is not known. Perhaps Jesus introduced Moses and Elijah to the disciples, or it might be that they received divine enlightenment.

Peter, the man always quick to speak and act on impulse, rushed in to suggest some form of lasting recognition for Jesus, Moses and Elijah. Although this was understandable and a noble thought, he made a terrible mistake and suffered divine rebuke because of it. Mark's account seems to be almost apologetic for Peter, **v6** *'He did not know what to say, they were so frightened.'*

What was Peter's great error? Simply this: by suggesting that some form of memorial (shelters or booths) be erected,[4] that placed Moses and Elijah on the same level as Jesus. Though

[4] 'These booths, made of plaited branches, were used at harvest times in the fields , but in the celebration of the Feast of Tabernacles, they came to be interpreted as a reminder of the tents which had been used in the wilderness (Lev 23:42f). The Gospel According to Mark. A & C Black (publishers Ltd) 1991. Hooker Morna D. p217.

Moses and Elijah were great men of God, they were just men!

In **v7** the Father's voice was heard from heaven, (according to Luke **9:34**, Peter was still speaking when the Fathers voice came as an interruption.) A cloud enveloped them; then the voice was heard, seemingly from the cloud. This was a cloud of glory, signifying the presence of God.

In the Old Testament the presence of God was often manifest in the form of a cloud. The cloud symbolized the 'Shekinah' or 'presence of God.' The Hebrew word 'Shekinah' literally means 'that which dwells.'[5] (**Ex 13:21-22; 33:7-11. Ezek 1:28; 11:23**.)

With authority and affirmation the words *'This is my Son, whom I love. Listen to him!'* are heard. According to Matthew **17:6** *'they fell face down to the ground.'* When they looked around, or up, the only person in view was Jesus **(v8)**. Peter and the others were solemnly reminded that the all important person to take up their attention was to be Jesus.

This was a lesson well learned, for the time would come when in his first sermon **(Acts 3:23),** Peter would say *'Anyone who does not listen to him will be cut completely off from among his people.'* The challenge for Peter, James and John on this mountain, is there for all who would follow Jesus – to fix their eyes on Him, giving Him His rightful and exalted place.

Not for the first time **(1:34, 44; 3:12; 5:43; 7:36; 8:26, 30)**, Jesus warned them, as they came down the mountain, not to tell anyone what they had seen **(v9).** This warning however, was not absolute, but only *'until the Son of Man had risen from the dead.'*

The reason for restraint in speaking openly about this was that the full significance of their experience would only be

---

[5] 'The Shekinah, the radiance, glory, or presence of God, 'dwelling' in the midst of His people, is used by Targumist and Rabbi to signify God Himself. The Shekinah, the nearest Jewish equivalent to the Holy Spirit, became with other Old Testament ideas or derivatives, Word, Wisdom, Spirit etc., a bridge between man's corporeality and God's transcendence.' New Bible Dictionary. IVP. March 1961. p1174.

understood following the resurrection. **Verse 10** affirms this, for they were still puzzled.

It seems from **vv11-13**, that although the disciples were beginning to understand God's plan much better, they were still uncertain with regards to the coming of Elijah as a forerunner to the Messiah, especially after this recent event.

Had Elijah come and they had missed him; or could his appearance on the mountain have been the fulfilment of this prophecy?

They would have been familiar with the prophecies from **Malachi 3:1, 4:5-6,** and taught that these prophecies should be fulfilled before Messiah appeared.

Jesus' response in **vv12-13** made it clear to them that Elijah, as a forerunner, had already come, and was, in fact, John the Baptist. This is clear from **Matthew 17:13** *'The disciples understood that he was talking to them about John the Baptist.'* Just as they had rejected John the Baptist (Elijah), so they would reject the Son of Man: as it was written. (For further comments on the Son of Man, see comments from **8:31**).

The healing of a boy with an evil spirit. 9:14-32

> *'When they came to the other disciples, they saw a large crowd around them and the teachers of the law arguing with them. As soon as all the people saw Jesus, they were overwhelmed with wonder and ran to greet him. 'What are you arguing with them about?' he asked. A man in the crowd answered, 'Teacher, I brought you my son, who is possessed by a spirit that has robbed him of speech. Whenever it seizes him, it throws him to the ground. He foams at the mouth, gnashes his teeth and becomes rigid. I asked your disciples to drive out the spirit, but they could not. 'O unbelieving generation,' Jesus replied, 'how long shall I stay with you? How long shall I put*

> *up with you? Bring the boy to me.' So they brought him. When the spirit saw Jesus, it immediately threw the boy into a convulsion. He fell to the ground and rolled around, foaming at the mouth. Jesus asked the boys father, 'How long has he been like this?' 'From childhood,' he answered. 'It has often thrown him into fire or water to kill him. But if you can do anything, take pity on us and help us.' 'If you can?' said Jesus. 'Everything is possible for him who believes.'*
>
> *Immediately the boy's father exclaimed. 'I do believe; help me overcome my unbelief!' When Jesus saw that a crowd was running to the scene, he rebuked the evil spirit. 'You deaf mute spirit,' he said, 'I command you, come out of him and never enter him again.' The spirit shrieked, convulsed him violently and came out. The boy looked so much like a corpse that many said, 'He's dead.' But Jesus took him by the hand and lifted him to his feet, and he stood up. After Jesus had gone indoors, his disciples asked him privately, 'Why couldn't we drive it out?' He replied, 'This kind can only come out by prayer. They left that place and passed through Galilee. Jesus did not want anyone to know where they were, because he was teaching his disciples. He said to them, 'The Son of Man is going to be betrayed into the hands of men. They will kill him, and after three days he will rise.' But they did not understand what he meant and were afraid to ask him about it.*

From the majesty and mystery of the mountain of Transfiguration, Jesus, James, Peter and John return to the other disciples, only to find them surrounded by a large crowd and teachers of the law **(v14)**. They are quite literally 'back down to earth again' following their heavenly experience.

During their absence, the other disciples had been caught up in a perplexing and demanding situation. A father had brought his son to them to be delivered of a spirit that *'robbed him of speech,'* and caused him to be convulsed into an uncontrollable state. It had clearly been a terrible condition for this father to witness and for his son to experience.

To add to the father's heartache, according to **Luke 9:38**, the boy was an only child.

The disciples had failed in their bid to deliver the boy from his condition, which was probably epilepsy! All those present were no doubt disappointed. However, we are told, in **v15**, when they saw Jesus *'they were overwhelmed with wonder and ran to greet him.'*

The reason for their wonder and amazement was attributed to His supernatural reputation, authority and charisma. His reputation was unscathed, unlike the disciples, He had never failed. They certainly welcomed His presence, and we may assume, were full of expectation.

Whether or not the radiance (or visible glory) from Jesus' person was still in evidence, as was the case when Moses descended from Mount Sinai, although likely, is open to speculation.

Amidst the disappointment and expectation of the crowd (including father and son), they had been arguing **(v16)**, '*What are you arguing with them about?' He asked'*.

From **vv17-18** we are told that the father of the boy spoke with Jesus, explaining the effects of his son's condition, and how His disciples were unable to drive out the spirit. During this time the disciples would probably have been taunted and ridiculed because of their failure and spiritual impotency. This was the substance of their argument!

In response, Jesus said **(v19)**, *'O unbelieving generation.'* One can sense the pain and indignation which Jesus must have felt. Jesus' rebuke seems to have been addressed to all who were present, including His disciples. **Verse 19** could be paraphrased *'Have you no faith? After all this time, can I not leave you to do anything?'*

Not for the first time, an evil spirit reacted to the presence of Jesus **(5:6)**, by throwing the boy into a convulsion **(v20)**.

Jesus then asked the boy's father how long he had been like this **(v21)**. Jesus already knew the answer, yet He showed care and compassion by taking an interest in such detail. It mattered to Him how long they had suffered, and He wanted the father to know this.

In **v22**, having told Jesus that his son has suffered since childhood, the man exhibits faith, albeit tentatively. *'If you can do anything, take pity on us and help us'* he said.

This man must have tried many potential cures, in fact, everything and anything to relieve his son of this illness, and surely at great expense – yet without effect. Is it any wonder that his faith is rather fragile?

To this, Jesus said in **v23** *'If you can?' Everything is possible for him who believes.'* There are no limits or boundaries to what faith can accomplish.

Jesus was implying that 'If and Faith' should not coexist. Faith dispels doubt.

Jesus' words drew the man into deeper faith **(v24)**. From *'If you can,'* it is now, *'I do believe, help me overcome my unbelief.'* Christians may well identify with the acknowledgement of such frailty of faith and sympathise with this man. This story teaches the value of true faith and demonstrates the power of it.

Those who seek to follow Christ have at their disposal the transforming power of God through the eye of faith. Not simply faith – but faith in who Jesus is, and what He can do.

Having already caught the attention of large numbers, Jesus became aware that even more people were now running to the scene **(v25)**. He immediately moved into action and rebuked the evil spirit, commanding it never to enter the boy again. This was to bring a lasting benefit of health to the boy – hence, *'never* *enter him again.'* Jesus was concerned not only for his present, but also for his future.

The evil spirit was not for giving up its place of abode lightly, and resisted by violently convulsing the boy – then came out **(v26)**. The boy was so physically drained of energy that, we are told, *'he looked so much like a corpse.'* How typically loving of Jesus! He took the boy by the hand and lifted him up to his feet – then the boy stood up **(v27)**. Mark alone provides us with a graphic description, both of the reaction of the evil spirit, and also of the tenderness of Jesus.

It was not unusual for Jesus to want privacy, away from the crowds and also to be with His disciples.

In **v28** they had no sooner entered the house, than His disciples asked Him the question that burned in their hearts, *'Why couldn't we drive it out?'* **(v29)**. Jesus' reply was short and simple, *'This kind can come out only by prayer.'*[6] To what extent the disciples were committed to prayer, at this stage is unknown, yet from this gentle and direct rebuke from Jesus, they are made aware of the deficiency of their prayer-life.

It was another learning curve for them. In this short narrative Mark reminds his readers of three important things.

- The value and effect of faith.
- The power and discipline of sincere prayer.
- The tenderness and compassion of Jesus.

Verses **30-32** bring a conclusion to this part of the narrative, and also a change of focus. Moving on from that place they passed through Galilee.

Mark informs that Jesus wanted to be away from all others except the disciples at this time, and provides the reason. This was to be a time set apart exclusively for the disciples' education **(v31a)**. Jesus had much to teach them; most of which they would not fully understand, yet it was vital that Jesus bring to their attention what would soon happen to Him.

[6] Some manuscripts have 'prayer and fasting' as does the Authorised Version.

Although the full weight of His teaching would be beyond their immediate understanding, it was important to bring these disturbing truths before them. The benefit to the disciples would actually be greater post resurrection, because then, they would recall what He taught beforehand and recognise the fulfilment of His predictions.

Out of the three 'passion predictions' recorded by Mark, this was the second; the others are found in **8:31** and **10:33**. Using the term 'Son of Man'[7] once again, Jesus spoke of His deliverance into the hands of men who would betray Him. They would kill Him and He would be raised after three days.

It was no great surprise that they did not understand what He meant (**v32**). These were the worst and most difficult words they could hear. That Jesus would die was unthinkable. They were still blind to the significance of His death, let alone and understanding of what being raised meant. It is impossible to appreciate their dilemma. Clearly, Jesus' teaching perplexed them, for they were afraid to ask Him about it. How much detail Jesus shared with them about His death and resurrection, or what other subjects He taught, is not known.

Who is the greatest? 9:33-37

> *'They came to Capernaum. When he was in the house, he asked them. 'What were you arguing about on the road?' But they kept quiet because on the way they had argued about who was the greatest. Sitting down, Jesus called the twelve and said, 'If anyone wants to be first, he must be the very last, and the servant of all.' He took a little child and had him stand among them. Taking him in his arms, he said to them, 'Whoever welcomes one of these little children in my name welcomes me; and whoever welcomes me does not welcome me but the one who sent me.'*

---

[7] For further consideration on the Son of Man, see comments from 8:31.

Competition, rivalry and the self exaltation of the disciples dominate this short event. The shortness of the narrative has little bearing on the importance of the lesson taught by Jesus.

Jesus and His disciples are found back at Capernaum, which for some time had been their base.

When settled in the house (possibly at home), Jesus invited them to share what they had been arguing about as they travelled **(v33)**.

Not only did Jesus know they had been arguing, but also the subject matter.

According to **v34** their response was one of silence.

This was not surprising, for they had been arguing about who was the greatest among them.

Shortly before this, they had shared in a unique and momentous occasion on the Mount of Transfiguration, where Jesus was the exalted one; the focus was on Him. How quickly this lesson had lost its place in their hearts! How fickle they were! Surely the disciples might have found something better to discuss, having just heard from Jesus of His sufferings, rather than their pecking order.

There is something very sad in the thought of Jesus going towards the Cross, while they are taken up with themselves and their own greatness. Although they had much to learn, their silent response was an indication that their consciences troubled them.

And so in **v35** Jesus gathered all twelve around him. Sitting in their midst (as teacher and superior), the Master conducted His seminar on the nature of true greatness. *'If anyone wants to be first, he must be the very last...'* This is a 'Kingdom Expression,' and stands in contrast to the secular mindset where to think highly of oneself is commendable and encouraged.[8]

---

[8] 'The world's philosophy is that you are 'great' if others are working for you, but Christ's message is that greatness comes from our serving others.' Scripture Press. 1991. Be Diligent. Warren W Wiersbe. p93

This new paradoxical way of thinking would not be easy for them to understand. Jesus had let them talk freely on the road, but now He redirects their thinking.

Their future ministry called for men with a 'servant spirit,' whose ministry pointed not to them, but to Christ. John the Baptist said, **Jn 3:30** *'He must become greater; I must become less.'* If, within the Kingdom of God, the disciples had any aspirations of greatness, then it would only come through humility and a servant spirit. It would come through preferring others before themselves, and serving with a view to exalting their Lord.

They would, in due course, make this discovery.

Furthermore, before them in the person of Jesus, was one who would, at the highest level, put this into practice. This is highlighted in **Philippians 2:4ff** *'Each of you should look not only to your own interests, but also to the interests of others. Your attitude should be the same as that of Christ Jesus....And being found in appearance as a man, he humbled himself and became obedient to death – even death on a cross.'*

Many years later Peter wrote *'Humble yourselves, therefore, under God's mighty hand, that he may lift you up in due course.'*

In **v36**, to reinforce His point, Jesus used a visual aid in the form of a little child. Mark brings before us a beautiful picture of Jesus, which is not found in the other gospels, *'Taking him in his arms,'*[9] The Greek word for *'in his arms,'* is ENAGKALISMENOS, and means *'holds in the crook of his arm.'* This points to tenderness and fondness, and is a reminder of the firm place children had in Jesus' heart. And so, with the disciples, probably arranged in a crescent around him, and with the child in his embrace, Jesus spoke to them.

---

[9] 'Jesus, with the child held to his bosom, is the living law of service, and the child nestling close to him, because sure of his love, is the type of trustful affection which we must evoke if we are to serve or help. This picture has gone straight to the hearts of men; and who can count the streams of tenderness and practical kindliness of which it has been the source.' Bible Class Expositions. Hodder & Stoughton. St Mark. Alexander MacLaren. p142

From **v37** Jesus informed them that even a little child, such as was before them, mattered to Him. Children occupied a lowly place in the world at that time; there would be no prizes for time invested with children.

By showing such affection for this child, Jesus was making the point that those who welcomed the least in society, also welcomed Him. Their future ministry should not be one of prejudice, but all-embracing.

Jesus also saw in children the simplicity of uncomplicated trust. Just as this child welcomed Jesus' embrace, so all who would do likewise, welcomed not only Him, but also His father.

This was not the only occasion when Jesus used a child as an example. (**Mk 10:14, 16. Matt 18:2-6. 19:14-15. 21:16**.)

For or against Jesus. 9:38-41

> *'Teacher,' said John, 'we saw a man driving out demons in your name and we told him to stop, because he was not one of us.' 'Do not stop him,' Jesus said. 'No-one who does a miracle in my name can in the next moment say anything bad about me, for whoever is not against us is for us. I tell you the truth, anyone who gives you a cup of water in my name because you belong to Christ will certainly not lose his reward.'*

Verse 38. There is a certain irony as John speaks here on behalf of the disciples.

Not long before this, it was these same disciples who had failed to deliver an evil spirit from a young epileptic boy, yet now they are critical of someone who has - and in the name of Jesus! The disciples, understandably, were caught up with following Christ and almost constantly on the move. This meant that they would not have seen the lasting fruit of Christ's ministry.

The likelihood is that John's observation was of someone who had come to faith, committed himself to Christ and His teaching, continued to mature and put into practice what he had witnessed from Jesus and His disciples. As the spokesman, it seemed that John's main reason for rejecting this man was simply, that he 'was not one of them.'

In **vv39-40** Jesus said *'Do not stop him.....'*

Following Jesus Christ is not something that springs from the old sinful nature, it cannot **(Rom 8:8)**. It is not a natural thing to speak for Christ or do miracles in His name, unless that person is a believer. Therefore, for someone to do as this man had done, indicated that a life-changing experience had taken place – he was for Jesus!

Jesus, in **v41**, concludes this brief discussion with his disciples by pointing to a solemn truth. When Jesus said *'anyone who gives a cup of water in my name,'* He was effectively saying that 'everything' that is done in His name by those who belong to Him, has eternal and lasting value.

There are many tasks in life that seem menial or insignificant, yet done for the Master and benefit of the recipient, will bring glory to Jesus' name. Bearing in mind the disciples' argument about true greatness, this was another way of affirming the previous lesson.

This is exemplified in **Colossians 3:23** *'Whatever you do, work at it with all your heart, as working for the Lord, not for men, since you know that you will receive an inheritance from the Lord as a reward.'*

Spiritual surgery. 9:42-50

> *'And if anyone causes one of these little ones who believe in me to sin, it would be better for him to be thrown into the sea with a large millstone tied around his neck. If your hand causes you to sin, cut it off. It is better for you to enter into life maimed than with*

> *two hands to go into hell, where fire never goes out. And if your foot causes you to sin, cut it off. It is better for you to enter life crippled than to have two feet and be thrown into hell. And if your eye causes you to sin, pluck it out. It is better for you to enter the kingdom of God with one eye than to have two eyes and be thrown into hell, where 'their worm does not die, and the fire is not quenched.' Everyone will be salted with fire. Salt is good, but if it loses its saltiness, how can you make it salty again? Have salt in yourselves, and be at peace with each other.'*

This passage presents a radical challenge for all who are serious about true discipleship, both personally, and in relation to other believers. Using the words 'little ones' in **v42**, Jesus was probably meaning 'little ones in the faith,' since he referred to *'little ones who believe.'* However, it is possible that Jesus also had in mind those children present in **v37**, and points to the responsibility not to lead the young astray or into sin.

Such was the seriousness of this, that those who would do such a thing would be better off drowned in the sea with a millstone tied around their necks (drowning was a recognised form of capital punishment by the Romans). The large millstone mentioned here would have been drawn by a donkey, and was the top-stone of two, between which the grain was crushed.

Where certain physical illnesses are concerned, there are occasions when a person may need to have a limb amputated in order to preserve the whole body. In the spiritual life the same can be true. This is what Jesus had in mind.

In **vv43-47** Jesus refers to three parts of the body – the hand, the foot and the eye. Why are these mentioned and not other parts of the body? Although we cannot be certain, and since all three play a vital role in bodily function, the following suggestions might be helpful.

- The HAND refers to what a person DOES.
- The FOOT is indicative of DIRECTION.
- The EYE is the gateway to DISCERNMENT.

Jesus is not suggesting that if a person commits a sin with any of his limbs that he severs it from his body. This teaching was for spiritual application. In other words, the aim is to deal with sin in a radical way, not to moderate or accommodate it, but undergo spiritual surgery where appropriate.

Sin is to the inner person what a cancerous tumour is to the body; therefore it calls for a surgical response. This is made clear in the apostle Paul's teaching in **Colossians 3:5-10**, *'Put to death, therefore, whatever belongs to your earthly nature: sexual immorality, impurity, lust, evil desires and greed, which is idolatry........'*

That this lesson should be taken seriously cannot be in doubt, otherwise Jesus would not have introduced the subject of hell.

Bishop J.C. Ryle comments *'There is no mercy in keeping back from men the subject of hell. Fearful and tremendous as it is, it ought to be pressed on all, as one of the great truths of Christianity.'*[10]

The word GEHENNA, which comes from the Hebrew word Ge-Hinnom (the valley of Tophet), is used for 'hell' and is found on twelve occasions in the New Testament, eleven of those in the synoptics, and in every instance it was Jesus who used it.

Within this section **(vv43-47)**,[11] certain truths are clear.

1) It refers to an actual place that can be entered (notice the words 'into' **v43, 45, 47**).

---

[10] Expository thoughts on the Gospels. Mathew and Mark. Evangelical Press. 1977. p193

[11] Verses 44 and 46 have been omitted since the manuscript evidence is against their inclusion in the text. This, however, does not affect the teaching of Jesus, or the record of Mark in any way, since v44 and 46 are.

2) It is eternal in duration (notice phrases - **v43** '*where the fire never goes out*' and, **v48** '*where their worm does not die, and the fire is not quenched*'.

3) It is a place to be avoided, a place of eternal punishment **(Mtt 25:46)**.

It is the place reserved for those who wilfully reject Jesus Christ through unbelief **(Jn 3:18)**. The concept of a 'literal hell' is not popular among some, and there is much that it is not understood in relation to it, yet, the fact remains that it was taught by Jesus Himself and should not be dismissed.

Verses 49-50. These verses are among the most difficult in the New Testament to understand. Commentators abound with their many and varied interpretations.

Verse **49** is generally accepted as a link verse and probably has as its background **Lev 2:13**, where it relates to sacrifices being offered with salt added to them. This could make sense with the content of **v50** in mind. That verse would seem in keeping with what has preceded **(vv42-48)**, for cutting sin out of one's life is a form of purification which leads to sanctification.

The gospel was first preached in an ungodly and heathen world, where Christians were called to be the salt of the earth – an influence for good **(Mtt 5:13)**.

The apostle Paul writes in **2 Cor 7:1** ' *....let us purify ourselves from everything that contaminates body and spirit, perfecting holiness out of reverence for God.'*

According to **v50** *'Have salt in yourselves,'* would refer to this inner purity of life that glorifies God and ministers to a lost world.

The last phrase *'and be at peace with each other'* points to the expectation of the sanctified life bearing witness in Christian fellowship, as a witness to the lost and a blessing to the saints.

10

Divorce. 10:1-12

'Jesus then left that place and went into the region of Judea and across the Jordan. Again crowds of people came to him, and as was his custom, he taught them. Some Pharisees came and tested him by asking, 'Is it lawful for a man to divorce his wife?' 'What did Moses command you?' he replied. They said, 'Moses permitted a man to write a certificate of divorce and send her away.' 'It was because your hearts were hard that Moses wrote you this law,' Jesus replied. 'But at the beginning of creation God 'made them male and female.' For this reason a man will leave his father and mother and be united to his wife, and the two will become one flesh. So they are no longer two but one. Therefore what God has joined together, let man not separate.' When they were in the house again, the disciples asked Jesus about this. He answered, 'Anyone who divorces his wife and marries another woman commits adultery against her. And if

she divorces her husband and marries another man,
she commits adultery.'

Jesus' Galilean ministry had now concluded and He was moving in a southerly direction to the region of Judea. In doing so He crossed the Jordan. From this time onward, the narrative moves towards its inevitable climax in Jerusalem, where Jesus' earthly ministry would culminate with His death on the cross.

By using the word 'again' in **v1**, Mark was making the point that wherever Jesus was, the people were increasingly close behind – His reputation had gone ahead of Him. When the crowds gathered around Him, '*as was his custom, he taught them.*' Jesus took every opportunity to teach the people.

Though many hungered for His words and were miraculously blessed by Him, there were others who were always out to trap Him. Such was this occasion, and no better opportunity than before these crowds.

The Pharisees wasted little time **(v2)** before they presented Him with a controversial test question, *'Is it lawful for a man to divorce his wife?'* This was a thorny subject among the Pharisees at that time. Even amidst their own ranks they were divided on this matter, yet their reason for asking this question was not so much for an answer, but to catch Jesus out.

The question of divorce and remarriage had been the subject matter for John the Baptist's denunciation of the conduct of Herod Antipas and Herodias **(6:17ff)**, which led to his violent death. Geographically, Jesus was near the jurisdiction of Herod and perhaps the Pharisees thought they could lure Him towards the same end as John – ironically using similar issues.

In **v3** Jesus answered their question by asking another. In doing so He referred them to Moses, *'What did Moses command you?'* They in turn, quoted from Deuteronomy **24:1-4**, where, if a man found anything indecent about his wife, he was permitted to write a certificate of divorce and send her out of the house. In those days a woman had no legal rights whatever, and was at the disposal of the male head of the family. For this reason it was the 'man' who divorced his wife.

The leading question at that time was not, could a man divorce his wife, but, what would be the grounds for it? In **v5** Jesus informed them that the reason for the Mosaic law of writing a certificate of divorce, was because of their own weakness - *'your hearts were hard.'* It was to provide a practical solution for difficult situations, that Moses, under the guidance of God, wrote this law.

In order not to get caught up with Pharisaic disputes relating to points of law, Jesus did not take their bait. In **vv6-9** He took them back to pre-law times to show God's ideal for marriage. He pointed as far back as creation, God creating male and female, in so doing, laying the foundation for heterosexual relationships as being the purpose of God.

In **Gen 2** we find three important pieces of information in relation to marriage.

1) The need for human companionship – *'It is not good for man to be alone* **(v18)**.*'*

2) The divine provision to meet this human need – *'Then the Lord God made a woman from the rib he had taken out of the man* **(v22)**.*'*

3) The institution of marriage – *'For this reason a man will leave his father and mother and be united to his wife, and they will become one flesh* **(v24)**.*'*[1]

Jesus affirmed the sanctity and uniqueness of marriage **(v9)** by stating that this was something God had done. The bond of marriage and seal upon it is ratified through these words – *'Therefore that which <u>God</u> has joined together, let man not separate.'*

---

[1] 'The Mosaic permission was a departure from the creation ordinance and from the practice to which it obligated men. The original constitution of the race as male and female is the basis of marriage. The creation of the two sexes is resolved in unity through marriage, as instituted by God.' The New London Commentary on the New Testament. The Gospel of Mark. Lane, William L. p356

Matthew 19 (also **5:32**) contain what has been described as the 'exception clause.' The content is similar to what Mark has recorded, with reference to the Scriptures in **Deuteronomy 24** and **Genesis 2**. Then in **Matthew 19:9** Jesus said *'I tell you that anyone who divorces his wife, except for marital unfaithfulness, and marries another woman commits adultery.'* This verse has been the subject of much debate and divided opinion. The problem seems to be not so much with the permission to divorce due to unfaithfulness, but marrying again.

Though the exception clause is viewed by some as an act of grace, because of the weakness of the flesh and failure in many marriages, it does not change the basic fact taught in God's Word, that in the eyes of God, marriage is indissoluble.

John Stott writes – *'His reason for adding the exceptive clause was to clarify that the only remarriage after divorce which is not tantamount to adultery is that of an innocent person whose partner has been sexually unfaithful, for in this case the infidelity has already been committed by the guilty partner. Jesus' purpose was emphatically not to encourage divorce for this reason, but rather to forbid it for all other reasons.'* [2]

Mark leaves no record of how the Pharisees responded to what Jesus said. However, from **vv10-12**, it is clear that the disciples required further clarification on this matter. Responding to the disciples in **vv11-12**, Jesus is quite emphatic; making it clear that the outcome of divorce and remarriage was adultery. In this connection Mark adds something that is not found in Matthew. He points out that Jesus applied the same rule to both husbands and wives, thereby showing them an equality not recognised in their tradition.

The subject of marriage and divorce has for many years been a difficult topic for the Christian Church to deal with. Within society, attitudes seem to have moderated with the passing of time, and sadly, Biblical principles are often viewed

[2] Issues Facing Christians Today. Collins – Marshall Pickering. John Stott. p294

as out of date or irrelevant because of the changing world in which people live.

The institution of marriage has suffered greatly and become no more than an option for many who have decided to live together. However, Biblical teaching is relevant for all people and throughout all ages.

The problems that lead to the break up of marriage are not so much found in the institution of marriage – as within the human heart. Due to the difficulties and breakups of many marriages, the Church has a responsibility to offer support and encourage the continuance of the marriage relationship where possible.

Biblical teaching, including love, forgiveness and reconciliation, which are core elements of the gospel, ought to have a greater priority in the Church's teaching programme.

Though some would see evidence of God's grace through Jesus' words in **Mtt 5:32** and **19:9**, it has to be affirmed that God's ideal is, that 'marriage should not be dissolved by humankind.'

Little children come to Jesus. 10:13-16

> *'People were bringing little children to Jesus to have him touch them, but the disciples rebuked them. When Jesus saw this, he was indignant. He said to them, 'Let the little children come to me, and do not hinder them, for the kingdom of God belongs to such as these. I tell you the truth, anyone who will not receive the kingdom of God like a little child will never enter it.' And he took the children in his arms, put his hands on them and blessed them.'*

Mark provides no detail as to the geographical or domestic location to this lovely narrative. The fact that time, place and other peripheral information are absent, takes nothing away from the beauty of the situation.[3] It does, however, seem fitting that children should have the centre-stage following the discussion on marriage.

The 'people' mentioned in **v13** were presumably parents or family. They brought their children to Jesus so that He might touch them. Most of these children were probably very young, because in Luke's account the word 'babies' is used **(18:15)**.

Jesus' reputation had gone ahead of Him, for there were many who had been healed, exorcised, fed or blessed by His kindness and teaching. In these and many other ways the uniqueness and deity of Jesus had become visible.

The people saw in Him, someone quite different from anyone they had ever seen or heard before. Obviously, they believed that the touch of Jesus invoked a special blessing, otherwise, why should they present their children before Him?

Seeing this, *'the disciples rebuked them'*. Why did they do this? Perhaps they were still concerned about their status (see **9:33-37**), or maybe they did not want Jesus to be troubled. They may even have viewed the children's arrival as an intrusion. Whatever their motives, they certainly did not seem to value children as much as their Master did, who had previously embraced them **(9:36)**.

Verse **14** informs that Jesus *'was indignant.'* The Greek word for 'indignant' is AGANAKTEO, and means *'to grieve, or feel violently irritated, to be vexed.'* Neither Matthew **(19:13)** or Luke **(18:15)** include Jesus' reference to indignation; only Mark.

The disciples' attitude clearly displeased Jesus. With the cruel shadow of the cross hanging over Him, it is quite touching and most remarkable that Jesus should express such kindness towards little children. This story not only informs us that Jesus cared for children, but that children also felt comfortable and welcomed in His presence.

[3] 'This section has been used from very early times to support the practice of infant baptism, and it has been suggested that the story itself reflects a controversy as to whether children should be baptised.' The Gospel according to Mark. A & C Black publishers Ltd) 1991. Hooker, Morna D p238

Jesus said *'Let the little children come to me, and do not hinder them,'* in other words, make way for these children; put no obstacle in their path. He then told them why – *'for the kingdom of God belongs to such as these.'*

In what sense did the Kingdom of God belong to them? (For further detail on the Kingdom of God, see **1:14-15**)

Normally children are very **'trusting,'** although there will always be the exception to the rule. Children believe what they are told, especially by their parents. They find no reason for doubt or disbelief. They have a simple uncluttered trust, especially very young children.

It must be likewise for those who seek to follow Jesus Christ. The rule of God and entrance into the kingdom of God are gained by faith alone. *'Therefore since we have been justified through faith, we have peace with God through our Lord Jesus Christ, through whom we have gained access by faith ......'* **(Rom 5:1-2).**

The sense in which the 'Kingdom of God belongs to children,' is that they show no merit of their own and model the way of faith and trust. In **v15** Jesus spoke of receiving the kingdom of God on this basis; in so doing declared the kingdom of God as something to 'enter into.' (see **John 3:3-5** where Jesus spoke to Nicodemus about 'entering the kingdom.')

Verse 16 paints a beautiful picture of Jesus and the children. Jesus did two things.

1) '*He took the children in his arms.'* In doing so He expressed His love for them. The children responded willingly to Jesus and received His intimate embrace. As a result they found themselves in a place of love and safety.

2) He '*put his hands on them and blessed them.'* These children were doubly blessed. Firstly, they could not have been nearer the Lord Jesus, and secondly, they received His touch.

The danger of earthly wealth. 10:17-31

'As Jesus started on his way, a man ran up to Him and fell on his knees before him. 'Good teacher,' he asked,'what must I do to inherit eternal life?' 'Why do you call me good?' Jesus answered. 'No-one is good – except God alone. You know the Commandments: 'Do not murder, do not commit adultery, do not steal, do not give false testimony, do not defraud, honour your father and mother.' 'Teacher' he declared, 'all these things I have kept since I was a boy.' Jesus looked at him and loved him. 'One thing you lack' He said. 'Go, sell everything you have and give it to the poor, and you will have treasure in heaven. Then come and follow me.'
At this the man's face fell. He went away sad, because he had great wealth. Jesus looked around and said to His disciples, 'How hard it is for the rich to enter the kingdom of God!' The disciples were amazed at His words. But Jesus said again, 'Children, how hard it is to enter the kingdom of God! It is easier for a camel to go through the eye of a needle than for a rich man to enter the kingdom of God.' The disciples were even more amazed, and said to each other, 'Who then can be saved?' Jesus looked at them and said, 'With man this is impossible, but not with God; all things are possible with God.' Peter said to Him, 'We have left everything to follow you!'
'I tell you the truth,' Jesus replied, 'no-one who has left home or brothers or sisters or mother or father or children or fields for me and the gospel will fail to receive a hundred times as much in this present age (homes, brothers, sisters, mothers, children and fields – and with them, persecutions) and in the age to

> *come, eternal life. But many who are first will be last, and the last first.'*

As Jesus made His way from the previous situation with the children, a man ran up to Him, obviously having heard that He was in that vicinity, and fell on his knees before Him.

The fact that all three synoptic writers bear witness to this story conveys the importance of the discussion that took place.

The additional information provided by Matthew and Luke is helpful and makes sense of the phrase *'the rich young ruler.'*

- Mark simply refers to him in **v17** as *'a man.'*
- Matthew in **19:20** writes *'the young man.'*
- Luke introduced him in **18:18** as *'a certain ruler.'*
- All three state that he had *'great wealth.'* **Mark v22; Mtt 19:22; Lk 18:23.**

Verses 17-22. This young man would, on the surface, seem to have it all - youth, wealth, prestige and position in society. He would, no doubt, be popular and friends would not be lacking. On the evidence of the gospels he had good manners and morals. There is every reason to consider him as rich, religious and respectable – he had it all - or did he?

He came running to Jesus, and falling to his knees, asked what he must do to inherit eternal life. In spite of all he possessed, he was still not satisfied – something was missing! It is not surprising that with this man's wealth and position, he said *'what must I do to inherit eternal life?'* He could afford to have things done! On this occasion, however, unlike countless others who came to Jesus, this young man eventually went away in a sad and unimproved state.

This story provides an interesting contrast with the previous one, where children were used as an example of the simplicity of faith, and this being the key to entering the kingdom of God.

Although the young man addressed Jesus rather superficially as *'Good Teacher',* he exhibited some measure of humility by falling on his knees. This would not have been easy for a person in possession of youth, wealth and position.

Using the word 'good' may have been an attempt to patronise Jesus, since Jewish Rabbis (according to tradition) did not like to be called 'good.' His question, however, could not have been straighter and to the point – *'what must I do to inherit eternal life?'* Matthew, in **19:16** includes the words 'good thing'. '*What good thing must I do to get eternal life?'*

No greater or more relevant question could have been asked! Most other things he could afford, work for, or arrange to have done – but not 'eternal life,' it could not be purchased. By using the word 'good things,' it is clear that his shallow understanding of salvation was based on self achievement or good works. Human effort! The apostle Paul writes in **Ephesians 2:8-9** *'For it is by grace you have been saved, through faith – and this is not from yourselves, it is the gift of God – not by works, so that no-one can boast.'*

This young man would have been taught by the Pharisaic scribes, and as a result, should have been familiar with the concept of 'life everlasting' from the Old Testament. Daniel, with the end times in view, writes in **12:2** *'Multitudes who sleep in the dust of the earth will awake: some to everlasting life, others to shame and everlasting contempt.'*

Though his understanding was limited, it is likely that having great prosperity in this life, he now looked for continuance of life following the grave. Perhaps he wanted the best of 'both worlds'.

In **v18** and in response to his question, Jesus asked *'why do you call me good, no-one is good except God alone?'* Jesus knew the answer to His own question, for He was the Son of God, and perfect in knowledge (**Jn 2:25** *' ......for he knew what was in man'*). So why did Jesus ask the question? Possibly to tease from him his understanding of who Jesus was! Jesus wanted him to stop and think!

Mark's leading purpose throughout his gospel – was to present the person of Jesus Christ as the Son of God, as the One whom men should follow and trust. Back in **8:27** Jesus asked His disciples *'Who do people say I am?'* Perhaps Jesus is saying to this young man *'Who do you say I am?'*

Continuing in **v19**, Jesus quoted the last six of the Ten Commandments which formed the basis for spiritual and moral life among the Jews. He gradually stretched him in such a way that ultimately exposed his Achilles heel.

The young man responded in **v20** with what he may have considered the perfect answer – *'Teacher,' he declared, 'all these I have kept since I was a boy.'* This might have seemed arrogant, yet he was probably being sincere. However, the fact that Matthew adds in **19:20** *'What do I still lack?'* indicates lack of fulfilment in his present religious state. That he was committed to his religious way of life was not in question, the real issue seemed to be, 'where did God come in his order of priorities? Was God really his God – or was wealth his god?

The outcome of the story leaves us in no doubt that 'gold was his god.' This being the case; he was in breach of the first commandment, *'You shall have no other gods before me.'*

Mark alone records in **v21**, one of the most wonderful statements in all Scripture, *'Jesus looked at him and loved him.'* The Greek word for 'looked' on this occasion is EMBLEPO, and means '*to look upon*'. It implies a close penetrating look. A look that goes beyond the physical body and sees the inner person – a kind of 'spiritual x-ray'. This was a look from one who had perfect understanding and complete knowledge: Jesus was God incarnate!

Jesus saw all his imperfection, his misguided sense of priorities, his lack of discernment, his emptiness, his great need and his sin – and loved him! Only Jesus could love like this! AGAPE is the Greek word used here for 'loved' and means

'Divine love'. It is the same word that is used to describe God's love toward His own Son, Jesus. This indicates the depth of Jesus' love for this young man.

Jesus' heart went out to him. He felt compassion and a sense of grief for him, because He knew what the outcome would be.

In the eyes of all who knew him he had everything, yet Jesus said *'One thing you lack.'* In a sense he had everything – yet nothing! In **Philippians 3:8** the apostle Paul, as he contrasted his past and present life, wrote *'I consider everything a loss compared to the surpassing greatness of knowing Christ Jesus my Lord, for whose sake I have lost all things. I consider them rubbish that I may gain Christ.'*

Jesus' challenge, '*go and sell everything you have and give it to the poor*,' must have come as a terrible shock. This was a step too far – he was not prepared to leave all and follow Jesus! He would not release his grasp of 'earthly treasure,' as a result - he would forfeit 'heavenly treasure'.

Verse 22 informs us that *'At this the man's face fell. He went away sad, because he had great wealth.'* What a sad conclusion! In **Matthew 6:21** Jesus said *'Where your treasure is, there will your heart be also.'* Again in **Luke 12:24** *'A mans life does not consist in the abundance of his possessions.'*

The challenge of discipleship given by Jesus in **8:34ff** had at its heart the need for self denial. The rich young ruler went away sad because he found it impossible to turn his back on his wealth, take up his cross and follow Jesus.

It should be pointed out, however, the root problem was not his 'wealth' but the place it had in his life. It was this man's god!

Verses 23-27. Jesus now turned His attention to His disciples. He did not say it was impossible for a rich man to enter the Kingdom of God, but that it was hard. Wealth often carries with it an 'independent spirit.' It can breed a 'self-sufficient' attitude that recognises little place for the rule and purpose of God in a person's life. In this sense, wealth is a relative concept. It need not be an 'abundance' of wealth alone that makes it hard to embrace the values of God's Kingdom – but a general comfortability that says, 'I don't need God.'

Materialism has proved to be a very sharp tool of Satan, blinding many to their true condition before a holy and righteous God. Material possessions have a way of fixing a person's heart to this world. **1 Corinthians 3:12** *'If any man builds on this foundation using gold, silver, costly stones, wood, hay or straw, his work will be shown for what it is, because the Day will bring it to light.'*

In **v24** the disciples were amazed at Jesus' words, for it was generally held among the Jews that wealth was an indication of God's pleasure. If a man was rich, God must have blessed him. The sentiment of the disciples in **v26** seemed to be – 'If this man cannot enter the kingdom of God – then who can?' Once again, Jesus, with a tone of endearment, had to stress that it was *'hard'* to enter the Kingdom of God. Not hard in terms of being beyond a person's reach, but hard, in that it called for humility and simple trust.

Using the picture of a camel going through the eye of a needle **(v25)**, was Jesus' way of helping the disciples understand the degree of difficulty for the rich to enter the Kingdom of God. The implication is that of degree of difficulty.[4]

Having 'looked' earlier at the rich young man, Jesus now set his 'gaze' upon His disciples **(v27)**. In one sweeping statement He declares that salvation is only possible on the basis of what God has done, not on human merit – *'With man this is impossible, but not with God; all things are possible with God.'* The man who trusts in himself and his possessions can never enter the Kingdom of God, but the man whose trust is in Christ

[4] 'In spite of its beautiful imagery, there does not seem to be good early evidence for the view that the eye of a needle is a postern-gate in the city wall, with a consequent need for the camel to kneel and be unloaded if he is to be pushed through. It is better to regard this forced explanation as a piece of Christian 'midrash' rather than exegesis, and see the metaphor as one of sheer impossibility.' New Testament Commentary. Tyndale. IVP 1983. Cole, R. Alan. p164-165

and His gospel of grace can freely enter. '*Jesus answered, 'I tell you the truth, no-one can enter the Kingdom of God unless he is born of water and the Spirit'* (**Jn 3:5**).

Verses 28-31. Peter had just witnessed a man's plain refusal to follow Jesus. This man was not prepared to relinquish his wealth in favour of following Jesus. Having assessed the situation, Peter wasted no time in drawing a contrast, and said to Jesus, *'We have left everything to follow you!'* Was this a form of self exaltation? Was it a fresh affirmation? There is possibly a third alternative. In the light of Jesus' response, it could be that Peter, as the spokesman, was asking what was in it for them – what reward! Matthew's account confirms this - **19:27** *'We have left everything to follow you! What then will there be for us?'*

Peter was right! Jesus made no attempt to correct him – they 'had left all to follow Him.' They may not have possessed as much as the rich young man, but the fact remained that whatever they had, they left it all to follow Jesus!

In **vv29-30** Jesus widened the issue by dealing with the principle in question. Whether it is the rich young man, the disciples or whoever; it made no difference. Those who leave family, possessions or anything else, for Jesus' sake and the gospel, will be rewarded infinitely. Whatever sacrifice is made by those who 'take up the cross and follow Christ,' will be far outweighed by the eternal gain of belonging to the family of God. *'Now if we are children, then we are heirs – heirs of God and co-heirs with Christ, if indeed we share in his sufferings in order that we may also share in his glory'* (**Rom 8:17**).

Verse 31. *'But many who are first, will be last, and the last first.'* These words provide a postscript to this section. The final standard of judgement is with God. There may be some who, because of their religious pedigree (like the Jews at that time), consider themselves to be safe in God's kingdom. Others, past and present, may view their inclusion in God's kingdom on the basis that God is a loving and gracious God.

The fact is this; man's sense of judgement is imperfect, some may be first in their own eyes, but not in God's. **Genesis 18:25** asks, ' *....will not the Judge of all the earth do right?'* God's values are often quite different from man's.

Jesus predicts His death. 10:32-34

> *'They were on their way up to Jerusalem, with Jesus leading the way, and the disciples were astonished, while those who followed were afraid. Again he took the Twelve aside and told them what was going to happen to him. 'We are going up to Jerusalem,' he said, 'and the Son of Man will be betrayed to the chief priests and teachers of the law. They will condemn him to death and will hand him over to the Gentiles, who will mock him and spit on him, flog him and kill him. Three days later he will rise.'*

This is now the third prediction of Jesus' death and resurrection and provides more detail than the previous two (**8:31, 9:31**). Mark's three passion predictions are a reminder to his readers that the death and resurrection of Jesus were part of God's purpose. The obedience of Jesus to His Father's will further endorses this fact. He was now openly making His way to Jerusalem.

Verse 32. Jesus was leading the way. He was a man driven on with a sense of purpose. His every step was a step of obedience; fulfilling His Father's will as He moved with unflinching determination towards Jerusalem, where the suffering of body and soul awaited Him.

As they witnessed Jesus striding courageously ahead of them, the disciples were astonished, and those behind them were afraid. Why should this be? Mark sheds no light on this. It is left to his readers to picture the scene, if at all possible, and sense the intensity of Jesus, as He absorbed in an ever increasing way, the reality of what lay ahead for Him. Perhaps the disciples, and those around had detected some form of change from Jesus' body language and demeanour.

Separating the Twelve from the others, (as He had done previously with some or all of the group).[5] He took them aside and told them (for the third time) what was going to happen to Him. Jesus had difficult things to share with them; He knew that they would not understand. Once again, referring to Himself as the Son of Man,[6] Jesus told them what Jerusalem would hold for Him **(vv33-34)**.

- Betrayed and handed over to the priests and teachers of the law. (Fulfilled in **14:53**)
- Condemn Him to death. (Fulfilled in **14:55-64**)
- Be handed over to the Gentiles. (Fulfilled in **15:1**)
- Mock Him and spit upon Him. (Fulfilled in **15:16-20**)
- Flog Him and kill Him. (Fulfilled in **15:15**)
- Three days later He would rise. (Fulfilled in **16:1ff**)

It was impossible for the disciples to comprehend all these things. How could they? These were hard truths to hear and, perhaps, a deeper understanding would only have meant further distress for them. At that time they were blind to the meaning of the cross. After Jesus' resurrection, however, these words would fall into place. Only then, would they understand. Even the promise of being raised after three days could not cushion the blow.

True greatness explained. 10:35-45

> *'Then James and John, the sons of Zebedee, came to him. 'Teacher,' they said, 'we want you to do for us whatever we ask.' 'What do you want me to do for you?' he asked. They replied, 'Let one of us sit at*

[5] Mark 3:13; 4:35-36; 5:37,40; 6:31,45; 7:17,33; 9:2.

[6] See 8:31ff for more information on the Son of Man.

> *your right and the other at your left in your glory.' 'You don't know what you are asking,' Jesus said. 'Can you drink the cup that I drink or be baptised with the baptism I am baptised with?' 'We can,' they answered. Jesus said to them, 'You will drink the cup I drink and be baptised with the baptism I am baptised with, but to sit at my right or left is not for me to grant. These places belong to those for whom they have been prepared.'*
> *When the ten heard about this, they became indignant with James and John. Jesus called them together and said, 'You know that those regarded as rulers of the Gentiles lord it over them, and their high officials exercise authority over them. Not so with you. Instead, whoever wants to become great among you must be your servant, and whoever wants to be first must be slave of all. For even the Son of Man did not come to be served, but to serve, and to give his life as a ransom for many.'*

Ordinary men for sure! Yet Jesus chose them, with all their imperfection and ignoble credentials, to be servants of His gospel. Post Resurrection and Pentecost, these men, filled with the Holy Spirit, would become God's instruments for the establishing of the New Testament Church, and turn the world upside down.

On this occasion, however, two of those closest to Jesus, James and John, set their sights on the place of privilege and rank. In doing so, they once again demonstrated their ignorance in relation to the true nature of Christ's Kingdom.

In **v35** James and John approached Jesus and asked Him for what amounted to a 'blank cheque'; *'we want you to do for us whatever we ask.'* Was this blatant cheek? Did they think that being part of Jesus' inner circle gave them the right to ask for an exalted position in His Kingdom? And so, Jesus asked

'What do you want me to do for you?' **(v36)**. He could have rebuked them, but treated them graciously, in a way that allowed Him to teach the essence of true greatness and the cost of genuine discipleship.

Their request in **v37**, to sit on either side of Jesus in His glory, was probably not their idea. According to Matthew's record of the event in **20:20**, it was their mother who came to Jesus with James and John; and *'kneeling down, asked a favour of Him.'* In **Matthew 20:21** we read *'She said.'* It may, therefore, be concluded that it was their mother who made the request on their behalf. However, James and John could have refused, but did not!

The words *'in your glory'* are expressed in Matthews account as *'in your Kingdom'* **(20:21)**. These terms are synonymous; there is no conflict in meaning. As previously mentioned, the disciples did not yet fully understand the true nature and concept of the Kingdom, their minds were, as yet, thinking on an earthly Kingdom, which they assumed Jesus would soon establish.

Jesus, in **v38**, made it clear that they were asking a question that was way out of their depth. His reply came in the form of a question which introduced two important words – cup and baptism! *'Can you drink the cup I drink or be baptised with the baptism I am baptised with?*

Firstly, the cup – what was its significance?

In the Old Testament the cup is mentioned in a number of passages,[7] and is usually associated with suffering or punishment under the hand of God. In the New Testament the cup is associated with Jesus' suffering, and the punishment He willingly received on behalf of others on the cross. Referring to His crucifixion, Jesus said to Peter in **John 18:11** *'Shall I not drink the cup the Father has given me?'*

---

[7] Ps 75:8; Is 51:17-23; Jer 49:12; Lam 4:21; Ezk 23:31-34

The drinking of wine from a cup was also the way instituted by Jesus as a way of remembering Him, referred to as the 'Lord's Supper or Communion.(**Lk 22:17ff**)'. In this connection, bread is broken and eaten to remember the broken body of Jesus. The cup of wine is then shared with the outpoured blood of Jesus in mind. These were symbolic.

In **Luke 22:20** Jesus said *'This cup is the new covenant in my blood, which is poured out for you.'* The shed blood of Jesus stood in contrast, and was the fulfilment of the shed blood of animal sacrifice, under the Old Covenant which operated during the Old Testament period.

The cup which Jesus spoke of in **v38** was for Him, a cup of immense suffering of body and of soul. Jesus' sufferings were entirely unique to Him, due to their Atoning purpose. Those who followed Him would also experience suffering for His sake (see comments from **8:34ff** on the challenge of discipleship).

Secondly, what is the significance of baptism?

The Greek word for baptism is BAPTISMA, and means to immerse, submersion, to dip. It was used for both John's and Jesus' baptism, which was by total immersion. The same word is used here in **vv38-39**, indicating the completeness and depth of Jesus' suffering – immersed in suffering! Jesus' own words in **Matthew 26:38** are helpful in this connection, *'My soul is overwhelmed with sorrow to the point of death.'*

Verses 39-40. In response to Jesus' question, James and John reply *'We can.'* Though no doubt sincere, their affirmation was based on little understanding. However, with the passing of time, they would willingly suffer for the sake of Christ and His gospel. Jesus acknowledged their reply, but said *'to sit at my right or left is not for me to grant.'* In these words, Jesus submits to the will and eternal purpose of His Father. This was a willing submission.

Verses 41-45. Having heard of James' and John's request, the other ten are concerned that they have missed out. Jesus called them all together. He had a lesson to teach them about the nature of true greatness. He pointed them to the attitude of Gentile rulers, who ruled with authority, and revelled in their position; treating others as subordinates. They liked to exercise authority; it was a form of self-exaltation.

Jesus said in **v42** *'Not so with you.'* Greatness was to be seen through the spirit of a servant. If they wanted to become great, they must learn to serve. The pathway for them, and all who would follow Jesus, must ever be the path of servanthood. It is the way of humility that makes way for the exaltation of Christ. In **John 3:30**, John the Baptist said *'He must become greater; I must become less.'* **Matthew 23:12** *'For whoever exalts himself will be humbled, and whoever humbles himself will be exalted.'*

These were 'Kingdom of God' values, and stood in contrast to the principles of the secular world around them at that time.

Jesus concluded this brief teaching session in **v45** by pointing to the supreme example of humility and servanthood – Himself! Using the title Son of Man, a title which only Jesus used of Himself, and previously considered,[8] He informed the disciples that *'even'* He did not come to be served, but to serve. In life and ministry Jesus was the model example of servanthood. Doctor Luke records these words of Jesus in **Luke 22:27** *'But I am among you as one who serves.'*

The highest form of service, however, expressed by Jesus, was to take place on the cross, where Jesus gave up His life as an atoning sacrifice, a substitute for sinners **(see 1 John 4:10)**. In doing so, we are able to understand the significance of these words *'and to give His life as a ransom for many.'* The word 'ransom' refers to the price of man's redemption. Yet, Jesus not only paid the ransom price – He was the price! The voice of Holy Scripture affirms these glorious truths. **1 Peter 1:18-19**

---

[8] See 8:31ff for more information on the Son of Man.

'For you know that it was not with perishable things such as silver or gold that you were redeemed ..... but with the precious blood of Christ ....' because, *'He himself bore our sins in his own body on the tree....'* **(1 Pet 2:24)**.

Blind Bartimaeus – spiritually and physically made whole. 10:46-52

> *'Then they came to Jericho. As Jesus and his disciples, together with a large crowd, were leaving the city, a blind man, Bartimaeus (that is, the Son of Timaeus), was sitting by the roadside begging. When he heard that it was Jesus of Nazareth, he began to shout, 'Jesus, Son of David, have mercy on me!' Many rebuked him and told him to be quiet, but he shouted all the more, 'Son of David, have mercy on me!' Jesus stopped and said, 'Call him.' So they called to the blind man, 'Cheer up! On your feet! He's calling you.' Throwing his cloak aside, he jumped to his feet and came to Jesus. 'What do you want me to do for you?' Jesus asked him. The blind man said, 'Rabbi, I want to see.' 'Go,' said Jesus, 'your faith has healed you.' Immediately he received his sight and followed Jesus along the road.'*

This is the final healing miracle in Mark's gospel and contains within it a double blessing. It is, without doubt, a beautiful story, worthy of meditation, admiration, and imagination. Evidence of saving and healing faith leap out - pointing to a man gloriously transformed. Bartimaeus was restored spiritually and physically. His life was turned around in every sense as he became a follower of Jesus.

Verse 46 informs us that Jesus and His disciples came to Jericho. Jericho was just fifteen miles from Jerusalem; the place towards which Jesus was resolutely moving. It was as

Jesus and His disciples were leaving this city, with a large crowd in attendance, that they passed by a blind man called Bartimaeus. He was sitting by the roadside begging. Because of his blindness he would have been at the bottom of the social scale and have little or no place in society. To survive, he had to beg.

By this time Jesus had a reputation; that is why the crowds were so large. No doubt Bartimaeus had heard many reports about Jesus. The compassion, words, message and miracles of Jesus would all have reached his ears. In a sense he was a man prepared for the arrival of Jesus. He had never seen Jesus, yet, according to what he had heard, had made up his mind with regards to who Jesus was. According to **v47** he heard that Jesus of Nazareth was coming. This man had no sight, yet possessed great insight. It can only be imagined just how excited he must have been – his greatest wish had come true!

He began to shout, but not '*Jesus of Nazareth*'. He shouted '*Jesus, Son of David, have mercy on me!*' What wonderful words indeed! This title was used exclusively for Jesus as the promised *'Messiah',* and is only used on this one occasion by Mark. By using this title, Bartimaeus demonstrated saving faith in Jesus as the Son of God, recognising Him as the Messiah.[9] Further evidence of this is found in his words *'have mercy on me,'* surely indicating his repentance for sin. There was only one who could forgive sin – Jesus, Saviour, Son of God, Messiah. Many sighted people were blind to this fact, but not Bartimaeus!

The crowds responded to this in **v48** by rebuking Bartimaeus. They told him to be quiet. Who did he think he was? He was just a beggar, of no importance, why should Jesus be interested in someone like him? But he shouted all the more, he would not be silenced! This man not only had faith – but was also persistent.

---

[9] 'Bartimaeus addressed Jesus as 'Son of David.' This was a standard title for the Messiah among the Jews, and had its basis in the Old Testament (e.g. in Jer 23:5,6), although our Lord taught later (12:35-37) that it was not fully adequate because he was God's Son, not simply David's.' Mark – Good News from Jerusalem. Christian Focus. 2003. Geoffrey Grogan.

What wonderful words are these, *'Jesus stopped'* **(v49).** *'Call him'* Jesus said. Humanly speaking Jesus should not have heard this man. Amidst all the hustle, bustle and noise, who could possibly have heard someone sitting down? Jesus not only heard him, but recognised that this was the voice of faith.

At this, those around called Bartimaeus and told him to cheer up and get up – *'He's calling you'* they said. He threw off his cloak, jumped to his feet and, probably with the help of others, made his way to Jesus **(v59).** Jesus called, and Bartimaeus responded – how simple!

In **v51** Jesus said to him *'What do you want me to do for you?'* What makes this question special, indeed unique, is the one who asked it. It was Jesus the Son of God, with whom nothing is impossible. *'All things are possible to those who believe'* **v27**. Having already asked for mercy and shown true faith – he now asked for his sight. He said *'Rabbi I want to see.'* Jesus said *'Go, your faith has healed you.'* Bartimaeus had experienced a double miracle – he received salvation and his eyesight was restored. One moment total blindness, the next unimpaired vision.

Mark informs his readers that his first act of obedience was to follow Jesus. Morna D Hooker comments, 'His faith in Jesus' power, his confession of His authority, and his willingness to follow Him all mark him out as a disciple; his response forms an interesting contrast to the poor showing of the Twelve in the previous story.'[10]

It seems fitting that this story should bring to a close this section of Mark's gospel. Mark leaves his readers with a wonderful picture of salvation. In this picture we also witness the deity of Jesus Christ, together with His wonderful love and compassion towards – just one man!

---

[10] The Gospel according to St. Mark. A&C Black (Publishers Ltd) 1991.

11

The King enters Jerusalem. 11:1-11

'As they approached Jerusalem and came to Bethphage and Bethany at the Mount of Olives, Jesus sent two of his disciples, saying to them, 'Go to the village ahead of you, and just as you enter it, you will find a colt tied there, which no-one has ever ridden. Untie it and bring it here. If anyone asks you, 'Why are you doing this?' tell him, 'The Lord needs it and will send it back here shortly.' They went and found a colt outside in the street, tied at the doorway. As they untied it, some people standing there asked, 'What are you doing, untying that colt?' They answered as Jesus had told them to, and the people let them go.

When they brought the colt to Jesus and threw their cloaks over it, he sat on it.' Many people spread their cloaks on the road, while others spread branches they had cut in the fields. Those who went ahead and those who followed shouted, 'Hosanna! Blessed is he who comes in the name of the Lord!' Blessed is the coming

> *kingdom of our father David! 'Hosanna in the highest!' Jesus entered Jerusalem and went to the temple. He looked around at everything, but since it was already late, he went out to Bethany with the Twelve.'*

The time had come for Jesus to enter Jerusalem, though probably not for the first time.[1] His' Galilean ministry was behind Him; no longer was there any restraint on making His name known; quite the opposite. This was the week of the great Passover festival – a momentous occasion! This was a high point in the Jewish calendar. These celebrations were to remember the great exodus from Egypt 1500 years earlier, when God intervened in a most miraculous ways to make their exodus possible. (**Ex 12:37-51**)

Jerusalem was packed with people who had travelled great distances. It was a hive of activity. Jewish people wanted to attend at least one Passover feast during their lifetime. It has been estimated that there could have been as many as two and a half million who made this pilgrimage.

Shouts of joy rang out as the crowds, including His disciples, engaged in an exultant procession. Some of those people even spread their cloaks and branches on the road before Him. They shouted *'Hosanna! Blessed is he who comes in the name of the Lord!'*

However, the joy and happiness that filled the air would soon change. How fickle and changeable they were, one moment exalting Jesus, the next, putting Him to death. Before the week was over, grief and sadness would possess many – some would even shout aloud 'Crucify Him!' The time was approaching for Jesus to offer up His life on the cross, thereby fulfilling His Father's purpose for the salvation of all who would believe.

---

[1] 'And when we read the fourth gospel we find Jesus frequently in Jerusalem. (John 2:13, 5:1, 7:10). We find in fact that he regularly went up to Jerusalem for the great feasts.' Daily Study Bible. Revised Edition. The Saint Andrew Press. 1979. William Barclay. p263

Almost three years had passed since the Spirit descended on Jesus like a dove, and the Father's voice was heard from heaven *'You are my Son, whom I love; with you I am well pleased'* **(1:10-11)**. At that time John the Baptist introduced Jesus as *'the Lamb of God'* **(Jn 1:29)**. Now, with thousands of bleating lambs shortly to be prepared for slaughter, together with all the hustle, bustle and excitement of the people, the Lamb of God who came to take away the sins of the world - entered Jerusalem!

How timely and God-planned! Jesus was the fulfilment of all that was about to take place – before their very eyes was the true Passover Lamb!

Verses 1-6. Before arriving at Jerusalem they approached Bethphage and Bethany at the Mount of Olives. Bethany was about two miles from Jerusalem and Bethphage a little closer, probably around half a mile. Bethany was also where Mary, Martha and Lazarus lived, which helps us to understand why Jesus would have previously visited Jerusalem. Both of these villages were on the slopes of the Mount of Olives and would have been likely places for pilgrims attending the Passover to lodge.

Two of the disciples were told by Jesus to go to the village ahead of them where they would find a colt tied up on which no-one had ever ridden. The fact that it was an unbroken colt would be in keeping with that reserved for sacred use. The use of the colt is also the fulfilment of **Zec 9:9** *'See your King comes to you, righteous and having salvation, gentle and riding on a donkey.'*[2] (Matthew specifically quotes this as fulfilled prophecy **(Mtt 21:4-5).**

Before going on their errand to fetch the colt, they were also told what to say should they be questioned **(v3)**. According to Mark the disciples did not question Jesus'

---

[2] 'To ride on a horse would have been disastrous. The horse was a military animal. To enter the city in that fashion would have fostered the notion that he was to be a conventional warrior Messiah expected by the Jews at this time, and, perhaps, that his immediate purpose was to free the people from Roman rule.' Mark. Good News from Jerusalem. Christian Focus. 2003. Geoffrey Grogan. p196.

instructions but acted in faith and obedience. They found the colt tied at a doorway. In the process of untying it they were questioned **(v5)**, to which they replied *'The Lord needs it and will send it back here shortly.'*

In this instance the deity of Christ is in evidence. Jesus knew what awaited the disciples, and by informing them, He demonstrated supernatural knowledge. William Barclay's suggestion that Jesus had previously arranged with the colt's owner to borrow it is speculative. Our Lord may have made this arrangement but it is uncertain.

Verses 7-11. In preparation for Jesus sitting on the colt the disciples threw their cloaks over it; then Jesus sat on it. In **v8** Mark informs his readers that *'many people'* spread their cloaks and branches on the road; only John in his gospel used the word 'palm' **(Jn 12:13)**. Matthew describes this as *'a very large crowd'*. Remembering that by this time Jesus had a reputation; together with the Passover crowds, there is every reason to envisage an extremely large and excited crowd. Bearing in mind Jesus' teaching and references to the Kingdom of God,[3] the people were being carried along on an emotional high.

The people's understanding of the Kingdom of God would have been varied. Though most thought of the Kingdom in earthly and political terms, there would surely be those who genuinely looked and waited for the Messiah. Whatever their understanding, they were full of expectation!

In **vv9-10** Mark quoted from **Psalm 118:25-26**. The scene before Mark's readers can only be imagined. Jesus was surrounded by people, shouting and crying out *'Hosanna!'* As the King seated on the colt, He approached Jerusalem. Meekness and majesty epitomise Jesus, an apt description of the character of Jesus and His Kingdom. The word *'Hosanna'* literally means 'save now' and introduces the concept of salvation.

Clearly there is a Messianic expectation in the words *'Blessed is he who comes in the name of the Lord!'* That Jesus

---

[3] Daily Study Bible. Revised Edition. The Saint Andress Press 1979. Chapters 1:15: 3:24: 4:11,26,30: 9:1,47: 10:14,15, 23-25.

is the subject of fulfilled prophecy here cannot be in doubt. The word *'blessed'* is a way of affirming the Divine person of Jesus, rather than conveying a blessing to others.

Verse 11 brings this section to a close with Jesus entering Jerusalem and going to the temple, but since it was late He went back to Bethany with the Twelve. The phrase *'He looked around at everything'* may seem insignificant, yet it informs the reader that Jesus carefully observed the temple area. The very next day, and with righteous indignation, Jesus would clear and cleanse that same area.

This story would be incomplete, however, without reference to additional information from **Luke 19:41**. *'As he approached Jerusalem and saw the city, he wept over it and said, 'If you, even you, had only known on this day what would bring you peace – but now it is hidden from your eyes.* Jesus' heart was full of sorrow and sadness for those who were blind to their spiritual need. He could scarcely contain His emotions, so that His feelings found expression through His tears.

How telling are the words - *'Jesus wept!'*[4] The Greek word used here is KLAIO, and means 'to sob deeply, to lament in the sense of mourning.' Amidst the crowd's acclamations of joy, Jesus grieved for their spiritual blindness, sin and unbelief. His tears are also a tender expression of love!

The Temple and the fig tree. 11:12-26

> *'The next day as they were leaving Bethany, Jesus was hungry. Seeing in the distance a fig-tree in leaf, he went to find out if it had any fruit. When he reached it, he found nothing but leaves, because it was not the season for figs. Then he said to the tree, 'May no-one ever eat from you again.' And his*

[4] Only on three occasions do we read of Jesus weeping. Jn 11:35. At the death of Lazarus. Lk 19:41. As Jesus entered Jerusalem. Heb 5:7 'He offered up prayers with loud cries and tears.'

> *disciples heard him say it. On reaching Jerusalem, Jesus entered the temple area and began driving out those who were buying and selling there. He overturned the tables of the money-changers and the benches of those selling doves, and would not allow anyone to carry merchandise through the temple courts. And as he taught them, he said, 'Is it not written: 'My house will be called a house of prayer for all nations.' But you have made it a den of robbers.'*
> *The chief priests and the teachers of the law heard this and began looking for a way to kill him, for they feared him, because the whole crowd was amazed at his teaching. When evening came, they went out of the city. In the morning, as they went along, they saw the fig-tree withered from the roots. Peter remembered and said to Jesus, 'Rabbi, look! The tree you cursed has withered!' 'Have faith in God,' Jesus answered. 'I tell you the truth, if anyone says to this mountain, 'Go, throw yourself into the sea,' and does not doubt in his heart but believes that what he says will happen, it will be done for him. Therefore I tell you, whatever you ask for in prayer, believe that you have received it, and it will be yours. And when you stand praying, if you hold anything against anyone, forgive him, so that your Father in heaven may forgive you your sins.'*

Mark employed a method in this section which he had previously done in chapter 5 where the narrative weaved between two stories - the raising of a dead girl and the healing of a woman. Likewise, there are two stories in this section. Mark began and ended with the story of the fig-tree. Wedged between was the cleansing of the temple.

The cleansing of the Temple. vv15-19.

Jesus then entered the *'temple area'* (**v15**), which was the outer court or court of the Gentiles. In doing so, He witnessed a sorry sight. The court of the Gentiles was the most outward part of the temple, which was a beautiful and elaborate structure. Other areas included the court of women, the priest's court, Israel's court, and the most sacred part of all – the holy of holies. The entire temple area would have measured about one thousand feet on each side and been surrounded by a massive outer wall.

The intended purpose of this court was as a place of prayer and preparation - **v17** *'a house of prayer for all nations.'* This was a quote from **Isaiah 56:7**. It may also be noted that Jesus *'taught them'* (**v17**). Mark records this fact but leaves his readers without any knowledge of the content of such teaching.

The court of the Gentiles was a very spacious area which had degenerated into a large outdoor market for buying, selling, and exchanging currencies and merchandise. Remembering that this was Passover week, it would be much busier than normal. Instead of the priests using this as an area of influence to the non-Jew, they used it as a means of transacting business.

Among others, the poor suffered greatly at their hands, they were robbed, hence in **v17** *'But you have made it a den of robbers.'* Pilgrims were defrauded as extortionate prices were charged for animals that were to be sacrificed as part of the Passover celebration.

As soon as Jesus entered Jerusalem and saw the terrible desecration of the outer court He reacted in a way that must have shocked the people; and possibly His disciples! According to **John 2:13-17** Jesus had already shown His thorough distaste for a similar situation during the earlier part of His ministry. Now, however, it is clear that with the passing of time the Temple custodians had reverted to their old ways.

By providing a few details Mark helps his readers to picture the scene. Jesus drove out the offenders, threw the tables with their contents over, no doubt causing great havoc and confusion. He would not even allow the priests to carry their goods through the court **(v15-16)**. Clearly Jesus was disturbed by all that He saw, and, not surprisingly, acted with righteous anger.

Why did Jesus react in this violent way?

- He saw the desecration of God's Holy place. There was no reverence, sense of God's presence or respect.
- He saw the exploitation of the pilgrims at the hands of priests who should have known better. Their actions were hypocritical, and stood in contrast to the ethics and principles of their faith.
- He saw in their behaviour a reflection of their true spiritual condition.

It is safe to assume that any other person acting in this way would have been arrested – yet Jesus was not just any other person, He was the Son of God. His actions bore the stamp of His Father's approval and His character radiated divine authority. Nevertheless, we read in **v18** that the chief priests and teachers of the law were looking for a way to kill Him, *'for they feared him.'* They felt threatened; having recognised how popular Jesus was with the people, for we read *'the whole crowd were amazed at him.'* They could not afford to have Him killed publicly for fear of an uprising by the people – so they started to examine their options.

Jesus' own words in **John 3:19** are quite telling in relation to their actions – *'This is the verdict: Light has come into the world, but men loved darkness instead of light because their deeds were evil.'* Their evil intentions exposed the darkness of their hearts and their wayward spiritual condition. Mark concludes in **v19** with '*When evening came, they went out of the city.'*

The fig tree. vv12-14, 20-26.

Verses 12-14. At the beginning of the next day Mark simply states *'Jesus was hungry'* (**v12**), in doing so he reminds his readers of the humanity of Jesus. As a human person Jesus experienced all the symptoms and emotions anyone else would. Pain, tiredness and hunger were all part of the human package which enabled Him to understand others **(Heb 4:15)**. Taking upon Himself a human body was part of Jesus' humiliation and necessary for His atoning sacrifice on the cross **(Phil 2:8)**.

This short story raises certain questions. Why was Jesus hungry, did He not have breakfast before leaving Bethany? Why did He expect to find figs on a tree that was not yet in season **(v13)**? Why would Jesus condemn the tree to a fruitless existence? Was He not out of character? The fact is that Mark tells this story not so much to raise questions – but simply to record what he saw. There is, however, a connection between this story and the cleansing of the temple – thereby making good sense of the two stories being interwoven.

When Jesus approached the fig tree He discovered that although it had leaves, it had no figs. There is no sound reason why Jesus would pronounce a curse on this tree as a form of punishment. There has to be another reason. The likelihood is that Jesus was acting out a parable (the message was in his actions), as was the case with some Old Testament prophets. Two examples are found in **Isaiah 20** and **Ezekiel 14**. This is often done in churches today by means of drama.

Jesus' actions were symbolic and focused on the nation of Israel who had failed to produce the appropriate fruits expected by her Messiah. As God's chosen people, Israel had failed to maintain the light and glory of God. The cleansing of the temple and the judgement on the fig tree were symbolic of Israel as a nation which had fallen under the judgement of God.[5]

---

[5] 'Equally important is the expectation that in the messianic age the fig tree will bear fruit. The fig tree is an emblem of peace and prosperity: hope for the future is expressed in terms of sitting in security under one's vine and one's fig tree (e,g. Mic 4:4; Zec 3:10) and gathering fruit from them.' The Gospel according to Mark. A & C Black (publishers Ltd) 1991. Hooker, Morna D. p262

Israel's spirituality could be summed up at that time from this fig tree lesson. Plenty of leaves but no fruit! An abundance of religious activity but empty of sincerity and truth!

According to **v14** the disciples heard Jesus cursing the fig-tree. Whether or not Jesus amplified on this fig-tree judgement is not made clear. It would be most unlikely, however, that the disciples would not seek a reason for Jesus' actions, for they stood in contrast to all they had seen and heard so far.

The fact that Jesus cursed the fig-tree in the presence of the disciples suggests that there was a lesson here for them. A lesson to remember! In **Matthew 23:3**, Jesus, speaking about the teachers of the law and Pharisees, said *But do not do what they do, for they do not practise what they preach.'*

Verses 20-26. Passing by that way again the next morning, the disciples saw that the fig-tree had withered to the roots **(v20)**. Peter, as the spokesman, said to Jesus *'Rabbi, look! The fig-tree you cursed has withered* **(v21)**.*'* Peter was astonished that in such a short time the tree should wither. In response, Jesus spoke to them about 'faith and prayer'.

The exhortation was to *'Have faith in God* **(v22)**'. This passage must be interpreted in conjunction with other scriptures. Can it really be that so long as a believer prays in faith, that his or her prayer will be answered, irrespective as to the request being made? If this was the case, then it would be the will of man that is brought about, and not necessarily the will of God. How then is **v24** to be understood? *'Therefore I tell you, whatever you ask for in prayer, believe that you have received it and it will be yours.'*

It is often said that the purpose of prayer is not to get man's will done in heaven, but to get God's will done here on earth. What would be a sound faith/prayer formula? Faith > Prompting of The Holy Spirit > Prayer > God's will on earth. Jesus said in **Matthew 6:9** *'This then, is how you should pray ...'*. **v10** *'your will be done on earth as it is in heaven.'* In the light of Jesus' teaching on prayer, the expression of faith surely finds at the heart of it the over-riding desire for God's will to be done. For God's way is perfect, even although the believer may struggle at times to make sense of it. God does know best!

This passage is not so much about the content of prayers – but rather, the believer's attitude in prayer. There are certain principles worth noting.

- Believers are to have faith in God and not to doubt.
- Believers are to make their requests without limitation or reservation.
- Believers should make their requests primarily for the glory of God, and with *'your will be done'* in mind **(Mtt 6:10)**.

The best possible answer to prayers will always be with God's will in mind. The reason for Jesus speaking of casting a mountain into the sea **(v23)** was to show that with God nothing is impossible. No request is too great! In **9:23** Jesus had previously made this point *'Everything is possible for him who believes.'*

In **v25** Jesus had one final lesson for the disciples. In a nutshell, they had not to allow anything to hinder their prayers; in particular, in relation to others.[6]

Jesus' authority questioned. 11:27-33

> *'They arrived again in Jerusalem, and while Jesus was walking in the temple courts, the chief priests, the teachers of the law and the elders came to him. 'By what authority are you doing these things?' they asked. 'And who gave you authority to do this?' Jesus replied, 'I will ask you one question. Answer me, and I will tell you by what authority I am doing*

[6] The NIV does not contain verse 26 'But if ye do not forgive, neither will your Father which is in heaven forgive your trespasses.' Although the Authorised Version includes this verse, it is omitted in some important manuscripts. This does not detract, however, from the truth expressed since it is also found in Matthew 6:15.

> *these things. John's baptism – was it from heaven, or from men? Tell me!' They discussed it among themselves and said, 'If we say, 'From heaven', he will ask, 'Then why didn't you believe him?' But if we say, 'From men . . . .' (They feared the people, for everyone held that John really was a prophet.) So they answered Jesus, 'We don't know.' Jesus said, 'Neither will I tell you by what authority I am doing these things.'*

Within the scope of just a few days much had happened in Jerusalem. Jesus had been welcomed into Jerusalem by the people with great joy, excitement and expectation. Having cleansed the temple He attracted much attention to Himself. His actions would have been the subject of much discussion. Not surprisingly, as Jesus once again made His way to the temple, a certain group of people wanted to speak with Him, in fact, to question Him.

This group, made up of chief priests, teachers of the law and the elders, were collectively known as the Sanhedrin. They were the council or supreme Jewish court who represented the Jews in matters pertaining to religion, law and justice; although their remit was somewhat wider. It was normal for the high priest to be their president.

On numerous occasions Jesus condemned the hypocrisy of the Pharisees and teachers of the law. An example of this is found in **Matthew chapter 23** where Jesus called them hypocrites, blind guides, blind fools and whitewashed tombs.

Not for the first time they were out to get Him! Seeing Jesus at the temple they came to Him **(v27)**. As they did previously **(10:2)**; they wanted to put Him to the test. *'By what authority are you doing these things?'* they asked Jesus.

What did they mean by *'these things'*? This must have referred to His recent activities in the court of the Gentiles. But not only this, for according to **Matthew 21:23** Jesus was teaching in the temple. **Luke** also, in **20:1** says that Jesus was preaching the gospel.

What right did Jesus have to exercise such authority? Who gave Him permission to act in such a way and teach the people? What were His credentials? Who did He think He was? Clearly, the Sanhedrin members saw an opportunity to discredit Jesus; the time seemed right to sort Him out. Although the Sanhedrin had the responsibility to investigate anyone who claimed to be sent by God, including Jesus, their motives on this occasion were not honourable. They were not seeking the truth but evidence to destroy Jesus. **(see v18)**.

In response to their question *'And who gave you authority to do this?'* **(v28)**, Jesus replied with another question. *'John's baptism – was it from heaven, or from men? Tell me!'* **(v30)**, Should they answer this question, then Jesus would answer their question. They were driven into a corner! If they held that John's baptism was from heaven, then why did they not obey his teaching? Many of them were proud and the farthest thing from their minds was to repent of their sins in public through John's baptism. This would have been a hard thing for them to do.

On the other hand if they said it was from men, they would be very unpopular with the people, *'They feared the people'* **(v32),** who believed that he was a prophet from God. Mark affirmed John's popularity with the people in **1:5** *'The whole Judean countryside and all the people of Jerusalem went out to him.'* Discussing their position and how they should respond **(vv31-33)**, they replied *'We don't know.'* They stood self-condemned.

This was a unique occasion. Rarely if ever, would these Jewish leaders be left without words. Mark's account of their discussion indicates that they refused to acknowledge the truth, both in relation to John the Baptist and Jesus. Jesus, therefore, provided no reason for His authority.

It might seem at first glance that Jesus could have said more than He did, yet with just a few chosen words from the lips of the Son of God, He silenced His critics. In doing so Jesus effectively declared that just like John the Baptist, His authority was from God. There was no need to elaborate; His words were simple and direct, manifesting the wisdom and power of God. Furthermore, it may be that Jesus did not consider their hypocrisy worthy of a more comprehensive response.

12

The parable of the tenants. 12:1-12

'He then began to speak to them in parables: 'A man planted a vineyard. He put a wall around it, dug a pit for the winepress and built a watchtower. Then he rented the vineyard to some farmers and went away on a journey. At harvest time he sent a servant to the tenants to collect from them some of the fruit from the vineyard. But they seized him, beat him and sent him away empty-handed. Then he sent another servant to them; they struck this man on the head and treated him shamefully. He sent still another and that one they killed. He sent many others; some of them they beat, others they killed.

He had one left to send, a son, whom he loved. He sent him last of all, saying, 'They will respect my son.' But the tenants said to one another, 'This is the heir. Come, let's kill him, and the inheritance will be ours.' So they took him and killed him, and threw him out of the vineyard. What then will the owner of the

> *vineyard do? He will come and kill those tenants and give the vineyard to others. Haven't you read this scripture: 'The stone the builders rejected has become the capstone, the Lord has done this, and it is marvellous in our eyes?' Then they looked for a way to arrest him because they knew he had spoken the parable against them. But they were afraid of the crowd; so they left him and went away.'*

Having left the delegation from the Sanhedrin with much to think about regarding His authority; Jesus then told them a parable. They would have been familiar with the Old Testament and this picture of the vineyard, which finds its background in **Isaiah 5:1-7**, would not be difficult for them to understand. It is presented by Isaiah as 'The song of the vineyard,' for the prophet may well have sung his message. The details of the vineyard, as recorded by Mark, are in keeping with the Isaiah account – the planting, the wall, the pit and the watchtower are all listed **(v1)**. Mark uses the plural: parables. On this occasion however, he records only one.

The principle employed was that of an owner renting out his vineyard to others, followed by regular collection of the rental, often paid in produce from the land. This was a practice common at that time. Because of their knowledge of Isaiah, together with that local practice, the meaning from the parable would come across loud and clear.

Verses 2-5. The owner of the vineyard is God and the vineyard itself is the people of Israel. The tenants of the vineyard are Israel's religious leaders. In essence the parable is straight-forward. At harvest time the owner sent a servant to collect what was due. The tenants decided to give the servant nothing and beat him up before sending him on his way. Another servant sent by the owner is also assaulted and sent away empty-handed. Yet another servant is sent, this time they killed him. The owner was incredibly patient and persistent, for

v5 says *'He sent many others; some they beat, others they killed.'*

The pattern was clear for Jesus' hearers to follow; they knew that for centuries God had communicated through numerous Old Testament prophets to His chosen people Israel – yet often without response or blatant rejection. It made no difference whether it was Daniel in great dignity, Jeremiah with his tears or Ezekiel's eloquence. (See **1 Kgs1:10: Ez 2:7: Is 5:24: 53:3: Jer 8:9: Jn 1:11**).

The parable reaches its climax in **vv6-8**. One final possibility remained for the owner – to send the only person he had left, his son, whom he loved. The owner was convinced that they would (in spite of their previous actions) listen to his son. Yet how wrong he was! Such was the evil in their hearts that they saw this as an opportunity to take possession of the vineyard by killing the heir.

Having finished telling the parable, but not yet explaining it, Jesus asked His audience **(v9)** *'What then will the owner of the vineyard do?'* They are in no doubt what their response should be – *'He will come and kill those tenants and give the vineyard to others.'* By giving this answer they condemned themselves. At that moment the penny had not yet dropped – for 'they' were the tenants!

Jesus then surprised them by quoting in **vv10-11** from **Psalm 118:22-23**. The capstone or cornerstone was usually the last stone to be fitted into the corner of a building. It was the most important stone and was a hallmark of the builder's work. Having already rejected God's revelation through the prophets, they would also reject Jesus who was the capstone.

In **1 Peter 2:6** we read *'See, I lay in Zion, a chosen and precious cornerstone, and the one who trusts in him will never be put to shame.'* Jesus was the Father's last word to them, His Son whom He loved. *'In the past God spoke to our forefathers through the prophets at many times and in various ways, but in these last days he has spoken to us by his Son, whom he* *appointed heir of all things, and through whom he made the universe'* (**Heb 1:1-2**).

When they realised that Jesus was telling this parable against them, and that they were the ones who would reject Him, they wanted to arrest Him (**v12**). Once again they feared the crowd and could not act out their true feelings of rejection. This parable not only exposed their attitude towards God's past revelation, but was also a deliberate challenge to the Jewish authorities because it contained the unmistakable claim of Jesus as the Messiah.

This parable contains other truths which point to the character of God.

- It is a reminder of the generosity and love of God.
- It is a reminder to the Church of its responsibility to the grace of God.
- It is a reminder of the wonderful patience of God.
- It is a reminder that God is also a God of justice.

Trick question about paying tax. 12:13-17

> *'Later they sent some of the Pharisees and Herodians to Jesus to catch him in his words. They came to him and said, 'Teacher, we know you are a man of integrity. You aren't swayed by men, because you pay no attention to who they are; but you teach the way of God according to the truth. Is it right to pay taxes to Caesar or not? Should we pay taxes or shouldn't we?' But Jesus knew their hypocrisy. 'Why are you trying to trap me?' he asked. 'Bring me a denarius and let me look at it. They brought the coin, and he asked them, 'Whose portrait is this? And whose inscription?' 'Caesar's', they replied. Then Jesus said to them, 'Give to Caesar what is Caesar's and to God what is God's.' And they were amazed at him.'*

Following Jesus' entrance into Jerusalem it is clear that opposition continued to build up against Him.

- **11:8** After cleansing the temple - *'They began looking for a way to kill Him.'*
- **11:28** Questioning His authority - *'By what authority are you doing these things?'*
- **12:12** Following the parable of the tenants - *'They looked for a way to kill him.'*
- **12:13** They attempted to trick Him – *'to catch him in his words.'*

The first thing to notice from this incident is who it was that came to Jesus. The Pharisees and the Herodians! A most unlikely combination! The Pharisees were teachers of the law and dedicated to uphold it. Jesus had previously described them as hypocrites and play-actors **(Mtt 23)**. They stood in opposition to the Roman authorities.

The Herodians were attached to Herod's family and were supporters of the Roman authorities.

These two parties held little in common. However, in their pursuit of this righteous man they were prepared to waive their differences. The Pharisees did not like Jesus because He exposed their hypocrisy. The Herodians were afraid that Jesus would create more political instability, thereby making it less likely that the Roman leaders would step down and be replaced by a descendant of Herod. These were reasons enough to stand together against Jesus.

Verse **13** informs the reader why they came to Jesus – *'to catch him in his words.'* Their purpose was to trap Jesus. They had schemed and plotted until they thought they had the perfect plan. The phrase *'to catch him'* is taken from the world of the hunter and conveys the idea of using the correct bait to ensnare chosen prey. Their cunning approach involved a threefold deceit which led to their question, *'Is it right to pay taxes to Caesar or not?* **(v14)**.

- **Flattery**. *'Teacher we know that you are a man of integrity.'* This may have fooled others but not Jesus. Appealing to His ego was a waste of time. *'But Jesus would not entrust himself to them, for he knew all men......he knew what was in a man'* (**Jn 2:24-25**).
- **Strength of character**. *'You aren't swayed by men, because you pay no attention to who they are.'* Jesus was not impressed by, nor did He bow down to human position or greatness. Before this deceitful group, stood one who was the King of Kings and Lord of Lords – there was no-one greater! **Hebrews 1:8** is clear in its statement of God's interface with Jesus; *'But about the Son he says, 'Your throne, O God, will last for ever and ever, and righteousness is the sceptre of your Kingdom.'*
- **Truth**. *'But you teach the way of God in accordance with the truth.'* They were telling Jesus that He was a teacher of truth – yet refused to obey His teaching. In **John 8:45** Jesus said *'Yet because I tell you the truth, you do not believe me.'*

Compliments may swell the heads of many – but not Jesus! Mark informed his readers that *'Jesus knew their hypocrisy. Why are you trying to trap me?'* (**v15**). Should they pay taxes to Caesar or not? If Jesus said yes, He would have shown allegiance to Caesar. If He said 'no,' He would have encouraged rebellion against Rome. This joint delegation thought they had put Jesus in an impossible no-win situation. Could Jesus get out of this?

With great simplicity and a masterly touch Jesus asked for a coin (denarius). The denarius had the image of Caesar's head on one side with the words 'Tiberius Caesar Augustus, son of the divine Augustus'. On the other side, Caesar's image is seated on the throne with the words 'highest priest'.

Having looked at the coin, Jesus' answer in **vv16-17** amazed them! *'Give to Caesar what is Caesar's and to God* *what belongs to God.'* This must have surprised them. His answer also emphasised the divisions in society at that time. Not only did it partly favour Caesar – but also introduced a responsibility towards God.

Jesus' answer was not evading their question but pointed towards a twofold responsibility for all men and women - both then and now. **Firstly**, it is right to pay taxes to those in authority, in this case Caesar.[1] **Secondly**, just as the image of Caesar was on the denarius, likewise, the image of God is upon all humankind – albeit distorted because of sin – yet bringing a responsibility towards God.

Although Christians have a responsibility to be good citizens and respect those in authority, there are exceptional occasions when obedience to those in authority and God may be in conflict. This was the case in **Acts 4:18-20** when the apostles were brought before the Sanhedrin and commanded not to speak or teach in the name of Jesus. Peter and John replied by saying *'Judge for yourselves whether it is right in God's sight to obey you rather than God.'*

The truth taught by Jesus to *'Give to God what is God's'* is relevant to all people of all ages. Those who seek earnestly to follow Jesus Christ may at times find it a battle to give God His rightful place in their lives. This was the way of self denial and the taking up the cross that Jesus spoke of in **(8:34-38)**.

Marriage and the after-life. 12:18-27

> *Then the Sadducees who say that there is no resurrection, came to him with a question. 'Teacher,' they said, 'Moses wrote for us that if a man's brother dies and leaves a wife but no children, the man must marry the widow and have children for his brother. Now there were seven brothers. The first one married*

[1] Not only did Jesus teach the rightness of believers having a responsibility to those in Government – in 1 Tim 2:2-3 the apostle Paul urged that 'request, prayers, intercessions and thanksgiving be made for everyone – for kings and all those in authority.'

> *and died without leaving any children. The second one married the widow, but he also died, leaving no child. It was the same with the third. In fact, none of the seven left any children. Last of all, the woman died too. At the resurrection whose wife will she be, since the seven were married to her?'*
> *Jesus replied, 'Are you not in error because you do not know the Scriptures or the power of God? When the dead rise, they will neither marry nor be given in marriage; they will be like the angels in heaven. Now about the dead rising - have you not read in the book of Moses, in the account of the bush, how God said to him, 'I am the God of Abraham, the God of Isaac, and the God of Jacob'? He is not the God of the dead, but of the living. You are badly mistaken!'*

Another test question is presented to Jesus. It was about the status of marriage at the future resurrection. The questioners on this occasion were the Sadducees and this was their only appearance in Mark's gospel. What is known of the Sadducees? Why did they ask such a question?

The Sadducees were aristocratic and wealthy; enjoying the comfort and privileges that life had to offer. Most of them were priests and the office of high priest was regularly held by a Sadducee. They had a reputation for harshness in relation to meting out justice.

They differed considerably from the Pharisees. The only Scriptures they would accept were the first five books of the Old Testament, known as the Pentateuch, and were ascribed to Moses. Many of the rules and regulations held dear by the Pharisees were dismissed by the Sadducees. They had little room for oral law or tradition. They did not believe in immortality, resurrection **(v18)**, spirits or angels **(see Acts 23:8-10)**.

Their test question was insincere and designed to try and reveal a flaw in the theology of those who believed in the resurrection. They had come up with a way, or so they thought, that would make nonsense of a resurrection. The irony of their question was that they were prepared to quote the resurrection which they didn't even accept. They built their case on the teaching of Moses from **Deuteronomy 25:5-10**,[2] where if a husband died, his brother would be responsible to marry his deceased brother's wife and have children to her. This practice would continue so long as there were other brothers left and so long as no child was born.

The situation presented by the Sadducees to Jesus in **vv19-23** was this: If a woman was widowed seven times, and as result had married all seven brothers, at the resurrection whose wife would she be? Their cunning, however, only revealed their ignorance of the Scriptures and the power of God! Had they been right, it would have been a blow both for Jesus and the Pharisees who believed in a resurrection. From **vv24-27** Jesus made two important points.

Firstly, in **v25** *'When the dead rise, they will neither marry nor be given in marriage; they will be like the angels in heaven.'* Earthly life is temporary and the institution of marriage is therefore limited to life on earth. Marriage, as men and women understand it, will cease to be at the end of this age. The risen will be like angels. Their question was swiftly emptied of its cunning – it was in fact, irrelevant!

Secondly, the Sadducees believed there was no evidence for immortality. How wrong they were, Jesus said *'You do not know the Scriptures* **(v24)** ......*'You are badly mistaken* **(v27)**!' From the writings of Moses which they held dear, Jesus quoted from **Exodus 3:6** – *'I am the God of your father, the God of Abraham, the God of Isaac, and the God of Jacob.'* The point made by Jesus is this; Moses did not write *'I was (*past tense*) the God of ....' 'but I am.'* Abraham, Isaac and Jacob, although

[2] This passage expresses the regulations governing what is known as 'Levirate marriage'.

physically dead, were referred to as being alive, because God *'is not the God of the dead, but of the living'* **(v27).** The Sadducees did not understand that the words of Moses were an affirmation of life after death.

The greatest commandment. 12:28-34

> *One of the teachers of the law came and heard them debating. Noticing that Jesus had given them a good answer, he asked him, 'Of all the commandments, which is the most important?' 'The most important one,' answered Jesus, 'is this, 'Hear, O Israel, the Lord our God, the Lord is one. Love the Lord your God with all your heart and with all your soul and with all your mind and with all your strength.' The second is this: 'Love your neighbour as yourself.' There is no commandment greater than these.' 'Well said, teacher,' the man replied. 'You are right in saying that God is one and that there is no other but him. To love him with all your heart, with all your understanding and with all your strength, and to love your neighbour as yourself is more important than all burnt offerings and sacrifices.' When Jesus saw that he had answered wisely, he said to him, 'You are not far from the kingdom of God.' And from then on no-one dared ask him any more questions.*

According to **v28** one of the teachers (according to **Matthew 22:34**, an 'expert') of the law who had been listening to the previous debate was impressed by the answer Jesus gave, and so it seemed a fitting time to ask another question.

Experts are usually expected to answer rather than ask questions, but not on this occasion. The reason for his question was twofold. Firstly to seek a genuine answer, and secondly to resolve a debate among the Jewish legalists who were always splitting hairs, in particular, in relation to the law and commandments. Warren W. Wiersbe writes 'The scribes had determined that the Jews were obligated to obey 613 precepts in the law, 365 negative precepts and 248 positive. One of their favourite exercises was discussing which of these divine commandments was the greatest.'[3]

The question was *'Of all the commandments, which is the most important?'* **(v28).** Jesus' response in **vv29-31** was comprehensive and dominated by the word 'love.' The first quotation came from **Deuteronomy 6:4-9** which was called the 'Shema'. This name comes from the first Hebrew word of the quotation and means 'hear'. This passage had a special place among the Jews. This would have been the first passage of the Old Testament taught by a mother to her child. It was that important!

The first and greatest responsibility for all men and women, said Jesus, was to *'Love the Lord your God* **(v30)**.*'* Before anyone or anything else in life, love for God was to be the first priority.

The question must then be asked, 'how are people to love God?' Jesus said *'with all your heart and with all your soul and with all your mind and with all your strength.'* In broad terms this refers to the absolute surrender of every fibre of a person's being to love and worship God.

William Hendriksen writes 'What is meant in all these passages is that man should love God with all the 'faculties' with which God has endowed him.'[4] Although care must be taken not to over-analyze, the following suggestions may be helpful.

- **Heart.** Is the core or wheel of a person's existence; the inner being.
- **Soul.** Points towards the seat of emotions, feelings and thoughts.

[3] Mark. 'Be Diligent' Scripture Press. 1991. p120
[4] Mark. NTC. Banner of Truth. 1976. p493

- **Mind.** Directs our attention to the intellectual aspect of life.
- **Strength.** This may be a reference to the physical energy expended.

God calls for a love that is not half-hearted or intermittent, and not based on mere circumstances or feelings. The challenge of this commandment is not dissimilar in principle to the words of the apostle Paul in **Romans 12:1** *'Therefore, I urge you, brothers, in view of God's mercy, to offer your bodies as living sacrifices, holy and pleasing to God – this is your spiritual act of worship.'* In other words; in the light of all that God has done, surely the least that men and women can do, is to offer everything!

In **v31** Jesus speaks of the second most important commandment *'Love your neighbour as yourself.'* This is a quotation from **Leviticus 19:18** and refers to love between fellow Jews. On this occasion, however, Jesus broadens the scope to include Gentiles, for love for others must be without boundaries. Loving one another was also evidence that a person was a true follower of Jesus (**see John 13:35**). These two commandments express the responsibility and challenge to love both God and mankind.

The questioner who was expert in the law was well pleased with Jesus' response (**v32**). Indeed, from **v33** he understood that love for God and others was more important than ritual obligations of the sacrificial laws – *'...... is more important than all burnt offerings and sacrifices.'* The apostle Paul writes in **Romans 13:9-10** *'Love your neighbour as yourself. Love does no harm to its neighbour. Therefore love is the fulfilment of the law.'* In **v32** he also affirms his belief in just one God, *'.... there is no other but him.'*

This man's reply also pleased Jesus (**v34**). As a result Jesus said *'You are not far from the kingdom.'* What telling words these were! By his response he recognised the superiority of inward spiritual life in contrast to that which was external.

He didn't say that burnt offerings and sacrifices were unimportant, but that the commandments relating to the supremacy of love were more important.

In what sense was this teacher of the law near the kingdom? Let us remember that it was Jesus, the One who knew the hearts of all men (**see John 2:25**), who said *'You are not far from the kingdom.'*

- He had knowledge of Scripture.
- He had an enquiring heart and desire to understand more.
- He had a discerning spirit.

Though Jesus' words to this teacher were complimentary and praiseworthy – it must be borne in mind that he was 'near' the kingdom. He had not yet entered the kingdom of God. The work of the Spirit may well have been active in his life, yet whether he ever entered the kingdom is not known. It is possible to be near, yet still far from the kingdom.

There was another teacher of Israel who came to speak with Jesus about this very subject. His name was Nicodemus and he possessed similar qualities. On that occasion Jesus said to him in **John 3:5** *'I tell you the truth, no-one can enter the kingdom of God unless he is born of water and the Spirit.'* Religious and moral credentials may be stacked a mile high, yet entrance into the kingdom of God, said Jesus, could only take place through 'spiritual new birth.' *'You should not be surprised at my saying, 'You must be born again'* (**Jn 3:7**).

Having silenced this group, largely hostile apart from one who was now nearer the kingdom; it is clear that either embarrassment possessed them or their courage fled, because *'no-one dared ask him any more questions* (**v34**).'

A question about the Christ. 12:35-40

> *'While Jesus was teaching in the temple courts, he asked, 'How is it that the teachers of the law say that*

> *the Christ is the son of David? David himself, speaking by the Holy Spirit, declared: 'The Lord said to my Lord: 'Sit at my right hand until I put your enemies under your feet.' David himself calls him 'Lord.' How then can he be his son?' The large crowd listened to him with delight. As he taught, Jesus said, 'Watch out for the teachers of the law. They like to walk around in flowing robes and be greeted in the market-places, and have the most important seats in the synagogues and the places of honour at banquets. They devour widows' houses and for a show make lengthy prayers. Such men will be punished most severely.'*

Verses **35-37**. Jesus was teaching in the temple courts and in the process He asked a question. According to **Matthew 22:41** He was addressing the Pharisees, but in Mark it is a *'large crowd'* **(v37)**. At that time, with just a few days to go before the shadow of the cross would stretch across Jesus' path, it was the right time to ask a question which would cause those present (including the Jewish teachers) to reflect on His true identity.

The background to the question is from **Psalm 110:1** and is not the easiest Scripture to understand. What did Jesus mean when He quoted David' words *'The Lord said to my Lord?'* (**v36**).[5] How are we to understand them? David was saying that 'God the Father was speaking with His pre-incarnate Son, the promised Messiah'. David placed on record an intimate moment between Father and Son. It is unlikely that David understood this because he was *'speaking by the Holy Spirit'* (**v36**).

Most of those in the crowd would have accepted the teaching of this Psalm and would have been familiar with David's words. The teachers of the law taught that the Christ (*Messiah*) would descend from David, yet David himself

---

[5] Reference to Psalm 110:1 is also made by Peter in Acts 2:34, 35, Paul in 1 Cor 15:25, and the author of Hebrews in 1:13; 10:13.

referred to Him as Lord. The question is this. How could He descend from David and also be his Lord?

In **v37** Jesus said *'David himself calls him 'Lord'. How then can he be his son?'* How could He be both son and Lord? Answer! Only if Jesus was the Messiah; which He was! In essence, Jesus was saying:

- He was a descendant of David.
- He was also the Lord of whom David spoke.
- He was affirming that He was the promised Messiah, though in a rather veiled way.

From the story of blind Bartimaeus **(10:46-52)** Jesus made no attempt to correct his words, *'Jesus, Son of David, have mercy on me.'* Indeed, Jesus responded to this title in such a way which affirmed His deity by showing mercy and healing.

Accepting the fact that the Messiah would come from the line of David,[6] the Jews would not have understood that the Messiah would be God in human form. Waiting on the Messiah as a prophet who would deliver them from earthly oppression was one thing – but not God in human form coming to establish His spiritual reign within the human heart.

Although Jesus did not explicitly state that He was the Messiah; by implication the inference is there. Later, no doubt, His hearers would reflect on His question and understand more fully. Jesus was not yet openly teaching that He was the Christ. This would come later **(see 14:61-62)**. It was not unusual for Mark to round off an event with the crowd's response; in this case **v37b** *'The large crowd listened to him with delight.'*

Verses 38-40. Having previously warned the people of the yeast of the Pharisees in **8:15**; Jesus now has a further warning, *'Watch out for the teachers of the law.'* He did so because of the power and influence these men exerted among the people. Many of these religious teachers ought to have been a glowing example to all who wanted to follow God, yet they did not

[6] See 2 Samuel 7:12. Micah 5:2. Psalm 78:68-72.

practise what they preached – they were hypocrites! Here lies a solemn warning for all who are in a position of Christian teaching and responsibility **(See James 3:1)**. Jesus summarised their hypocrisy in four ways.

- **Their clothes (v38)**. They liked to impress people by the way they looked. Walking around in long flowing robes which were neither fit to work in or hurry – it was no more than ostentatious swaggering. They pointed to no-one other than themselves. Meeting others in the market-places gave them the opportunity to express their self-prominence.
- **Place of honour (v39)**. The market-place was not the only opportunity to glorify self. When they gathered for worship their attention was still very much on themselves, not on God – for they sought the prominent seats in the synagogue.[7] These seats would have been at the front where no-one could fail to see them. Likewise, on social occasions the place of honour was their target.
- **Widows (v40)**. The thought behind '*They devour widows*' is that these Jewish teachers took advantage of certain women who would grant them hospitality. Women who had little themselves provided more than they could afford and were made to feel obliged to do so.
- **Prayers (v40)**. Lengthy prayers were a form of spiritual self-exaltation. The Pharisees were notorious for this and knew how to impress others. It has been suggested that their prayers were offered to men rather than God. The parable of the Pharisee and the Tax-collector in **Luke 18:9-14** is typical. The Pharisee stood up in the temple and prayed about himself *'God, I thank you that I am not like other men ....'*

---

[7] 'No form of Christian service we undertake should ever be thought of in terms of status. It is a privilege and is just as much due to the grace of God as is our salvation itself (Eph 3:8, 9)'. Mark. Good news from Jerusalem. Christian Focus. 2003. Geoffrey Grogan. p217

This prideful and egotistic behaviour does not glorify God and incurs the judgement of God. Jesus said *'Such men will be punished most severely* **(v40)**.*'*

Giving! little can be much. 12:41-44

> *'Jesus sat down opposite the place where the offerings were put and watched the crowd putting their money into the temple treasury. Many rich people threw in large amounts. But a poor widow came and put in two very small copper coins, worth only a fraction of a penny. Calling his disciples to him, Jesus said, 'I tell you the truth, this poor widow has put more into the treasury than all the others. They all gave out of their wealth; but she, out of her poverty, put in everything – all she had to live on.'*

This was only one of a few occasions where gospel material is recorded only by Mark and Luke. Mark introduces his readers to a rare picture of Jesus sitting down. Jesus chose to sit in the temple area near where the people placed their offerings. There were thirteen chests, shaped like trumpets, which were placed around the court of women. The offerings were placed in them. Why Jesus sat there is unknown. The fact that he did, however, means that Mark's readers would be privy to lessons drawn from Jesus' observations.

Although individuals may be rich, it is no guarantee that they will give in appropriate measure. On this occasion Jesus observed that certain rich people put in *'large amounts* **(v41)***'*. However, He drew a contrast between the large amounts given by those who were rich and the very small amount given by a poor widow (this contrast is in keeping with the mention of a widow in the previous section).

Although the large amounts given by the rich cannot be discounted, the fact remains that it was unlikely to have affected the quality of their lifestyle. In **v44** Jesus said *'They all gave out of their wealth.'* The point being, that it was not so much what they gave – but what they had left! Once again, their giving was typical of their pomposity and pride as expressed earlier in **vv38-40**. In their case the 'large amounts' had little bearing on their true spirituality.

Verse 42 introduces a considerable change! *'But a poor widow came and put in two very small copper coins, worth only a fraction of a penny.'* There was no ostentation or self-exaltation; no 'look at me' attitude! This poverty stricken widow expressed her worship in a most sacrificial way, she *'put in everything – all she had to live on* **(v44)**.*'*

Jesus made it clear that this woman, by giving this small amount, actually put in more than all of the others put together. Being a widow meant that she had no regular income; it must have been a continual struggle to make ends meet! Yet in all this, there is little doubt where God stood with her – He had the place of pre-eminence.

In this short event we see in Jesus, perfect humanity and deity, setting His wonderful gaze upon ordinary people, taking time to sit and observe. This can only be imagined! The Greek word for 'watched' in **v41** is THEOREO, and literally means 'to gaze or behold'.

This story serves as a useful tool in relation to worship and money, for a person's attitude to money has a remarkable way of revealing the content of their heart.

Jesus said in **Matthew 6:21** *'For where your treasure is, there your heart will also be.'* It is not surprising then that Jesus called His disciples to Him and brought this challenging lesson before them **(v43)**.

13

The Temple building. 13:1-4

> *'As he was leaving the temple, one of his disciples asked him, 'Look Teacher! What massive stones! What magnificent buildings!' 'Do you see all these buildings?' replied Jesus. 'Not one stone here will be left on another; every one will be thrown down.' As Jesus was sitting on the Mount of Olives opposite the temple, Peter, James, John and Matthew asked Him privately, 'Tell us, when will these things happen? And what will be the sign that they are all about to be fulfilled?'*

The contrast and lessons taught from the rich, who gave from their abundance, and the poor widow from her poverty, were now behind Jesus and His disciples as they leave the temple area. As they were walking away the disciples' attention was captured by the magnificence of the temple buildings; **v1** *'What magnificent buildings!'*

These buildings were famous for their outstanding grandeur and known as 'Herod's Temple'. The enormous size, the stone, the white marble and the gold facade, must have presented a most imposing spectacle.[1] Building construction commenced around 20 BC, and it is thought that although the main structure was completed within ten years work continued until its completion around AD 64.

To the Jew, nothing would seem as stable as this building. It was the symbol of God's presence with His people and it must have come as a great shock when Jesus said **(v2)** *'Not one stone will be left on another; every one will be thrown down.'* Although this was virtually a new building, Jesus' prophecy to the disciples was of its destruction.

Verses 3-4. Having arrived at the Mount of Olives which lay to the east of Jerusalem, and was higher than it, they would have had a spectacular view over the city and the temple. It was therefore the ideal setting for Jesus to sit down and speak with His disciples, including Peter, James, John and Matthew who were the questioners on this occasion.

Their enquiry was natural and expected *'Tell us, when will these things happen? And what will be the sign that they are all about to be fulfilled?'* Little did they understand that as soon as AD 70, the glory and majesty of the temple would disappear with its complete and utter destruction. For this reason, Jesus did not give them a direct answer, but used the occasion and the location to speak about signs and events that would precede the end of the age. Since the temple was a symbol of the nation, it was fitting, yet tragic, that its destruction would be the result of Israel's spiritual decline.

Be vigilant! Look for the signs. 13:5-13

> *'Jesus said to them: 'Watch out that no-one deceives you. Many will come in my name, claiming, 'I am*

---

[1] For further information and detail on Herod's Temple see The Illustrated Bible Dictionary. IVP. 1994. Part 3. p1525

> *he,' and will deceive many. When you hear of wars and rumours of wars, do not be alarmed. Such things must happen, but the end is still to come. Nation will rise against nation, and kingdom against kingdom. There will be earthquakes in various places, and famines. These are the beginning of birth pains. You must be on your guard. You will be handed over to the local councils and flogged in the synagogues. On account of me you will stand before governors and kings as witnesses to them. And the gospel must first be preached to all nations. Whenever you are arrested and brought to trial, do not worry beforehand about what to say. Just say whatever is given you at the time, for it is not you speaking, but the Holy Spirit. Brother will betray brother to death, and a father his child. Children will rebel against their parents and have them put to death. All men will hate you because of me, but he who stands firm to the end will be saved.'*

Verses 5-8. Throughout every generation since the resurrection, there have been those who claimed to have some special insight or knowledge into the time of Jesus' personal return. All have proved false. God's timetable for the return of His Son is known only to God Himself. Not even Jesus was privy to such knowledge **(v32)**.

On this occasion however, Jesus spoke to His disciples about certain circumstances, or signs, which would precede His personal return. In **v5** He said '*Watch out that no-one deceives you.'* The time would come when many would seek to deceive. False teachers with false doctrine would appear – some even claiming to be Christ Himself **(v6)**.

There have always been deceivers, and always will be, until the time when Christ Himself will return in a manner which Mark partially describes later in **vv26-27**. This was a warning to be 'spiritually alert and vigilant'; not to be easily fooled. The problem with deceivers both then and now is their resemblance to the 'real thing.' The Greek word used here for 'deceives' is PLANAO, and means 'being led into error' – don't be led astray.

In **vv7-8** Jesus told them that wars and rumours of wars would also take place. These things would happen, at times with such ferocity and evil, and on such a scale that men and women might think the end is in sight. However, Jesus encouraged His disciples not to be alarmed – these things must and will take place. The extent of such violence would be witnessed with nation rising against nation and kingdom against kingdom. Civil and world wars would erupt with consequences too horrible to envisage. Evil at the highest level would find expression through man's inhumanity against man.

There would also be 'natural events' such as earthquakes and famines. These would undoubtedly have a devastating effect upon humanity, yet Jesus informed His disciples that when these things take place – it would only be the beginning, *'These are the beginning of birth-pains'* **(v8)**. Worse would come before the glorious personal return of Christ – just as He promised.

Verses 9-13. Jesus never said it would be easy to follow Him, quite the reverse (see **8:34-38**)! The beginning of **v9** brings a repetitive warning *'Be on your guard'* for it concerns sufferings they were about to face. Persecution on a personal level awaited those who would faithfully follow Jesus Christ. Interrogation and physical punishment would take place in the synagogues, which indicates punishment from the Jewish authorities. They would also have to stand before the Gentiles; being called upon to bear witness to those in positions of authority (governors and kings).

The words *'On account of me'* in **v9** are important, for they draw attention to the personal nature of a Christian's faith. It was not simply faith in a new teaching, system or tradition, but faith and commitment in the person of Jesus Christ the Son of God. The days would soon come when the disciples would literally have to take their stand for Jesus Christ. As it was for them, so has it been for many who have taken up their cross to follow Jesus Christ.

Verse 10 is recorded only by Mark and makes reference to the preaching of the gospel to all nations. Shortly before He was taken up into heaven, Jesus, in **16:15**, would commission them to *'preach the good news to all creation.'* It may well be that Mark's inclusion is with the end times in mind. In other words, before Jesus' personal return the gospel must be preached to *'all nations'*.

In **v11**, the certainty that the disciples would face arrest, trial and suffering is not in doubt. Jesus stated this as a matter of fact: He said *'whenever you are'*. Thinking ahead on their behalf He told them not to be concerned about what they should say at such times. Jesus spoke prophetically to them, for He referred to something yet to take place. When their time of trial would come, words would be given them from the Holy Spirit. This is a rare reference to the Holy Spirit in Mark and was a means of encouragement because of what lay ahead.

Following Pentecost they would receive the Holy Spirit into their lives in a new way (**Acts 1:8**). The Holy Spirit would make His home in their physical beings. He would inhabit and empower them so that they would become temples in which the Spirit would live (**1 Cor 6:19-20**).

Looking towards the signs that point to the end of the age, Jesus, in **v12**, presents a terrible picture.

- Family structure which was the foundation of society would crumble.
- Self preservation would supersede loyalty between parents and children.
- Brothers would betray each other, even to death.
- Such would be the devastation of that age.

There would also be widespread hatred against those who followed Christ **(v13)**. The ministry of Jesus was one of compassion, grace and mercy – always seeking to bless, heal and encourage. Those who preached His Name, likewise, sought to bless others. Yet as they preached the gospel and ministered on Christ's behalf – they would face hatred and persecution.

In **John 15:18** Jesus is quoted as saying *'If the world hates you, keep in mind that it hated me also.'* Again in **John 16:2** *'....a time is coming when anyone who kills you will think he is offering a service to God..'* Such is the darkness within the human heart; *'This is the verdict: Light has come into the world, but men loved darkness instead of light because their deeds were evil'* **(Jn 3:19)**.

The phrase in **v13** *'but he who stands firm to the end will be saved'* is not a reference to salvation depending on human effort (see **Eph 2:8-9**). Leon Morris writes 'It is not surprising that, in a man-centred age, some writers put their emphasis on what man may be expected to do. It must be insisted upon that the Gospels speak of an election in which God, not man, is sovereign.'[2]

Times of trial and difficulty are often a means of testing the sincerity and genuineness of a person's faith. There may be many who 'fall away' not because of the severity of their persecution, but because their faith was never established in the finished work of Christ. The inference in this phrase is that those who persevere to the end (even if that be death) will be saved, because their faith was the real thing. These words are, therefore, meant to be a form of encouragement to continue and hold on – even amidst difficult times.[3]

---

[2] The Cross in the New Testament. The Paternoster Press. 1965. P19

[3] 'Trial is never welcome, but it can test and purify, and in the future it certainly was to do this for the Christian church, so that those of true faith might be revealed by their positive reaction to it.' Mark. Geoffrey Grogan. Good News from Jerusalem. Christian Focus. 2003. p227

Desolation and devastation. 13:14-20

> *'When you see the 'abomination that causes desolation' standing where it does not belong – let the reader understand – then let those who are in Judea flee to the mountains. Let no-one on the roof of his house go down or enter the house to take anything out. Let no-one in the field go back to get his cloak. How dreadful it will be in those days for pregnant women and nursing mothers! Pray that this will not take place in the winter, because those will be days of distress unequalled from the beginning, when God created the world, until now – and never to be equalled again. If the Lord had not cut short those days, no-one would survive. But for the sake of the elect, whom he has chosen, he has shortened them.'*

Having introduced His hearers to predictions about wars and catastrophes (**vv5-8**) and prophecies of persecution (**vv9-13**), Jesus then pointed towards future disaster. He described this in **v14** with the phrase *'the abomination that causes desolation.'* This expression comes from the book of Daniel where it is found three times (**Dan 9:27; 11:31; 12:11**). In the parallel passage from **Matthew 24:15** Daniel is specifically mentioned.

The word 'abomination' refers to that which was 'deeply disgusting and repugnant to God.' It is generally accepted that this prophecy was fulfilled in the desecration of the Temple by Antiochus of Syria in 168 B.C. and is recorded in First Maccabees 1:54.

A further fulfilment is related to the destruction of Jerusalem and its Temple in AD 70. From the parallel passage in **Luke 21:20** we read *'When you see Jerusalem being surrounded by armies, you will know that its desolation is near.'* Jerusalem did fall at the hands of Titus (who was to become the Emperor of Rome) with his besieging army.

At that terrible time the people crowded into Jerusalem from the countryside. This gave Titus the opportunity to starve the city into subjection. According to Josephus (the Jewish historian AD 37-100) in his fifth book 'The War of the Jews,' 97,000 were taken captive and 1,100,000 died by slow starvation and the sword. What took place was truly an abomination to the Lord, for the Temple was desecrated and the city destroyed. **Verses 15-18** help us to understand the swiftness of such devastation, and the effect upon every-day life.

It would seem in the light of these historical events and the central theme of this passage, that this prophecy can be related to several events both past and future. In keeping with Jesus' words as recorded by Mark, future fulfilment of this prophecy would be a sign that the second coming of Christ was near. In **v19** Jesus left His hearers in no doubt as to the unimaginable severity of such times, '.... *those will be days of distress unequalled from the beginning, when God created the world, until now – and never to be equalled again.'*

Although still with the destruction of Jerusalem in mind – this verse would seem to have a particular focus on future times immediately preceding Christ's personal return.

It is clear from **v20** that God has a specific time scale in mind. He will not let such torment, wickedness and suffering go on endlessly. God's love and mercy are in evidence here, for it is with those whom He has set apart for salvation in mind, that He has shortened this period of suffering and tribulation. Even in the midst of wrath, God remembers mercy (**Hab 3:2**).

Counterfeit Christs will appear. 13:21-23

> *'At that time if anyone says to you, 'Look, here is the Christ!' or 'Look, there he is!' do not believe it. For false Christs and false prophets will appear and perform signs and miracles to deceive the elect – if that were possible. So be on your guard; I have told you everything ahead of time.'*

To be forewarned is to be forearmed. And so Jesus warned His hearers that in the last days before His second coming, there would be those who claimed to be Christ. To convince others they would perform signs and miracles as a means of deception. When this takes place these counterfeit prophets and Christs will do so under the power of Satan – all part of his plan of cunning and deceit. The apostle Paul writes in **2 Corinthians 2:11** *'For we are not unaware of his schemes.'* They will not be the real thing!

Men and women may be impressed or even persuaded at that time, but not the elect. The idea that the Messiah will be discovered *'here or there'* (**v21**) suggests a human figure, not a heavenly one descending to earth. This idea may have referred originally to Jewish expectation of a Messiah. However, Christ will not appear from earth but from heaven above (**vv26-27**).

A key phrase comes from **v23** *'So be on your guard.'* God's people must be on their guard against all forms of heresy. Heresy is to be found in every age. False prophets will bring false doctrine. Their erroneous teaching will add to, subtract from and distort the truth. False Christs would bring false hope, whose words would prove futile and empty. For Christ's hearers at that time and all who seek to be faithful to Him and His Word today – the all-important thing is to know Christ and His Word. For it is through knowledge of the truth that error and heresy will be discerned.

The Son of Man returns in great power and glory. 13:24-27

> *But in those days following that distress, 'the sun will be darkened, and the moon will not give its light; the stars will fall from the sky, and the heavenly bodies will be shaken.' At that time men will see the Son of Man coming in clouds with great power and glory. And he will send his angels and gather his elect from*

the four winds, from the ends of the earth to the ends of the heavens.'

In this chapter a terrible picture of suffering, persecution and devastation has been presented by Jesus, as signs, events and circumstances that would take place at a certain time in history. These would all culminate with the second coming of Jesus, fulfilling His own prophecy *'I will come back.'* (**Jn14:3**).

To cap what He has already said, Jesus points to cosmic disasters that will herald the arrival of the Son of Man. **Verses 24-25** tell of things beyond human understanding.

- The sun will stop shining.
- The moon will give no reflecting light.
- Stars will plummet from the sky.
- The heavenly bodies will be shaken.

How are these things to be understood? Should they be taken as symbolic or can they be accepted literally? Either may be the case. However, there is no reason why they ought not to be taken literally. This would be in keeping with the rest of Jesus' teaching in this chapter (see also **2 Pet 3:5-13**). Furthermore, it would seem that the course of historical events will have been run, moving on to the winding up of history. In **Isaiah 65:17** we read *'Behold, I will create new heavens and a new earth. The former things will not be remembered, nor will they come to mind.'*

Verses 26-27 declare a truly momentous occasion. Never a shadow of doubt! At the Father's prescribed time His Son will descend from heaven with great power and glory. If at His birth, death and resurrection there was glory – how much more will His second coming be drenched in unimaginable and universal glory.

We do well to remember that at the time of Jesus speaking these words, the cross was on the horizon. A few days later He would be crucified and on the third does rise again. From this it is abundantly clear that Jesus spoke with authority and certainty. He had already instructed His disciples regarding these facts (**10:32-34**). And so with equal certainty Jesus points to a future time when He would return. The event is never in question. A number of certainties emerge.

Jesus' return will be visible. Verse 26 *'At that time men will see the Son of Man coming ..'* This would not be a secret event or with a limited audience, even those who crucified Him would witness the occasion. And in **Revelation 1:7** *'Look, He is coming with the clouds, and every eye will see Him, even those who pierced Him.'* To His disciples, as Jesus sought to comfort them shortly before His departure, He said *'And if I go and prepare a place for you, I will come back and take you to be with me'* (**Jn 14:3**).

Jesus' return will be sudden and unexpected. 1 Thessalonians 5:2 warns *'For you know very well that the day of the Lord will come like a thief in the night.'* There will be no opportunity for those dwelling in unbelief or uncertainty to reconsider their position – no time for a swift change of view or theology. Hence the words of Jesus in **13:33** *'Be on your guard! Be alert! You do not know when that time will come.'*

Jesus' return will introduce a time of gathering. Verse 27 *'And he will send his angels and gather his elect from the four winds, from the ends of the earth to the ends of the heavens.'* This will be a time when those who are in Christ will be gathered to Christ. From every corner of heaven and earth His children will come.

Although Mark's account is limited, Paul in **1 Thessalonians 4:16ff** writes *'For the Lord himself will come down from heaven, with a loud command, with the voice of the archangel and with the trumpet call of God, and the dead in Christ will rise first. After that, we who are still alive and are left will be caught together with them in the clouds to meet the Lord in the air. And so we will be with the Lord forever.'* To add words to the above would only detract from a sense of being lost in wonder, love and praise at such a prospect.

Be ever watchful. 13:28-31

> *'Now learn this lesson from the fig tree. As soon as its twigs get tender and its leaves come out, you know that summer is near. Even so, when you see these things happening, you know that it is near, right at the door. I tell you the truth, this generation will not pass away until all these things have happened. Heaven and earth will pass away but my words will never pass away.'*

Having used the fig-tree earlier in Mark's account as a symbol of judgement (**11:12-14; 20-21**), Jesus now teaches His disciples another lesson from the same kind of tree (**v28**). The lesson is not difficult to follow. When a person observes the branches of the fig-tree getting tender, it indicates that the sap is about to produce fruit, beginning with the leaves. This is a clear sign that summer is approaching. Likewise, it will be with the second advent of Christ. Having already informed His hearers what these signs will be; Jesus tells them that His coming will soon follow them (**v29**).

Much discussion has taken place regarding the precise meaning of **v30**, for it can scarcely mean those alive at that point in history. Clear understanding of this verse is difficult. The Greek word for 'generation' is GENEA, and may be translated as 'race, stock or family'. Jesus used this word several times as a reference to the Jewish nation (**8:12, 38; 9:19**). With this in mind, it may well be that Jesus is referring to the Jewish nation.

Verse 31 is a statement of fact regarding the permanency of Jesus' teaching. Although heaven and earth will cease to exist as mankind understands it, His words will remain. This being the case we have confirmation as to the value, validity and authority of Jesus' words.

The day and hour unknown. 13:32-37

> *'No-one knows about that day or hour, not even the angels in heaven, nor the Son, but only the Father. Be on guard! Be alert! You do not know when that time will come. It is like a man going away: he leaves his house and puts his servants in charge, each with his assigned task, and tells the one at the door to keep watch. Therefore keep watch because you do not know when the owner of the house will come back – whether in the evening, or at midnight, or when the cock crows, or at dawn. If he comes suddenly, do not let him find you sleeping. What I say to you. I say to everyone: Watch!'*

This closing section leaves the reader in no doubt at all about two things.

Firstly, no-one knows the precise time of Christ's personal return. Over the years many have engaged in speculation regarding times and dates, countless predictions have been offered but to no avail. The opening words of Jesus in **v32** make the point crystal clear *'No-one knows about that day or hour.'* Speculation is thoroughly unprofitable and a waste of time. It is enough to trust in God.

That only the Father is privy to this information is not easy for us to understand. Since there is equality within the blessed Trinity we may wonder why Jesus, as the Father's Son, does not know. When Jesus said that even He did not know the time of His second coming, He was in fact, affirming His humanity.[4] Holy Scripture provides no reason for this, simply a statement of fact. The emphasis on this verse is not on Jesus' lack of knowledge, but rather on the fact that no-one knows – only God the Father.

---

[4] The fact that even the Son according to his human nature, did not know, is in harmony with Phil 2:7 'He emptied himself' New Testament Commentary. Banner of Truth. 1976. William Hendriksen. p541

Secondly, *'Be on your guard! Be alert!'* said Jesus in **v33**. Christians must be morally alert, doctrinally faithful and committed to the way of faith. To live in a constant state of readiness was the challenge Jesus brought to His hearers. The challenge to all who follow Him is to live in such a way that the Lord's personal return, though sudden and swift, should be expected. In this chapter words such as *'When you hear'* **(v7)**, and *'when you see'* **(v14)** are a clear call to constant vigilance.

The final illustration from **v34ff** may be understood in this way. The master or owner of the house represents Christ. Following His death, resurrection and exaltation to heaven, Jesus would be visibly absent for an unspecified time. Those left in charge of the house were given particular responsibilities to carry out until the owner returned. They represent the Church - expanding, continuing to grow and minister as God's children, within the kingdom of God, in the power of the Holy Spirit.

The final challenge to the Church in **vv36-37** was to avoid laxity at all costs, *'do not let him find you sleeping.'* The fact that Jesus said '*What I say to you I say to everyone'* tells us that He wanted to affirm that the admonition to be 'watchful and alert,' was not just to His disciples at that time, but to all who truly belong to Christ. It was to all those He would gather from every corner of earth and heaven, when time as we understand it comes to an end at His second advent.

14

Jesus anointed at Bethany – love's extravagance. 14:1-11

'Now the Passover and the Feast of Unleavened bread were only two days away, and the chief priests and the teachers of the law were looking for some sly way to arrest Jesus and kill him. 'But not during the Feast,' they said, 'or the people may riot.' While he was in Bethany, reclining at the table in the home of a man known as Simon the Leper, a woman came with an alabaster jar of very expensive perfume, made of pure nard. She broke the jar and poured the perfume on his head.

Some of those present were saying indignantly to one another, 'Why this waste of perfume? It could have been sold for more than a year's wages and the money given to the poor.' And they rebuked her harshly. 'Leave her alone,' said Jesus. 'Why are you bothering her? She has done a beautiful thing to me. The poor you will always have with you, and you can help them anytime you want. But you will not always have me.

> *She did what she could. She poured perfume on my body to prepare for my burial. I tell you the truth, wherever the gospel is preached throughout the world, what she has done will also be told, in memory of her.'*
> *Then Judas Iscariot, one of the Twelve, went to the chief priests to betray Jesus to them. They were delighted to hear this and promised to give him money. So he watched for an opportunity to hand him over.'*

Approximately one third of Mark's gospel is taken up with the last week of Jesus' life - and much of this with His death. At the beginning of this gospel Mark announced who the gospel was all about **(1:1)** *'The beginning of the gospel about Jesus Christ, the Son of God.'* The word gospel means 'good news.' How then can it be that Mark concentrates a seeming disproportionate focus on Jesus' death, if what he has in mind is 'good news'? What is so good about death?

Death is not one of life's favourite topics. Rarely will a person find a biography that gives much space to a person's death. Birth, life, attainments, achievements, influences and much more will all occupy most of what is written. Yet with Jesus Christ it is quite different, following His birth narratives, very little is written about Him prior to the beginning of His public ministry at around the age of thirty.

More than any other in human history, Jesus was born with the leading purpose of dying. His death, however, was by means of crucifixion as an atoning sacrifice for the sin of mankind. God's great plan for His Son was to be fulfilled through His death and resurrection. His sacrificial death was for the benefit of others by reconciling them to God. *'But now he has reconciled you by Christ's physical body through death to present you in his sight, without blemish and free from accusation'* **(Col 1:22)**. The death of Jesus was therefore 'good news' for mankind. Chapters **14-15** are taken up with the passion story.

Matthew and Mark placed this event just before the last Supper, while John placed it a week earlier, just before the triumphal entry. This is not a problem, since the main purpose of the gospel writers was not to provide an exact chronological account of Christ's life, but to give an accurate record of his message.

Verses 1-2 introduce a familiar theme with the authorities determined as ever to destroy Jesus (**3:6; 11:18; 12:12**). With the passing of time, and in spite of all they had witnessed from the ministry and life of Jesus, the chief priests and teachers of the law had not softened or relinquished their desire to be rid of Jesus. Though eager to kill Jesus, they dared not attempt this with so many people around.

The Feast of the Passover and of Unleavened Bread were closely linked. Although, according to history, they were separate, they had virtually merged by this time. The details of both are recorded in **Exodus 12**.[1] Since (**Deut 16:16**) God had commanded all male Jews to attend these Feasts (usually with their families), this meant that Jerusalem would have been almost full to capacity at this time. A thriving, bustling and noisy city! Many travelled great distances to celebrate these Feasts.

Verses 3-9. Alexander McLaren writes 'We might almost suppose that Mark had an artist's eye for the power of contrast to heighten effects, when he framed this sweetest story of uncalculating and lavish love, in the black surroundings of the preceding and following paragraphs. How fair it shows the calculating, cold-blooded hatred of the rulers and the treacherous covetousness of Judas. The vulpine shrewdness of the one and the greed of the other look uglier by the side of the

[1] 'The Passover was one of the three compulsory feasts. The others were the Feast of Pentecost (or Unleavened Bread) and the Feast of Tabernacles.' Daily Bible Study. Revised Edition. The Saint Andrew Press. 1979. William Barclay. p325

woman's self-giving offering; and it gains even added tenderness and beauty from their hideousness.'[2]

Wedged between hatred of the enemy and treachery of a friend this beautiful story displays the extravagance of love. The setting was in Bethany at the house of Simon the leper. Little is known about Simon other than he may well have been a friend of Mary, some even speculate that he was the husband of Mary, and was dead by this time. The fact that Mark named him as Simon the Leper, introduces the possibility that he had been healed by Jesus, otherwise he would have been an outcast in society.

According to **v3** those present were reclining at the table (having their meal) when an unnamed woman entered. By doing so she acted against the protocol of that day,[3] yet must be forgiven for this, because she was a passionate woman with a mission. In John's record of this event he named the woman as Mary.

We have here a wonderful outburst of love! 'Love talk' can be cheap, words come easily at times, but this woman's love found expression in the most practical and sacrificial way. This jar of very expensive perfume would have been equal in value to one year's salary (**v5**). The design of the jar would probably have been globular with a long narrow neck.

With a love that knew no limit she broke the jar and poured it over Jesus' head. Although all around would enjoy the aroma, the anointing was for Jesus only. Nothing was held back. This was extravagance! This was worship! This was gratitude indeed! Her actions spoke louder than words! C.H. Spurgeon writes 'The beauty of this woman's act consisted in this – that it was all for Christ.'

Though unlikely to have been the same event (although some scholars suggest it is), Luke's words in **7:47** are nevertheless appropriate, *'Therefore, I tell you, her many sins*

---

[2] Bible Class Expositions. Hodder & Stoughton. St Mark. p153-154. (Published/printed date not recorded)

[3] In those days it was considered inappropriate for a woman to enter a male gathering while they were eating.

have been forgiven – for she loved much. But he who has been forgiven little loves little.'

In **v4** those present are unnamed by Mark. However, Matthew and John shed light on this (**Mtt 26:8** and **Jn 12:4**). Those present were Jesus' own disciples. The spokesperson was Judas Iscariot, their treasurer, who was later to betray Him. Their response to the Lord's anointing by Mary was disappointing. Rather than see the beauty of her actions they were caught up with 'money matters'. Were they really interested in the poor? If they had been, they could have taken action to raise funds and help at any time. *'Why this waste of perfume?'* they asked. By over-valuing the perfume they were actually devaluing their Lord; was Jesus not worth such extravagance? And so they rebuked Mary harshly (**v5**).

Jesus' response was to tell them to leave her alone (**v6**). Clearly they were unable to discern the significance of what Mary had done. However, we must not be too hard on them, for it is unlikely that even Mary fully understood. It was simply, yet profoundly, her way of demonstrating how much she loved Jesus. Just like the poor widow in **12:42** who gave her all (although only two copper coins), Mary was also giving her all. The lesson being that it is not so much the value of the gift, but the attitude of the giver towards Christ that counts.

In spite of Jesus' obvious concern for the poor, He sided with Mary, *'She has done a beautiful thing'* (**v6**). What she did was a good thing, praiseworthy and significant beyond her understanding at that time. The poor they would always have with them (**v7**), as Jesus pointed out, but they would not always have His physical presence.

Within a few days He would suffer at the hands of wicked men and be crucified. It was with this in mind that Jesus identified her actions as something 'beautiful' (literally a 'good thing'). What she did was not a waste – but an investment! This anointing was a symbolic preparation for His burial. Jesus' words in **v8** *'She did what she could'* are telling indeed, and present a challenge to all who follow Jesus. Nine times in seven verses Jesus made reference to this woman.

What Mary did was not impulsive, but planned and well intended for, judging by its value, such perfume must have taken considerable time to accumulate. It is safe to suggest that she must have gone without many things for the sake of this sacrifice. This act of love typified the place Mary had for Jesus in her life, and it is not surprising that Jesus stated **(v9)** *'wherever the gospel is preached throughout the world, what she has done will also be told, in memory of her.'* Mary's actions were compatible with her character:-

- **Luke 10:39.** Mary sat at the Lord's feet and listened to what He said.
- **Luke 10:42.** Mary has chosen what is better, and it will not be taken from her.
- **John 11:32.** Mary fell at His feet.
- **John 20:11.** Mary stood and wept outside the tomb.

Verses 10-11. What a contrast in characters! From one who could not get near enough to Jesus, to another who was so near, yet so far! Geoffrey Grogan writes 'To be one of the twelve, to spend months on the road with Him, to hear His words, to watch His works of love and power, and, most of all, to contemplate His character, to be so close to Jesus physically and yet to be so very far from Him spiritually, what a horror is this!'[4]

Judas is described in **v10** in two ways; as one of the Twelve and a betrayer. What a terrible combination, almost inconceivable! That he was a traitor is in no doubt, but what his motives were are uncertain, Mark provides no further information. The thought of doing this for the amount of money involved does not seem a valid reason. Some political reasons have also been suggested; yet the fact remains - we just don't know!

---

[4] Mark. Good News from Jerusalem. Christian Focus. 2003. p241.

Chapter **14** begins with the chief priests and teachers of the law looking for a way to arrest Jesus and have Him put to death. In **v11** the narrative returns to them and reveals their delight that Judas would be their accomplice and do the dirty work for them. No doubt there had to be a time-scale for this due to the problems of the Passover crowd, and the fear that Jesus would take over. An agreement was made; it was then left with Judas to wait for the appropriate time. Delight in such an evil deed is a grave reminder of the unholy potential of the human heart.

Preparation for the feast. 14:12-16

> *'On the first day of the Feast of Unleavened Bread, when it was customary to sacrifice the Passover lamb, Jesus' disciples asked him, 'Where do you want us to go and make preparations for you to eat the Passover?' So he sent two of his disciples, telling them, 'Go into the city, and a man carrying a jar of water will meet you. Follow him. Say to the owner of the house he enters, 'The Teacher asks: Where is my guest room, where I may eat the Passover with my disciples?' He will show you a large upper room, furnished and ready. Make preparations for us there.' The disciples left, went into the city and found things just as Jesus had told them. So they prepared the Passover.'*

The first Passover day may be identified as the 14 Nisan (our March-April). The normal procedure was to select a lamb four days earlier and have it thoroughly examined before slaughtering it on the 14th day of the month (**Ex 12:3-6**). The lambs were killed during the afternoon, then after sunset (regarded by Jews as the beginning of a new day i.e. 15 Nisan), the Passover meal was eaten. Arrangements for occasions such as this were never done in haste or without much thought and planning, and so, in **v12** the disciples asked Jesus where they were to prepare for the Passover. Although Mark does not identify the disciples, Luke names them in **22:8** as Peter and John.

As was the case in **11:1-6**, the possibility of natural planning and of our Lord's supernatural knowledge are in evidence. Jesus was in control of both. The information about whom the disciples should expect to meet, together with the fact of the upper room being furnished and ready, affirm this (**v13**). It may also be noted that it would have been most unusual for a man to be carrying the jar of water; according to local culture it would normally have been a woman. The man would, therefore, have stood out.

By following this man the disciples would be led to the house where the prepared room would be found (**v14**). The fact that there was a 'guest room,' described as 'a large upper room,' indicates that the owner was a man of some substance (**v15**). The room being on the second level would be ideal for quietness and privacy, and was usually accessed by means of an outside stair. Peter and John would duly convey the request of Jesus, whom they were to describe as 'The Teacher.' According to **v16** everything happened as Jesus had told them. So they prepared for the Passover.

Prophecy of the betrayer. 14:17-21

> *'When evening came, Jesus arrived with the twelve. While they were reclining at the table eating, he said, 'I tell you the truth, one of you will betray me – one who is eating with me.' They were saddened, and one by one they said to him, 'Surely not I?' 'It is one of the Twelve,' he replied, 'one who dips bread into the bowl with me. The Son of Man will go just as it is written about him. But woe to that man who betrays*

> *the Son of Man! It would be better for him if he had never been born.'*

All was now ready, and so Jesus and the Twelve arrived and settled down to their evening meal. The meal itself was full of meaning and detail. It was framed within a liturgy, the core of which was the Passover prayer of the family head, and the recitation of the Hallel (or Hallelujah) Psalms (**Ps 113-118**). Food, spices, bread, herbs and the lamb, which would be central, were all rich in meaning in relation to their exodus many years before (**1490 BC**).

The word *'reclining'* in **v18** refers to the posture they adopted as they ate, and was a symbol of their liberation from their slavery in Egypt. This stood in contrast to their departure from Egypt, when, due to their haste, they stood to eat.

There is never an easy way to share bad news, especially when the teller knows that it will not be understood. It was during this special meal that Jesus chose to tell them that one of them would betray Him. The words in **v18** *'one who is eating with me'* only increases the sense of awfulness, for in most cultures eating together is associated with close friendship and fellowship. It was not to be an outsider, but one of His own! Mark tells in **v19** that they were *'saddened.'* Surely an understatement! They must have been horrified! Every one of them declared their innocence *'Surely not I'* they said.

No mistake had been made, *'It is one of the Twelve'* said Jesus (**v20**). Yes! One who had walked, talked and prayed with Jesus; one who had been privy to the purpose of God and the nature of the Kingdom – such a one would betray Him.

Amidst this dark moment, it is well to remember that even this act of treachery by Judas (although unnamed by Mark on this occasion), would not overrule the sovereign purpose of God; rather it was used as part of His divine plan. This is clear from **v21**, where Jesus affirmed that it was all in accordance with what had been written about Him. This however, in no way exonerates Judas. He could not escape the responsibility for his actions.[5] Jesus said, *'It would have been better for him if he had not been born.'*

Once again Jesus used the title 'Son of Man' of Himself (see **8:31ff** for further details). Using this title in **v21** points to the highest form of servanthood. Chapter **10:45** is helpful; *'For even the Son of Man did not come to be served, but to serve, and to give his life as a ransom for many.'*

The Lord's Supper. 14:22-26

> *'While they were eating, Jesus took bread, gave thanks and broke it, and gave it to his disciples, saying, 'Take it; this is my body.' Then he took the cup, gave thanks and offered it to them, and they all drank from it. 'This is my blood of the covenant which is poured out for many,' he said to them. 'I tell you the truth, I will not drink again of the fruit of the vine until the day when I drink it anew in the kingdom of God.' When they had sung a hymn, they went out to the Mount of Olives.'*

This time of eating was also a time of remembering. They looked back to a time when lambs were slain and the blood painted on the door-posts so that the angel of death might pass over each house (**Ex 12:7**). They remembered this as their deliverance and redemption at that time. Now, in the midst of His disciples, Jesus pointed to Himself as the fulfilment of what they looked back to. The old was soon to finish and the new begin.

In **John 1:29**, John the Baptist said of Jesus *'Look, the Lamb of God, who takes away the sin of the world.'* His death

[5] 'Here is the mystery of divine sovereignty and human responsibility. They often meet in the Bible story, and, of course, in the life of the Christian believer today, but they have never had a more significant meeting than in the story of the crucifixion of Jesus.' Mark. Good News from Jerusalem. Christian Focus. 2003. Geoffrey Grogan. p245

on the cross would be a single sacrifice for sin for all time (see **Heb 7:27**).

In **vv22-23** Jesus took the bread and the cup, gave thanks, and then passed each element to His disciples to eat and drink. In doing so He instituted what is known as the 'Lord's Supper'. The bread and the wine were two elements already present; in themselves there was nothing special about them, other than the fact that Jesus gave them new significance. When Jesus said in **v22** *'This is my body,'* He was not suggesting that the bread literally became His body – only, that the bread was symbolic of His body to be offered on the cross.

Within hours Jesus would be crucified, His body broken and His blood shed. By eating bread and drinking wine from the cup, this was to be the new way of remembering Jesus, called the 'new covenant.' Although Mark (**v24**) and Matthew (**26:28**) simply record the word 'covenant,' Luke uses the words 'new covenant' in **22:20**. The word 'covenant' means 'agreement.' This new agreement was based upon the finished work of Christ (**Jn 19:30**).

A fuller version of the Lord's Supper is found in **1 Corinthians 11:23ff**. On that occasion not only is the act of remembering, the focal point, but the need to engage in self-examination beforehand is also emphasised. This act of remembrance was not to be taken lightly or without personal reflection, for it pointed to the most sacred and greatest act in history.

At the time of Mark writing his gospel this would have been the normal practice of Jesus' followers. Instead of looking back to what happened in Egypt centuries before, they would look back to the cross. Jesus' self-sacrifice is seen as the new act of redemption, establishing a new covenant between God and His people.

Verse 25 looks ahead to the future. This would be the last time Jesus would share in the 'Lord's Supper' with them on earth. His words *'I will not drink again of the fruit of the vine* *until the day when I drink it anew in the Kingdom of God'* refer to the wedding supper of the Lamb described in **Rev 19:9**. Heaven will be the venue - not an upper room. What a time that will be for Christ and His Church!

This great inaugural occasion came to a close by the singing of a hymn of praise (**v26**) before moving to the Mount of Olives. The hymn was probably taken from **Psalms 113-118** as previously cited in this chapter.

Peter's denial foretold. 14:27-31

> *'You will all fall away,' Jesus told them, 'for it is written: I will strike the shepherd, and the sheep will be scattered.' But after I have risen I will go ahead of you into Galilee.' Peter declared, 'Even if all fall away, I will not.' 'I tell you the truth,' Jesus answered, 'today – yes, tonight – before the cock crows twice you yourself will disown me three times.' But Peter insisted emphatically, 'Even if I have to die with you, I will never disown you.' And all the others said the same.'*

The Mount of Olives was familiar territory - for it was there that Jesus spoke about the destruction of Jerusalem and His second advent in Chapter **13**. Now, as they made their way to this same place, Jesus had something to say which would shock His disciples. What Jesus was about to share with them was further evidence of His deity. He foretold exactly what would soon happen with regards to them and Himself. Though the focus is on Peter's denial, Jesus also made reference to His death and resurrection.

To whom was Jesus speaking when He uttered the words *'You will all fall away'* (**v27**)? Was it half-hearted Pharisees or some would-be followers? Certainly not! It was to those who were closest to Him - men who had left all to follow Him, who had witnessed the miraculous and hung upon His every word for three years. They had left their occupations and families in favour of their allegiance to Jesus.

When Jesus needed His disciples most, they were to desert Him. How much the failure of those closest to Him must have hurt Him is beyond understanding, yet even human weakness and hard-heartedness are part of God's divine plan.

In **v27** Jesus quoted from **Zechariah 13:7** which was a prophecy about His own death and the dispersion of His disciples. The language is that of the shepherd and his sheep. Having just referred to His death, Jesus now says in **v28** *'after I have risen.'* How wonderful, and with what certainty! No qualification was required, it was simply a fact that He would rise again; it was never in question. It is interesting to note that in Mark's gospel Jesus never taught His disciples about His death without also referring to His resurrection (**8:31; 9:9, 10, 31; 10:34**).

In the eastern world the shepherd would always go ahead of his sheep, and so what Jesus said here is in keeping with the imagery of the shepherd and his sheep. Though they would not have understood at the time, this was a promise of a reunion and fellowship after His resurrection. *' .... I will go ahead of you into Galilee.'*

Verses 29-31. Peter had a reputation of being quick to speak and eager to act. At times he was over confident and impulsive. His response in **v29** *'Even if all fall away, I will not,'* was setting himself above others. He had a false sense of his own strength. How fitting are Paul's words from **1 Cor 10:12** *'if you think you are standing firm, be careful that you don't fall.'* Perhaps Paul was aware of Peter's early days.

By using the words *'I tell you the truth'* Jesus was strongly affirming what He was about to say to Peter. He made it crystal clear, that on that very night, before the cock crows twice,[6] Peter would disown Jesus three times (**v30**). The Greek word used for 'disown' is APARNEOMAI and means 'to affirm that one has

[6] In v30 some early manuscripts do not have twice.

no connection with a person.' How terrible! What an indictment on Peter, and how heart-breaking for Jesus!

Mark informs his readers in **v31** that Peter is 'emphatic' in his response. There seemed to be no way that Peter would accept Jesus' prophetic word. He is certain that he could never do such a thing; declaring that he would rather die with Jesus than turn his back on Him. That Peter is sincere and meant what he said is not in question. In his defence, it must be remembered that at times he was daring and bold while others kept behind the safety barrier.

- In the garden he raised his sword to protect Jesus **(Mtt 26:51)**.
- On the Mount of Transfiguration he said *'I will make three shelters.'* **(Mk 9:5)**.
- He ventured out of the boat to walk on water (**Mtt 14:29-30**).
- His confession of Christ (**Lk 9:20**).

What Peter had yet to discover was the weakness and frailty of his own heart. '*The spirit is willing but the body is weak'* (**v38**). Peter is often remembered because of his denial, yet Mark records in **v31** *'And all the others said the same.'* Though it was Peter who uttered the words and made the pledge, the others agreed with him.

Gethsemane – a place of anguish. 14:32-42

> *'They went to a place called Gethsemane, and Jesus said to his disciples, 'Sit here while I pray.' He took Peter, James and John along with him, and he began to be deeply distressed and troubled. My soul is overwhelmed with sorrow to the point of death,' he said to them. 'Stay here and keep watch.' Going a little further, he fell to the ground and prayed that if*

> *possible the hour might pass from him. 'Abba, Father,' he said, everything is possible for you. Take this cup from me. Yet not what I will, but what you will.'*
>
> *Then he turned to his disciples and found them sleeping. 'Simon,' he said to Peter, 'are you asleep? Could you not keep watch for one hour? Watch and pray so that you will not fall into temptation. The spirit is willing, but the body is weak.' Once more he went away and prayed the same thing. When he came back, he again found them sleeping, because their eyes were heavy. They did not know what to say to him. Returning the third time, he said to them, 'Are you still sleeping and resting? Enough! The hour has come. Look, the Son of Man is betrayed into the hands of sinners. Rise! Let us go! Here comes my betrayer!'*

The Place. Gethsemane was the place! It was situated some distance outside Jerusalem in the Mount of Olives. Most of these gardens were owned by wealthy people, it is therefore quite likely that Jesus was friendly with such people. The fact that Judas knew where to find Jesus also indicates that Jesus was in a regular habit of being there (**Lk 22:39; Jn 18:2**).

The name 'Gethsemane' means 'olive press.' Never was there such an apt definition. Not until this time (so far as Scripture records) had Jesus undergone such intense pressure. As the olives were crushed to pulp, so, in His inner being, Jesus also experienced being crushed. Anguish and agony escalated in His soul as the reality of the cross became ever nearer.

This is a passage worthy of deepest reverence, for it intrudes into the private agony of Jesus. C.H. Spurgeon writes 'Here we come to the holy of holies of our Lord's life on earth.'

The narrative before the reader is rich, deep and full of passion; yet to comprehend it in any measure, is bordering on the impossible. The author is aware that commenting on this event using mere words is almost to devalue the sanctity of our Lord's experience.

The People. Jesus and His disciples arrived at Gethsemane (**vv32-33**), He instructed them to stay at that place and pray. Leaving eight behind (Judas was absent), He took James, Peter and John with Him; they were to become known as His inner circle. It was these three who also accompanied Jesus on the Mount of Transfiguration (**9:2ff**) and at the home of Jairus (**5:37**). The inclusion of Peter, following Jesus' prediction of his denial, is remarkable. Not surprisingly, this points to the love, forgiveness and transforming grace of the Lord Jesus.

Although Jesus was the Son of God, He was also fully human, yet without sin. As a man, He welcomed their friendship and companionship. No doubt He would draw strength from their presence.

It must have come as a terrible shock for these three men to witness Jesus so deeply distressed and troubled; probably for the first time. There were occasions, however, when He had shown distress for other people and other reasons (ie Lazarus). Jesus' words in **v34** *'My soul is overwhelmed with sorrow to the point of death'* must have staggered them. Jesus felt so distressed that it seemed as though death was upon Him. Even the use of powerful verbs such as 'deeply distressed', 'troubled' and overwhelmed', all fall short of adequately describing Jesus' torment of soul.

Why should Jesus have expressed Himself in such a way? The shadow of the cross was now stretching over Him. He now sees more clearly what lay ahead for Him on the cross. It was not the act of dying or physical suffering which was the source of His anguish. History tells of men and women who died for noble and ignoble causes, and often calmly. On the cross Jesus (the sinless one - **1 Peter 2:22**) would take upon Himself the sin of humanity; but more than that! He would 'become sin' on behalf of others; He would take the full blown weight of sin upon Himself.

- *'God made him who had no sin to be sin for us'* (**2 Cor 5:21**).
- *'Surely he took up our infirmities and carried our sorrows .... he was pierced for our transgressions'* (**Is 53:4-5**).

To attempt any explanation of how Jesus felt at this time is quite beyond human understanding.[7] Instructing James, Peter and John to keep watch, He moved on to be alone with His heavenly Father. According to Luke, in **22:41** *'He withdrew about a stone's throw beyond them.'* In **vv43-44** of Luke's account, two things are recorded which highlight the severity of our Lord's inner struggle.[8]

Firstly, *'An angel from heaven appeared to him and strengthened him'*. Heavenly support was there in His hour of need. At this critical moment, He was safe in His Father's eternal purpose, even though, in that purpose, the progress to the cross was essential.

Secondly, *'And being in anguish, he prayed more earnestly, and his sweat was like drops of blood falling to the ground.'* The Greek work for 'anguish or agony' is AGONIA. This is the only time it is used in the New Testament, it denotes 'severe emotional strain'. The words *'sweat was like drops of blood'* are also significant. Medical experts suggest that, on certain occasions, when the body is undergoing immense inner anxiety, it is possible for blood to seep through the skin, so that sweat takes on the colouring of blood.

The Prayer. With the intensity and sorrow of His soul bearing heavily upon Him, Jesus fell to the ground and cried out to His Father. His prayer was for the removal from His circumstances *'if possible the hour might pass from Him'* (**v35**). Deity and humanity find expression here. As the Son of Man

[7] 'Jesus' suffering and death are not merely events compassed by men, but rather the fulfilment of a purpose deep in the counsels of God.' The Cross in the New Testament. Paternoster Press. 1967. Leon Morris. p27.

[8] 'A number of MSS omit these verses and RSV puts them in the margin; but the probability is that they should be included. They are well attested and should be accepted.' Luke. Tyndale New Testament Commentaries. IVP. 1984. Leon Morris. p311-312.

He prayed for deliverance *'take this cup from me,'* yet as the Son of God, He immediately submitted to the sovereign purpose of His Father God, *'Yet not what I will but what you will'* (**v36**).

In the person of Jesus Christ we have a wonderful example of submitting to the sovereign purpose of God – amidst the darkest struggle.

Verses 37-42. Returning to His disciples, Jesus found them sleeping. To Peter, the one who had just pledged his allegiance, even to death, He said *'are you asleep?* Three times Jesus found them asleep, saying in **v41** *'are you still sleeping and resting?'* In Matthew's gospel it is recorded that Jesus also prayed the same prayer three times (**26:36ff**). Yet Jesus understood their weakness; this was a trying and difficult time for them, *'The spirit is willing but the body is weak'* He said. They had left all to follow Him, they were sincere, they did love Him, but they were entering into a new realm, and would learn much about themselves in the days to come. It is often the case that more is learned through weakness than success.

Jesus brought His rebuke to a close (**v41**). Divine purpose and human treachery were about to meet. Jesus said *'The hour has come .... Here comes my betrayer'* He was now ready to face the suffering which He knew awaited Him. His words in **v42** *'Rise! Let us go!'* expressed His obedience and surrender to the will of His Father. The cup of suffering awaited Him and He was willing to drink it.

Confrontation in Gethsemane. 14:43-52

> *'Just as he was speaking, Judas, one of the Twelve, appeared. With him was a crowd armed with swords and clubs, sent from the chief priests, the teachers of the law, and the elders. Now the betrayer had arranged a signal with them: 'The one I kiss is the man; arrest him and lead him away under guard.' Going at once to Jesus, Judas said, 'Rabbi!' and*

> *kissed him. The men seized Jesus and arrested him. Then one of those standing near drew his sword and struck the servant of the high priest, cutting off his ear. 'Am I leading a rebellion,' said Jesus, 'that you have come out with swords and clubs to capture me? Every day I was with you, teaching in the temple courts, and you did not arrest me. But the Scriptures must be fulfilled.' Then everyone deserted him and fled. A young man, wearing nothing but a linen garment, was following Jesus. When they seized him, he fled naked, leaving his garment behind.'*

The momentum of the occasion raced ahead. Jesus was still speaking when Judas and his violent entourage arrived (**v43**). Judas, who was absent due to his sinister scheming with the authorities, now led the pack. How sad that one of the Twelve should blatantly and apparently, eagerly, lead the way. The fact that this crowd carried both swords and clubs was unusual. Those carrying swords were undoubtedly the soldiers acting officially on behalf of the Sanhedrin. Those wielding clubs probably joined in with the official group along the way.

Jesus would be identified with a kiss! It is difficult to imagine one who had spent so much time with Jesus, now betraying Him in such a way. *'The heart is deceitful above all things and beyond cure. Who can understand it?'* (**Jer 17:9**).

In this dark and fateful night, under the flickering torches, Judas made his appearance with the crowd following. He wasted no time, *'Going at once to Jesus'* he identified Him with the word *'Rabbi'* and kissed him (**v45**). How Judas could come face to face with Jesus is unthinkable – yet such was the depth to which he stooped. The kiss led to Jesus' arrest; *'The men seized Jesus and arrested him'* (**v46**).

One of the disciples, who had witnessed this event, responded in defence of his Lord. He took out his sword and cut off the ear of the high priest's servant (**v47**). Although Mark does not name this disciple, John does, in **18:10**. It was Peter, who else? Without a shadow of doubt, and in spite of his failures, Peter was a brave man. By acting in this way he risked his own life, and could easily have been struck down by the soldiers. Only in the gospel of Luke do we read that Jesus touched the man's ear and healed him (**22:51**).

How paradoxical Peter was! One moment he was laying his life on the line for Jesus – the next denying that he ever knew Him! Though many followers of Jesus will never face the unique challenges that confronted Peter - perhaps in him, we have a picture of 'everyone'. In Peter, the raw, the simplistic and heartfelt courage that is vulnerable was in evidence. Such is the nature of faith!

Verses 48-50. Jesus' response to the crowd was one of rebuke. Why should such a threatening and potentially violent mob be needed to secure His arrest? Perhaps, like Peter, they expected His disciples to resist His arrest and fight. In the light of **John 18:36** *'My kingdom is not of this world. If it were, my servants would fight to prevent my arrest,'* they had misunderstood the true nature of His kingdom. Jesus, however, reminded them that He was not leading a rebellion (**vv48-49**). Having witnessed His behaviour and teaching in the temple courts, this should have been clear to them.

Jesus made no attempt to resist arrest – He had already submitted to His Father's will and acknowledged (**v49**) that Scripture must be fulfilled (see **Isaiah 53**). Although the mob thought they were in control, the fact was that they were only doing what God allowed them to do. God was in control! The authority, accuracy and precision of Holy Scripture was being acted out at this moment in history.

Jesus' prophecy, *'You will all fall away'* (**v27**) was fulfilled in **v50**. How terrible it must have been for Jesus at this time. At His moment of great need He was abandoned by those closest to Him. And what must His disciples have been thinking? Their hopes, dreams and ambitions were now in tatters (or so they thought).

Why Mark includes the incident of **vv51-52** is uncertain. There would seem to be no obvious theological significance and no direct connection with the disciples. The only relevance may be that Mark described him as one who was 'following Jesus'. Perhaps he was a secret disciple! Seeing Jesus being unexpectedly seized, he panicked, and ran in such haste that part of his clothing was left behind.

Some scholars raise the question; was this young man John Mark the author of this gospel? Though this is possible, there is no way of being certain.

Jesus before the Sanhedrin. 14:53-65

> *'They took Jesus to the high priest, and all the chief priests, elders and teachers of the law came together. Peter followed him at a distance, right into the court yard of the high priest. There he sat with the guards and warmed himself at the fire. The chief priests and the whole Sanhedrin were looking for evidence against Jesus so that they could put him to death, but they did not find any. Many testified falsely about him, but their statements did not agree. Then some stood up and gave this false testimony against him. 'We heard him say, 'I will destroy this man-made temple and in three days will build another, not made by man.' Yet even their testimony did not agree.*
> *Then the high priest stood up before them and asked Jesus, 'Are you not going to answer? What is this testimony that these men are bringing against you?' But Jesus remained silent and gave no answer. Again the high priest asked him, 'Are you the Christ, the Son of the blessed One?' 'I am,' said Jesus. 'And you will see the Son of Man sitting at the right hand*

> *of the Mighty One and coming on the clouds of heaven.' The high priest tore his clothes. 'Why do we need any more witnesses?' he asked. 'You have heard the blasphemy. What do you think?' They all condemned him as worthy of death. Then some began to spit at him; they blindfolded him, struck him with their fists, and said, 'Prophesy!' And the guards took him and beat him.'*

Ensnared at last! The Sanhedrin's long awaited desire to trap Jesus was now in place. With the assistance and treachery of Judas, Jesus now stood before them (**v53**).

The normal venue for such a gathering as this would have been a special hall on the temple mount. However, on this occasion it was at the home of the high priest (**v54**). In order to accommodate the Sanhedrin (possibly 70 in total), it must have been a very large building. The fact that it had a courtyard endorses this. Although Mark does not name the high priest, Matthew's account tells us that it was Caiaphas (**26:57**).

Although all of His disciples had deserted Him (**v50**), Peter, it seems, had mustered up some courage and followed at a distance. Having entered the courtyard he even dared to sit with the guards. He was either brave or naive! Shortly before this, he had just raised his sword against them. Whatever his reasons for being there, it was in keeping with Jesus' prophecy regarding his denial (**v30**). The scene was now set!

Verses 55-59. How to fulfil their burning desire, which was to kill Jesus, was the Sanhedrin's present dilemma. They looked for evidence – but found none! Grasping at straws they listened to false testimony against Jesus, but their stories did not match up. [9]

Eventually, false witnesses brought evidence that, supposedly, was blasphemous against the temple. In doing so

[9] 'Mark presents the whole scene as a travesty of justice. According to the Mishnah (M. Sanh. 4.1), a trial on a capital charge should begin with a statement of the reasons for acquittal, not with reasons for convictions: here, however, the judges' minds are made up from the outset, since they are determined to put him to death.' The Gospel According to Mark. A & Black (publishers Ltd) 1991. Morna D Hooker. p358

they misquoted Scripture, possibly from **13:2**, but more likely from as recorded by John in **2:19** *'Destroy this temple, and I will raise it again in three days.'* In **v58** the false witnesses added *'man-made'*. Mark informs his readers that, in spite of their best efforts, there was still no accuracy in their statements (**v59**).

Verses 60-62. Perhaps with a sense of impatience and exasperation the high priest stood up (**v60**) and asked Jesus directly *'Are you not going to answer?'* Jesus' response in **v61** was one of silence, which emphasised His innocence. What He had heard was not worth responding to. They knew that their accusations were contrived to suit their predetermined agenda. In a sense, there was nothing for which Jesus must respond.

The high priest could not keep himself back from what he really wanted to ask Jesus, saying in **v61** *'Are you the Christ, the Son of the Blessed One?'* It is quite probable that the high priest knew that Jesus accepted the title 'Christ' from His followers (**Jn 1:49**). 'Are you openly declaring yourself to be the Son of God - the long awaited Messiah?' That was the question he was asking.

Jesus' reply is unequivocal: *'I am'* (**v62**). This was the first time in public that Jesus had clearly unveiled who He was. It stands in contrast to the restricted nature of His identity during His three years of ministry. The time was now right, however, for Jesus to acknowledge His deity – the cross was now in sight!

Jesus not only acknowledged His true identity but referred to an event beyond His suffering. The reference to His second coming *'And you will see the Son of Man sitting at the right hand of the Mighty One and coming on the clouds,'* is meant to convey two things to them.[10]

- Suffering will not have the last word. The Son of Man will return in triumph.
- This information, within its context, is addressed to Jesus' enemies who will find themselves judged because of their refusal to acknowledge Him.

[10] For further information on the Son of Man see comments on 8:31-33.

Verses 63-65. Why did the high priest tear his clothes (**v63**)? He considered Jesus to have committed blasphemy. This became the recognised gesture used at the end of a trial when the accused was convicted of blasphemy. Caiaphas (the high priest) did not even question Jesus' affirmation of deity; all present heard the words, *'I am'* from Jesus' own lips. Enough was enough! They had waited to hear these words for some time; yet, it was only in God's time that Jesus would use this self-designation.

The penalty for blasphemy was death; and so they all condemned Him as worthy of death (**v64**). The terrible and brutal way in which Jesus was treated in **v65**, in particular the words 'spit and struck,' echo the prophetic words of **Isaiah 50:6** *'I offered my back to those who beat me, my cheeks to those who pulled out my beard; I did not hide my face from mocking and spitting.'* They challenged Jesus to prophesy, but only as a form of ridicule. Jesus had already prophesied in **v62**, but it was not what they wanted to hear. What was really in the hearts of those present; now found expression in a most violent way – once again fulfilling the prophetic voice of Scripture (**Isaiah 52:13-53:12**).

Peter's denial of Jesus. 14:66-72

> *'While Peter was below in the court-yard, one of the servant girls of the high priest came by. When she saw Peter warming himself, she looked closely at him. 'You also were with that Nazarene, Jesus,' she said. But he denied it. 'I don't know or understand what you are talking about,' he said, and went out into the entrance. When the servant girl saw him there, she said again to those standing around, 'This fellow is one of them.' Again he denied it. After a little while, those standing near said to Peter, 'Surely you are one of them, for you are a Galilean.' He*

> *began to call down curses on himself, and he swore to them, 'I don't know this man you are talking about.' Immediately the cock crowed the second time. Then Peter remembered the word Jesus had spoken to him: 'Before the cock crows twice you will disown me three times.' And he broke down and wept.'*

This is a dark passage indeed! The reader witnesses the tragic fall of one who promised so much. Fortunately for Peter, this event did not have the final say, and was, in ways difficult to understand - part of God's sovereign purpose.

The courtyard in which Peter now sat would become a place of deep sadness and regret for him. It is difficult to believe that one so daring and outspoken for Christ, should now engage in such blatant denial of his Lord. Perhaps the seed for this was sown earlier in his failure to control himself in the garden and also by following Jesus at a distance (**vv47, 54**). Yet, Peter's audacity must also be commended – for simple prudence should have taught Peter to lie low, but he didn't!

As Peter sat warming himself by the fire he was recognized by a servant girl who *'looked closely at him'* (**vv66-67**). She accused Peter of being *'with that Nazarene, Jesus.'* These words were condemnatory! It wasn't a question, but an accusation. Peter was cornered, and responded with his first denial. He acted in ignorance, denied any knowledge of Jesus, turned away from his accuser, and walked towards the courtyard entrance (**v68**).

But the servant girl wasn't finished with Peter and spoke to others with a view to convincing them also (**v69**). For the second time Peter denied Jesus (**v70**). He was now on the slippery slope, going beyond the point of no return. At this moment in time, Peter's soul must have been in horrendous turmoil.

Verses 70-72. Gossip in the courtyard gained momentum, and so, others standing near Peter, said to him convincingly *'Surely you are one of them, for you are a Galilean.'*

The die was cast. Peter had been recognized and also betrayed by his accent that he was a Galilean (the Judeans did not like the Galileans). He knew that he could not worm his way out of this predicament, and so in **v71**, he cursed himself (not Jesus) and swore to them.

Immediately following his third denial (**v71**) the cock crowed for the second time. It was at this precise moment in time that Peter remembered Jesus' prediction that he would deny Him three times. It is no wonder that this tough, hardened ex-fisherman broke down and wept (**v72**). It is not possible for us to understand how he must have felt. Remorse and regret must have consumed him in the hours and days that followed. He was a broken man!

R. Alan Cole comments 'It is the fashion nowadays to make excuses for Peter, as some do for Judas, even if we do not go to the lengths of imputing good motives to either; and in so far as it means that we see our own weakness in him, that may be good. But unless we see the heinousness of sin, we cannot understand the bitterness of his remorse, nor depth of his repentance, nor the riches of grace in his restoration. The point is not to analyse by what easy steps the fall came, but to realize the terrible nature of the fall. Light thoughts on sin ultimately lead to light thoughts on redemption, and ultimately rob the cross of its glory.'[11]

Peter is always remembered for his thrice denial of the Lord. However, we do well not to forget that when Jesus restored him in **John 21:15-17**, he three times declared his loyalty to Jesus in ever increasing measure. Peter learned much from his weakness and failures

Following the Lord's ascension, Peter not only became a brave and courageous apostle, fearlessly declaring the gospel, but he also wrote two New Testament letters – 1st and 2nd Peter. Not surprisingly, in **1 Peter 3:15** we read *'But in your hearts set apart Christ as Lord.'*

---

[11] Mark. Tyndale New Testament Commentary. IVP 1983. p231.

There is a general consensus that Peter ended his life as a martyr, laying down his life for Jesus. Tradition tells that he refused normal crucifixion and was crucified upside down.

15

Jesus on trial before Pilate. 15:1-15

> *'Very early in the morning, the chief priests, with the elders, the teachers of the law and the whole Sanhedrin, reached a decision. They bound Jesus, led him away and turned him over to Pilate. 'Are you the king of the Jews?' asked Pilate. 'Yes, it is as you say,' Jesus replied. The chief priests accused him of many things. So again Pilate asked him, 'Aren't you going to answer? See how many things they are accusing you of.' But Jesus still made no reply, and Pilate was amazed.*
> *Now it was the custom at the Feast to release a prisoner whom the people requested. A man called Barabbas was in prison with the insurrectionists who had committed murder in the uprising. The crowd came up and asked Pilate to do for them what he usually did. 'Do you want me to release to you the king of the Jews?' asked Pilate, knowing that it was out of envy that the chief priests had handed Jesus*

> *over to him. But the chief priests stirred up the crowd to have Pilate release Barabbas instead. 'What shall I do, then, with the one you call king of the Jews?' Pilate asked them. 'Crucify him!' they shouted. 'Why? What crime has he committed?' asked Pilate. But they shouted all the louder, 'Crucify him!' Wanting to satisfy the crowd, Pilate released Barabbas to them. He had Jesus flogged, and handed him over to be crucified.'*

Jesus had already stood before the Sanhedrin at a hastily convened meeting the previous night, the conclusion being that He was guilty of blasphemy. As a result, those present condemned Jesus as worthy of death (**14:64**).

In **v1** Mark's words *'Very early in the morning,'* indicate that little time had passed since their previous deliberations. In fact, according to Jewish timescale, it was still within that same day. Urgency seemed to be the order of the day!

Since the Sanhedrin had no power themselves to carry out the death penalty (**see Jn 18:31**), they had Jesus bound and turned Him over to the Roman governor, Pilate. They wanted Jesus dead, but needed the Roman authorities to do their dirty work.

Pilate wasted no time in questioning Jesus (**vv2-5**); *'Are you the king of the Jews'* he asked. Jesus acknowledged this fact (only in relation to His kingdom, not as a threat to the established authorities), and from there the chief priests continued to accuse Him of many things. To the other accusations, which Mark does not name, Jesus remained silent (**v5**).[1] There are times when silence can be a better option than to utter words. On this occasion Jesus' silence was that of submission to His Father's sovereign purpose.

Although, according to the Sanhedrin, Jesus stood guilty of breaking their Jewish laws, the Romans would not put Him to

---

[1] This was also the fulfilment of prophesy. Isaiah 53:7 *'He was oppressed and afflicted, yet he did not open his mouth.'*

death for these reasons. In Luke's account **(23:2)**, we find that the accusation of *'subverting our nation'* is made against Him. Two reasons were suggested to support their claim; opposing the paying of taxes and claiming to be a king. These represented political charges; if true, Pilate would then have authority to act.

Verses 6-8. The twisted nature of this unjust saga then took a peculiar turn. There was a custom during the time of the Feast that allowed them to request the release of a prisoner.[2] The people requested Pilate to implement this form of amnesty which was their right. Mark informs his readers that at that time, a man called Barabbas was in prison for insurrection and murder. Not much is known about Barabbas; for there were many such insurrectionists. Nothing is known other than what the Gospels reveal.

Verses 9-15. Pilate was fully aware that Jesus had been dealt with unjustly by the Jewish hierarchy. They were envious and wanted rid of Him (**v10**). Behind the scenes the chief priests were stirring up the crowds, steering them according to their own will, or so they thought (**v11**).

Pilate was under great pressure. The Sanhedrin wanted him to do their evil deed. At the same time the people were making their will known and calling for the release of Barabbas instead of Jesus. The irony of this is quite incredible, if not unbelievable! Jesus was being accused of insurrection (rising up against the state), yet their call was to release Barabbas, whose crime was the same - plus murder (**see Luke 23:19**).

In this, we have a picture of a wider truth which lies at the heart of the gospel. Jesus, acknowledged as innocent, is put to death, while Barabbas, justly condemned to death for his crimes, goes free. The only one fit to live, was the only one fit to die.

---

[2] 'While political amnesties and release of prisoners have often been used as gestures of goodwill and to mark times of celebration, the specific custom presupposed here and in the other three gospels is not attested by any independent evidence. Thus while there is no exact parallel to the custom reported in the gospels, it is not improbable that Pilate found a similar concession politically expedient.' The International Greek New Testament. The Gospel of Mark. Paternoster 1993. R.T. France p629

In **v12**, having made their choice of Barabbas, Pilate then asked the crowd what he should do with Jesus, hoping they would see common sense and call for His release. Their response is truly terrifying! '*Crucify Him*' they shouted. Not surprisingly, Pilate questioned their wishes, stating that Jesus was innocent (**v14**)! The crowd did not change their mind but shouted even louder *'Crucify Him.'* This crowd is likely to have been different from those who welcomed Jesus one week earlier.

The words of **v15** *'Wanting to satisfy the crowd, Pilate released Barabbas to them'* are sad beyond measure. Not finding any charge proven against Him, Pilate had Jesus flogged and handed over for crucifixion.

Flogging was no small thing. It was so severe that it often killed the person. Those it did not kill were sometimes driven to madness. The person was bent over in order that his skin might be stretched and bones exposed. The implement used (a scourge) was a long leather thong, studded with sharpened pieces of lead and bone. It tore the person's back to shreds.

The complete injustice of Jesus' trial made absolutely no sense out-with the sovereign purpose of God. Jesus implied this in **John 19:11** *'You would have no power over me if it were not given to you from above.'*

Although Mark's account is rather brief, we discover from **Luke 23:4, 14, 22** that Pilate declared Jesus to be innocent three times. Luke provides more detail than Mark does, including the fact that Pilate tried to set Jesus free (**v22**), but the pressure from the people was too great. Clearly, Pilate was involved in his own personal struggle. His actions, however, express a cowardly evasion of responsibility.

Without any doubt, the trial of Jesus was surely the greatest miscarriage of justice ever recorded. This is equivalent to a present-day high court judge examining all the evidence, declaring the person before him to be innocent; then sentencing him to death. Quite absurd!

Jesus mocked and ridiculed by the soldiers. 15:16-20

> *'The soldiers led Jesus away into the palace (that is, the Praetorium) and called together the whole company of soldiers. They put a purple robe on him, then twisted together a crown of thorns and set it on him. And they began to call out to him, 'Hail, king of the Jews!' Again and again they struck him on the head with a staff and spat on him. Falling on their knees, they paid homage to him. And when they had mocked him, they took off the purple robe and put his own clothes on him. Then they led him out to crucify him. '*

In just a few verses Mark highlights the barbarism of the Roman soldiers. Having just been flogged; Jesus in an already weakened and painful state, now faced the onslaught of men who were experts in brutality and killing. According to **v16** the '*whole company of soldiers*' had been called together. No doubt they would try and outdo one another in their abuse of Jesus.

In their attempts to mock Jesus as king they stripped Him and took a soldier's scarlet robe, placed it on Him and acted out a royal situation, where the Emperor would have worn a majestic royal scarlet robe. He would also have worn a crown of great value and significance, indicating status and position. How different was the crown they pressed upon Jesus' sacred brow; it was a crown of thorns, long and razor sharp, tearing into His flesh.

The mockery then began! They bowed before Jesus and hailed Him as *'King of the Jews'*. Their cruelty in word and deed was also a way of despising all Jews, for they had no time for them. They stood before the King of Kings and Lord of Lords, oblivious to His true identity and struck Him on the head with a staff. Mark tells us that they '*struck him again and again'*

(**15:19**). The words of Isaiah the prophet, writing about 750 years BC, prophetically inform us that *'his appearance was so disfigured beyond that of any man and his form marred beyond human likeness'* (**52:14**).

When they had finished beating Him beyond recognition and leaving their humiliating spit upon Him, they put His own clothes back on, and led Him out to crucify Him. Spiritual darkness and the depraved state of their souls, are sadly in clear evidence!

One day, these same men, together with countless others will witness this same Jesus returning in all His true glory, splendour and power. *'Look, he is coming with the clouds, and every eye will see him, even those who pierced him'* (**Rev 1:7**). Still with the future in mind, Paul writes in **Philippians 2:10-11** *'that at the name of Jesus every knee should bow, in heaven and on earth, and every tongue confess that Jesus Christ is Lord, to the glory of God the Father.'*

The crucifixion of Jesus. 15:21-32

> *A certain man from Cyrene, Simon, the father of Alexander and Rufus, was passing by on his way in from the country, and they forced him to carry the cross. They brought Jesus to the place called Golgotha (which means the place of the skull). Then they offered him wine mixed with myrrh, but he did not take it. And they crucified him. Dividing up his clothes, they cast lots to see what each would get.*
>
> *It was the third hour when they crucified him. The written notice of the charge against him read: THE KING OF THE JEWS. They crucified two robbers with him, one on his right and one on his left. Those who passed by hurled insults at him, shaking their heads and saying, 'So! You are going to destroy the temple and build it in three days, come down from the*

> *cross and save yourself!' In the same way the chief priests and teachers of the law mocked him among themselves. 'He saved others,' they said, 'but he can't save himself! Let this Christ, this king of Israel, come down now from the cross, that we may see and believe.' Those crucified with him also heaped insults on him.'*

It was normal for criminals to carry their own cross. This was usually the main cross-beam, although historians are divided on whether this refers to the cross-beam alone, which would have been fixed to the centre post at the place of execution.

Mark does not explain why Jesus did not carry His own cross; however, the probable and common sense reason is that He was physically too weak following His scourging. Scourging normally took place on the way to crucifixion, but in Jesus' case, not so. Had Jesus also been scourged on His way to execution, humanly speaking, it would have killed Him before He reached the cross.

According to **John 19:17** Jesus carried His own cross. How then can this be squared with Matthew, Mark and Luke's account where it is recorded that Simon of Cyrene was compelled to carry Jesus' cross? One possibility is that Jesus carried His own cross for a very short distance until He was physically unable. William Hendriksen supports this theory, and comments 'Jesus, too, carried his own cross (**John 19:16, 17**), but not for long. Sheer physical exhaustion made it impossible for him to carry it very far.'[3]

And so in **v21**, we are introduced to the one who would bear the weight of the cross to the place of Jesus' crucifixion. He was Simon of Cyrene and had two sons, Alexander and Rufus. The fact that his sons are mentioned by Mark is probably an indication that they were known to Mark's readers. They had obviously no connection with what was happening since they were on their way in from the country.

---

[3] New Testament Commentary. Banner of Truth. 1976. p648.

It was both Jewish and Roman practice to carry out executions (stoning and crucifixions) beyond the inhabited area of a town. The place where Jesus was crucified was outside the city, but near the wall (**Jn 19:20**). In **v22** Mark named the place as 'Golgotha' which was a hill bearing the resemblance or shape of a skull.

Verses 23-24. Jesus, we are informed, was offered wine mixed with myrrh, but refused it. The drinking of wine mixed with myrrh was probably offered by women from Jerusalem, who may have been sympathetic towards Jesus. If taken, this would act as a pain-killing potion.[4]

Jesus' refusal to drink is seen as wanting His mind to remain clear and unclouded during His great act of Redemption upon the cross. Mark provides little detail regarding the actual crucifixion, simply stating, *'And they crucified him* (**v24**).*'* Perhaps there is value in brevity, for no matter the wisdom and eloquence expressed through mere words, it would not be possible to enter into the depth of Jesus' sufferings. And so, the greatest event in human history is not described in detail by Mark – only recorded with just four words!

Having removed His clothing before crucifixion, Mark tells that they cast lots and divided the clothes among them. In so doing, Mark quoted from **Psalm 22:18,** thereby fulfilling its prophetic intent.

Verses 25-27. Mark's reference to Jesus' crucifixion taking place at the third hour (**v25**) is problematic, since John in **19:14** gives the sixth hour as the time. Normally, the third hour would mean nine o'clock in the morning. The three hours of darkness would then have been from noon until three o'clock in the afternoon. It is probable that John used the Roman civil day time computation as he had done on a few other occasions (**Jn 1:39; 4:6; 4:52**). The fact of the crucifixion, however, is what mattered, and was far more important than the exact time!

---

[4] 'The custom of offering a pain-killing drink to those condemned to death is mentioned in the Talmud (B. Sanh. 43a), where it is said to be based on Prov. 31.6.' The Gospel according to St Mark. A & C Black (publishers Ltd) 1991. Morna D Hooker. p372-373

All four gospels agree that the written notice which was nailed above Jesus stated that He was THE KING OF THE JEWS (**v26**). It was normal for the notice, which stated the crime, to be carried ahead of the person being crucified, then nailed to the cross. Although crucified as a criminal – Jesus was actually a king!

In Jesus' case the words are significant. Though the words were usually meant to be derogatory, they affirmed that through crucifixion Jesus was the Messiah. Pilate could have written 'He claimed to be,' but as previously stated, he could find no charge against Him worthy of death (**Lk 23:14-15**).

Verse 27 fulfilled the prophecy of **Isaiah 53:12** *'he poured out his life unto death, and was numbered with the transgressors.'*[5] Once again Mark is brief, stating only that two robbers were crucified with Him, one on either side. Luke, in his gospel, provides further helpful detail (**Luke 23:39-43**).

The conversation that took place (as recorded in Luke) between the two criminals and Jesus is remarkable, and contains the very essence and purpose of the gospel. One man rebuked Jesus and challenged Him to save Himself and others if He truly was the Christ. This in turn caused the other criminal to chasten him with a challenge to 'fear God.' In so doing, he acknowledged his own guilt and also the innocence of Jesus.

The end product was - that one man, having demonstrated faith in Jesus, departed from this life having received salvation and entered the kingdom of God. Jesus promised that he would be with Him in paradise that same day – how wonderful! (**Lk 23:43**). The other, because of his unbelief – did not! Here we have a solemn reminder of the simplicity of salvation and also the wonderful grace of God.

Verses 29-30. Others passing by continued in their ridicule and unbelief. Shaking their heads they said *'Come down and save yourself!'* The prophetic words of **Psalm 22:7** are fulfilled

---

[5] Some manuscripts do not have v28 *'And the Scripture was fulfilled, which saith, And he was numbered with the transgressors.'* Authorised Version.

by their irreverent taunts! They were the Devil's advocate for sure.

Jesus was on that cross because it was to be the means of salvation for all who would believe. He was there as an expression of love and in submission to the eternal purpose of His Father. He did not come into this world to save Himself, but *'to give his life as a ransom for many'*. (**10:45**) To come down would have been pleasing for Satan, but disastrous for a lost world in need of salvation. The cross of Jesus was where all would be accomplished. His life, words and works – all aimed towards the cross. **John 12:27** records *'.. it was for this very reason I came to this hour.'* The cross was the place of victory. Jesus would not come down from it. He must finish His work!

To add insult to injury, the chief priests and teachers of the law continued with their ungodly and blasphemous mockery (**vv31-32**). Their own unbelieving words condemned them, *'come down now from the cross, that we may see and believe.'*

The essence of salvation is found in faith in Christ alone – Jesus said *'blessed are those who have not seen and yet have believed'* (**Jn 20:29**). The apostle Paul writes in **Ephesians 2:8ff** *'For it is by grace you are saved, through faith'*. How blind they were! Teachers of the Old Testament Scriptures – yet they failed to discern its Messianic message. Their hardened hearts left no opportunity for the way of faith.

The death of Jesus. 15:33-41

> *'At the sixth hour darkness came over the whole land until the ninth hour. And at the ninth hour Jesus cried out in a loud voice, 'Eloi, Eloi, lama sabachthani?' – which means, 'My God, my God, why have you forsaken me?' When some of those standing near heard this, they said, 'Listen, he's calling Elijah.' One man ran, filled a sponge with wine vinegar, put it*

> *on a stick, and offered it to Jesus to drink. 'Now leave him alone. Let's see if Elijah comes to take him down.' he said. With a loud cry, Jesus breathed his last.*
>
> *The curtain of the temple was torn in two from top to bottom. And when the centurion, who stood there in front of Jesus, heard his cry and saw how he died, he said, 'Surely this man was the Son of God!' Some women were watching from a distance. Among them were Mary Magdalene, Mary the mother of James the younger and of Joses, and Salome. In Galilee these women had followed him and cared for his needs. Many other women who had come up with him to Jerusalem were also there.'*

In **v33** Mark tells that from the sixth to the ninth hour darkness came over the whole land (from 12 o'clock until 3pm). Attempts have been made to explain this period of darkness by some natural phenomenon, such as an eclipse of the sun or a sudden thunder storm. These, plus other theories, however, present more difficulties than they solve.

That this period of darkness happened when it did, is remarkable, and has to be seen as something that God brought about. The nature and purpose of the entire event is shrouded in God's eternal purpose. Why then should such an intense and unforgettable period of darkness be relegated to a natural explanation? There is no need!

There are seven sayings or cries of Jesus on the cross. The cry in **v34** *'My God, my God, why have you forsaken me?'* is the fourth and central cry, and it comes at the conclusion of this period of darkness. This was a *'loud cry'* and came from the very core of His innermost being – it was a cry from the soul!

Only Matthew and Mark record this cry, in fact, neither of them records any of the others. **Psalm 22** provides the background to this cry, referred to at times as the 'Psalm of the cross'. When Martin Luther, the great 16th century reformer, meditated on this Psalm, it is recorded that he remained sitting upright and abstained from food for a long time.

In all history there was only one solitary instance in which God forsook a heart that had not forsaken Him – and it was to be that of His only Son. The relationship between the Father and the Son can never be understood by humankind. In the Father and the Son we have the perfect relationship.

For the first time ever, Jesus did not feel the love, smile, favour and nearness of His Father. Something had happened! What was it that had clouded their perfect fellowship? What had come between them? The answer is found in **2 Corinthians 5:21** *'God made him who had no sin to be sin for us, so that in him we might become the righteousness of God.'*

This should have been the brightest time of the day, yet for Jesus it was the darkest. The One who knew nothing but perfection and absolute purity had taken upon Himself the sin of mankind. Jesus did not simply pay the price of sin (which He did), but dealt with it personally by 'becoming' that sin. **1 Peter 2:24** *'He himself bore our sins in his body on the tree ...'* and in **Isaiah 53:4** *'Surely he took up our infirmities and carried our sorrows .... he was pierced for our transgressions, he was crushed for our iniquities.'*

On the cross He became a substitute for sinners and at the same time an expression of the Father's love. How paradoxical this may seem; yet, this was the grace of God towards a lost world. What God hated most, He allowed His Son to become! Such was the measure of His love for sinners!

The prophet Habakkuk helps us to understand the Father's attitude towards sin when he writes *'Your eyes are too pure to look on evil. You cannot tolerate wrong'* **(Hab 1:13)**. Vincent Taylor writes 'The depth of the saying are too deep to be plumbed, but the least adequate interpretations are those which find in it a sense of desolation in which Jesus felt the horror of sin so deeply that for a time the closeness of His communion with the Father was obscured.'[6]

The forsakenness and isolation that Jesus experienced was caused by His sin-bearing on the cross. His Father could not look on sin; which Jesus, at that time, had become. Jesus sensed the pain of isolation in a way that can never be understood. That the Father's presence was withdrawn is the measure of the horror of Jesus' death. This shows, as nothing else does, the true cost of the atoning work of Jesus.

Great care ought to be exercised not to search for logical understanding of this fourth cry. Leon Morris comments, 'The cry of dereliction must not be watered down. It is a shocking statement, and we must beware of trying to render it innocuous.'[7]

In the garden the angels strengthened Him – but on the cross, He was alone!

Verses 35-37. Jewish sources held to the popular belief that Elijah would come in times of critical need to protect the innocent and rescue the righteous. And so, those standing by, probably Jews, interpreted Jesus' cry as calling out to Elijah, which He was not.

One man, we are told in **v36** filled a sponge, put it on a stick and offered it to Jesus. This would have been 'soldier's wine,' which was quite coarse, and not the type previously mentioned in **v23**. According to **John 19:30** Jesus took some of this drink; probably just wetting His lips.

Verse 37 is both terrible and triumphant, *'With a loud cry, Jesus breathed His last.'* Jesus died! The Messiah, the King of kings and Lord of lords was now dead. But the manner of His death was different from any other human being. What did Jesus say about His death?

- *'No-one takes it from me, but I lay it down of my own accord'* **(Jn 10:18)**.

---

[6] The Gospel According to Mark. Second Edition. The MacMillan Press Ltd. 1980. p594.

[7] The Cross in the New Tesament. Paternoster Press. 1967. p47-48.

- *'He bowed his head and gave up his spirit.'* **(Jn 19:30)**.
- *'Jesus called out with a loud voice, 'Father into your hands I commit my spirit.' When he had said this, he breathed his last.'* **(Lk 23:46)**.

Jesus was in control of His own death. He was born of human flesh for the purpose of laying down His own life. Throughout all the sadness and tragedy associated with death, including His own (for His followers were devastated), there was divine purpose. For Jesus, death would not have the final say! In **John 19:30** the words *'It is finished'* are uttered by Jesus, indicating the completion of purpose. Jesus' death was victorious!

When did the Old Testament period finish and the New begin? It may be suggested that in **v38** we have the answer. The elaborate and ornate curtain (veil), which hung in the temple, was a means of separating the most holy place from the inner sanctuary. Only the high priest would enter behind this curtain once a year on the Day of Atonement.

Behind this curtain was the place where God's presence would be experienced, but the ordinary people could not be part of this.

And so, this curtain (as thick as a carpet), was torn from top to bottom. Being torn from the top indicated that God had initiated this. The spiritual significance was that no longer would there be a barrier to the presence of God. With the death of Jesus as a once-for-all sacrifice for sin, the old covenant, with all its rules and regulations regarding animal sacrifice, was now at an end (see **Hebrews 9:26; 10:11-12; 19-20**).

The tearing of this curtain pointed to a new way called the 'New Covenant' (see comments on **14:24**). Jesus was now the way, the truth and the life. The way of faith in Christ for salvation was now open to all who would believe. No longer did a high priest have to represent the people. Jesus is the great high priest. In **John 14:6** Jesus said *'No-one comes to the Father except through me.'*

There stood before Jesus a centurion, probably the one who supervised the crucifixion (**v39**). He had witnessed all that had been said and done. Mark tells that he *'saw how he died.'* This man would have witnessed many crucifixions, and be an expert at carrying them out, but he recognised something entirely unique about Jesus' death. Though we are not privy to his thoughts, we are told what his conclusion was, '*Surely this man was the Son of God.'*

His words were significant. His statement of faith summarises the theme of this gospel. That Jesus Christ was the Son of God, was one of Mark's important themes (**1:1, 11; 3:11; 5:7; 9:7; 14:61-62**). The cross is surely the place where faith begins – it certainly was for this centurion!

Verses 40-41. What a beautiful picture on such a sad occasion. A group of women, who, according to John's account included Jesus' mother, were there, and had witnessed all that had happened. Mark informs his readers that these women were followers of Jesus. They had cared for Him, supporting Him throughout His earthly ministry.

In spite of the strong pledge of allegiance from His disciples to stay with Him (**14:31**), it was this group of faithful and dedicated women who were present to the end. Evidence of their true devotion to Jesus is that they continued. How fitting that Scripture bears testimony to their faithful presence within sight of the cross.

Jesus' burial. 15:42-47

> *'It was Preparation Day (that is, the day before the Sabbath). So as evening approached, Joseph of Arimathea, a prominent member of the Council, who was himself waiting for the kingdom of God, went boldly to Pilate and asked for Jesus' body. Pilate was*

> *surprised to hear that he was already dead. Summoning the centurion, he asked him if Jesus had already died. When he learned from the centurion that it was so, he gave the body to Joseph. So Joseph bought some linen cloth, took down the body, wrapped it in the linen, and placed it in a tomb cut out of rock. Then he rolled a stone against the entrance of the tomb. Mary Magdalene and Mary the mother of Joses saw where he was laid.'*

The atoning work of Jesus on the cross was now complete. Jesus' sin-bearing suffering was now over, and the awfulness of the occasion, with all the jibes, taunts and ridicule were now at an end.

Jesus died at 3pm on Friday afternoon and the next day was the Sabbath. The new day (the Sabbath) started at 6pm on that same evening. This meant that any preparation for the Sabbath must take place before that time; there was no time to waste. Mark's words in **v42** *'So as evening approached,'* have a certain urgency about them, for unless Jesus' burial takes place soon, before 6pm, His body would have to be left until after the Sabbath.

Being both a Jew and a member of the Council (**v43**) meant that Joseph of Arimathea (a village some 20 miles from Jerusalem) moved quickly to secure the body of Jesus. What is known about this man?

- He was a prominent member of the Council (**15:43**).
- He had a good reputation. In **Luke 23:50** he is described as a 'good and upright man'.
- He was a 'man of God's Word' for he was waiting for the kingdom (**15:43**). This indicates that he was a Jew who was sincerely looking for the Messiah.
- He was also a 'rich man' (**Mtt 27:57**).

That some scholars suggest that Joseph was not necessarily sympathetic towards Jesus, is difficult to accept, for both Matthew and John describe him as a disciple (**Mtt 27:57** and **Jn 19:38**). Furthermore, in **Luke 23:50-51** we read that as a Council member he *'had not consented to their decision and action.'*

In John's account (**19:39**), Joseph was accompanied by Nicodemus, who earlier in John chapter three, came to speak with Jesus at night. He also was a rich man (see **Jn 19:39**).

These two men, by asking for Jesus' body were making their feelings, and their faith, public. This was an act of courage. Being members of the Jewish Sanhedrin, they may have been secret disciples – but no longer! They were men in waiting! They appeared just at the right time to perform a wonderful act for Jesus, and were instrumental in fulfilling the prophecy of **Isaiah 53:9** *'He was assigned a grave with the wicked, and with the rich in his death.'* It is possible that they were the first 'post crucifixion' believers to take their stand for Jesus.

Verses 44-45. Only Mark includes the content of these verses. The fact of Pilate's surprise that Jesus was already dead is significant, for he then asked for the centurion to verify that Jesus was actually dead. There was no need to break his legs as often happened to accelerate death. And so the prophetic word on **Psalm 34:20** was fulfilled *'he protects all his bones, not one of them will be broken'* (see **Jn 19:36**). Pilate then granted their request to go and take Jesus' body.

Here we have evidence that Jesus was dead, and not from one of His supporters. This counters the heresy that Jesus only 'appeared' to be dead.

Verses 46-47. Although Mark's account is rather brief regarding the placing of Jesus' body in the tomb, **Matthew 20:60** tells that this was Joseph's own tomb, which was cut out of rock and was new. We also learn from **John 19:39** that Nicodemus, who accompanied Joseph, brought a mixture of spices, aloes and myrrh, weighing about 75lbs.

The cost involved to do this would have been beyond the reach of most people. No expense was spared in preparation of Jesus' burial by these men. As previously stated, although these men were not prominent disciples, this final act for Jesus, in His death, was commendable. Having prepared the body, they sealed the tomb. Mark tells that *'they rolled the stone against the entrance of the tomb.'* The likelihood is that others helped them to do this.

This section concludes with the record of Mary Magdalene and Mary the mother of Joses looking on, observing *(saw)* the exact place where the tomb was.[8] Luke's record highlights the fact that they watched as His body was laid in the tomb (**23:55**).

[8] *'Saw: Greek 'were watching';* the imperfect perhaps suggests that they had remained all the time at the place from which they saw the crucifixion.' The Gospel of St Mark. Pelican New Testament Commentaries. 1963. D.E. Nineham. p435

16

The fact of Jesus' resurrection. 16:1-8

'When the Sabbath was over, Mary Magdalene, Mary the mother of James, and Salome bought spices so that they might go to anoint Jesus' body. Very early on the first day of the week, just after sunrise, they were on their way to the tomb and they asked each other, 'Who will roll the stone away from the entrance of the tomb?' But when they looked up, they saw that the stone, which was very large, had been rolled away. As they entered the tomb, they saw a young man dressed in a white robe sitting on the right, and they were alarmed. 'Don't be alarmed,' he said, 'You are looking for Jesus the Nazarene, who was crucified. He has risen! He is not here. See the place where they laid him. But go, tell his disciples and Peter, 'He is going ahead of you into Galilee. There you will see him, just as he told you.' Trembling and bewildered, the women went out and fled from the tomb. They said nothing to anyone, because they were afraid.'

The death and burial of Jesus were now over. The indisputable facts are recorded in Holy Scripture and the annals of history. Yet, had this to be the final record of the life of Jesus Christ, there would be no Gospel at all. The apostle Paul writes in **1 Corinthians 15:14** '*And if Christ has not been raised, our preaching is useless and so is your faith.'* The resurrection of Jesus Christ stands at the very heart of the Gospel. The Christian message without a resurrected Christ would be no more than a tale of woe, offering no hope and no salvation.

This concluding chapter provides a triumphant ending to Mark's account of the life, death and resurrection of Jesus Christ. Although it is an ending, it was also a new beginning, leading to the birth of the New Testament Church.

Verses 1-8. Reference to the Sabbath day being over, indicated that it was now after 6pm on the Saturday evening. Not surprisingly, it was the women who journeyed to the tomb. What a wonderful testimony to these women. Their love for their Saviour was in evidence by their presence at the cross, and now at the tomb. The men were nowhere to be seen!

As previously mentioned (see comment on **15:42**), Jesus was buried in haste due to the Sabbath fast approaching, and so it seemed appropriate that further care of His body should be taken. This information is given in **v1** that the women brought spices to anoint Jesus' body, thereby finishing off the embalming. It is not certain at what exact time the women arrived at the tomb. That it was after the Sabbath is clear, yet Mark records in **v2** that it was *'Very early on the first day of the week, just after sunrise.'* This means that they went to the tomb as soon as possible; in the early hours before dawn.

As the women neared their destination, they questioned among themselves who could roll the stone from the tomb entrance. When Nicodemus and Joseph laid Jesus' body in the tomb, it is possible that they would also have had assistance.

The stone used for this purpose would have been similar to a large mill stone, which would be rolled into a pre-cut groove in the ground. Once in place, it would require great effort to push it out of the groove. According to **v4** it was *'very large.'* And so, in **v3** the women ask themselves *'Who will roll the stone away from the entrance of the tomb?'* Arriving at the tomb their concerns were unnecessary, because the stone had been rolled away.

Acting on the fear of the chief priests, Pilate had the tomb sealed and guards placed at it (**Mtt 27:65-66**). In fact, Pilate said *'make the tomb as secure as you know how.'*[1] This made no difference, because God intervened. According to Matthews account it was an angel of the Lord who moved the stone. As a result the guards shook with fear to such an extent that it left them as though they were dead (**Mtt 28:4**).

Mark wanted to keep things simple and did not elaborate as Matthew did. As the women entered the tomb, they were 'alarmed,' for they saw a young man sitting, dressed in a white robe. He was possibly the angel who moved the stone! He had news for them – the most wonderful news they could ever hear, yet at this moment in time they were unable to comprehend it. Their hearts were still absorbed in deep grief, their world had just collapsed, their hopes and dreams had been shattered. They were in no fit state to understand.

What glorious news! *'Don't be alarmed,'* the angel said. *'You are looking for Jesus the Nazarene, who was crucified. He has risen! He is not here. See the place where they laid him* (**v6**).*'*

The angel had made two things plain.

- The person who lay here was the same One who had been crucified.
- He was no longer there because He had risen! Just as He said He would (**10:32-34**).

Without a resurrection Jesus would never have been remembered. Mark was brief, but he made his point!

---

[1] According to Matthew 28:11-15 the chief priests and the elders bribed the soldiers to lie - saying that Jesus' body had been stolen while they slept.

Not only had Jesus risen, but the women were told to go and tell His disciples and Peter. Peter is mentioned specifically because he denied that he was a disciple. Jesus was going ahead to Galilee and there they would see him (**v7**). These words echo Jesus' words from **14:28**.

The fact that these women had actually seen Lazarus who had been raised from the dead made no difference – they were still struggling to come to terms with the news of Jesus' resurrection. And so, Mark tells that they were *Trembling and bewildered.'* They were totally confused, they did not know what to make of all this, and so they fled from the tomb (**v8**).

The concluding section (**vv9-20**) is not included in some of the early manuscripts. Although Mark may have been the author, and this cannot be ruled out, the style and vocabulary would seem to be quite different from the rest of the gospel.[2] The narrative itself is, however, in keeping with the other gospel records, and is, therefore, included in the canon of Scripture.

The concluding section. 16:9-20

When Jesus rose early on the first day of the week, he appeared first to Mary Magdalene, out of whom he had driven seven demons. She went and told those who had been with him and who were mourning and weeping. When they heard that Jesus was alive and that she had seen him, they did not believe it. Afterwards Jesus appeared in a different form to two of them while they were walking in the country. These returned and reported it to the rest; but they did not believe them either.

[2] Eusebius, writing in the fourth century, said that the best MSS ended at v8. These verses were, however, apparently known to Tatian in about AD 140, and Irenaeus, writing in about AD 180, quotes from them and assumes them to be written by Mark. The Gospel according to Mark. A & C Black (publishers Ltd) 1991. Morna D Hooker. p389.

> *Later Jesus appeared to the eleven as they were eating; he rebuked them for their lack of faith and stubborn refusal to believe those who had seen him after he had risen. He said to them, 'Go into all the world and preach the good news to all creation. Whoever believes and is baptised will be saved, but whoever does not believe will be condemned.*
> *And these signs will accompany those who believe: in my name they will drive out demons; they will speak in new tongues; they will pick up snakes with their hands; and when they drink deadly poison, it will not hurt them at all; they will place their hands on sick people, and they will get well.' After the Lord Jesus had spoken to them, he was taken up into heaven and he sat at the right hand of God. Then the disciples went out and preached everywhere, and the Lord worked with them and confirmed his word by the signs that accompanied it.'*

Verses 9-14. How wonderful it is to read '*When Jesus rose early on the first day of the week'*. It is never in question, never in doubt, simply stated as a fact. A fuller picture of Jesus appearing to Mary Magdalene is found in **John 20:11-18**, which is full of emotion and tenderness.

Being absorbed with grief and having made her way to the tomb with the purpose of anointing Jesus' body, Mary did not expect an empty tomb, let alone a resurrection. A special moment of recognition took place when Jesus said *'Mary'*. When she heard Him speak her name she recognised Him immediately.

The first thing Mary did was to obey Jesus by returning to tell the others, who, according to **v10**, were *'mourning and weeping'*. This woman, who had witnessed Jesus' death and burial, was now the first to see the resurrected Christ; it was a just reward, for she loved Jesus deeply. It can only be imagined (or perhaps not) how she felt as she raced back to tell the others - her shattered world had now righted itself - because Jesus was alive!

How disappointing it must have been for Mary when the disciples refused to accept her testimony about Jesus (**v11**). In spite of all they had been taught on earlier occasions by Jesus about His death and resurrection – they still did not understand!

In **vv12-13** there is a similar pattern of unbelief. The background comes from **Luke 24:13-35** where Jesus walked with two disciples on the Emmaus road. Following their special moment of recognition, they returned to the other disciples and shared their experience; but they did not believe them either!

According to **Luke 24:16** the two disciples were kept from recognising Jesus. Here in **v12** this is explained in another way, *'Jesus appeared in a different form.'* What is meant by a 'different form' we cannot be certain. However, it would seem that this new form enabled Jesus to disappear from their sight, as in **Luke 24:31.** In **John 20:26** Jesus also appeared before His disciples while Thomas was with them, without coming through the door, which was locked.

Though the disciples' unbelief may be excused before Jesus' death, it would now seem that Jesus expected that to change. In **v14** as Jesus was eating[3] with the whole body of disciples (**Jn 20:19ff**), *'He rebuked them for their lack of faith and stubborn refusal to believe.'*

Why? Because they would not accept eye witness accounts of an event which they ought to have been anticipating from those they knew and surely trusted. The testimony of their friends ought to have reminded them of Jesus' earlier teaching about His resurrection. Jesus had previously rebuked them for their besetting sin of unbelief (**9:19**).

Verses 15-18. Having rebuked the disciples for their unbelief, Jesus now commissioned them to go into all the world

[3] It may be noted that Jesus' new resurrection body was able to receive food. See also John 21:9-10 and Luke 24:42-43.

and preach the good news.[4] Earlier in **13:10** and **14:9** Jesus told them that the gospel must be preached to all nations. Now that they had witnessed the death, and especially the resurrection of Jesus, they now had a gospel to preach. Prior to this they had nothing to say. Very soon Peter, filled with the Holy Spirit and fresh from his restoration, would say in his first sermon, *'God has raised this Jesus to life.'* (**Acts 2:32**)

In **v16** Jesus made it abundantly clear that those who remain in unbelief will be condemned. The challenge of the gospel is to 'believe and be baptised.' Baptism took place as a result of repentance and belief in Jesus Christ as Saviour and Lord. Baptism in itself cannot produce salvation, yet the act of baptism is a 'telling forth' to all who witness it, that a person has come to faith in Christ.*'Repent and be baptised, every one of you'* **(Acts 2:38)** and **(2:41)** *'Those who accepted his message were baptised.'*

This verse is not suggesting that baptism was essential for salvation, but that it was the expected response of genuine faith in Christ.

Signs would accompany those who believed (**vv17-18**). What was the significance of them? By saying *'In my name'* these signs should not be attributed to the believers, but rather to the activity of God, and for His glory.

Other than the drinking of deadly poison, all the other signs mentioned here are recorded in **Acts 5:16; 2:4; 28:3-5** and **28:8.** That these signs would happen every time the gospel was preached cannot be assumed; but would be in accordance with God's purpose.

Alan R Cole writes: 'Whether or not such evidential manifestations were intended to be continuous in the life of the Church, or restricted to this period, or sporadic, must be considered in the light of the rest of the New Testament; in view of the uncertain textual evidence for this longer Conclusion, no dogmatic assumptions should be made from it alone.'[5]

---

[4] The great commission is recorded in Matthew 28:18-20. Mark 16:15-16. Luke 24:46-47. John 20:21. Acts 1:8.

[5] Tyndale. New Testament Commentary. IVP. 1983. p262.

Verses 19-20. Irrespective as to the textual difficulties with this final section in Mark's gospel, there could be no more fitting event than what is set before us. *'After the Lord Jesus had spoken to them, he was taken up into heaven and he sat at the right hand of God.'* This is a short account of the Lord's ascension. A fuller description is found in **Acts 1**, where Luke avers that the disciples were eyewitnesses – *'he was taken up before their very eyes ....they were still looking intently up into the sky as he was going'* (**Acts 1:9-10**)

The Lord Jesus ascended to heaven having made provision for the salvation of all who would believe in Him. In **v19** we are told that Jesus *'sat at the right hand of God.'* This is a wonderful expression!

Why did Jesus sit down at His Father's right hand?

- Because He had finished His work – it was complete! He left nothing undone which His Father had planned.
- He commenced His heavenly ministry as our Great High Priest. His love, care and compassion continue through His priestly role. Never-ending, night and day He brings His children and their needs before His Father. The priestly ministry of Jesus is fully explained in the epistle to the Hebrews.

Jesus' work was finished on earth, but the work of the disciples was just beginning.

Verse 20 brings an end to Mark's gospel with the disciples engaging in their preaching ministry. That blessing accompanied their ministry was in evidence – *'the Lord worked with them and confirmed his word by the signs that accompanied it.'* No longer men of unbelief but men of faith, relying on the power of God.

The ministry which the apostles set in motion continues today, empowered by the same Holy Spirit. It is the same message; the same power; the same purpose; bringing many souls into the kingdom of God, building His Church until *'This same Jesus, who has been taken from you into heaven, will come back in the same way you have seen him go into heaven.'* **(Acts 1:11)**

BIBLIOGRAPHY

- Achtemeier, Paul J. Proclamation Commentaries. Mark. Fortress Press. Second Edition 1986
- Anderson, Hugh. The Gospel of Mark. New Century Bible. Marshall, Morgan & Scott. 1976.

- Barclay, William. Daily Study Bible. Revised Edition. The Saint Andrew Press. 1979.
- Branscomb, B. Harvie. The Gospel of Mark. Hodder and Stoughton Ltd. 1948.
- Brown, David. The Four Gospels. A Commentary, Critical, Experimental and Practical. The Banner of Truth Trust. 1969.

- Cole, R. Alan. Tyndale. New Testament Commentary. IVP 1983.
- Collins Dictionary of the English Language. 1981. William Collins Sons & Co Ltd. Glasgow.
- Cranfield, C.E.B. The Gospel According to Mark. Cambridge University Press. 1959

- English, Donald. Bible Speaks Today. Message of Mark. I.V.P 1993

- France, R.T. The New International Greek Testament Commentary. The Gospel of Mark. 1993. Paternoster Press. Published jointly in USA with Wm B. Eerdmans Publishing Co. 2002.

- Grogan, Geoffrey. MARK. Good News from Jerusalem. Christian Focus. 2003.

- Hastings, James. The Great Texts of the Bible. St Mark. T & T Clark. 1910.
- Hendriksen, William. New Testament Commentary. Banner of Truth. 1976.
- Hooker, Morna D. The Gospel according to St Mark. A & C Black (publishers) Ltd 1991

- Ladd George E. A Theology of the New Testament. Erdmans Publishing Co. 1971.
- Lane, William L. The New London Commentary on the New Testament. The Gospel of Mark. Marshall, Morgan & Scott 1974.
- Lockyer, Herbert. All the Apostles of the Bible. Zondervan Publishing House. 1972.

- Lockyer, Herbert. All the men of the Bible. Pickering & Inglis. Zondervan. 1958

- MacLaren, Alexander. Bible Class Expositions. Hodder & Stoughton. St Mark.
- Marshall, I.H. Bible Study Book. Scripture Union.
- Moule, C.F.D. The Gospel According to Mark. The Cambridge Bible Commentary. 1975.

- New Bible Commentary. IVP. March 1961.
- Nineham D.E. The Gospel of St Mark. Pelican New Testament Commentaries. 1963

- Ryle, J.C. Expository thoughts on the Gospels. Evangelical Press. 1977.

- Schweizer, Eduard. The Good News According to Mark. London S.P.C.K. 1971.
- Scroggie, W.G. A Guide to the Gospels. Pickering & Inglis 1972.
- Stein, Robert H. The Synoptic Problem. Baker Book House Company. USA. 1992 .
- Stott, John. Issues Facing Christians Today. Collins – Marshall Pickering. 1990.
- Swete, H.B. The Gospel According to St Mark. MacMillan and Co., Limited. 1898

- The New Bible Dictionary. Inter-Varsity Fellowship. 1962.
- Taylor, David Bruce. Mark's Gospel as Literature and History. SCM Press Ltd. 1992.
- Taylor, Vincent. The Gospel According to Mark. Second Edition. The MacMillan Press Ltd. 1980.

- Vine's Expository Dictionary of Old and New Testament Words. Thomas Nelson Publishers. 1997.

- Wiersbe, Warren W. Be Diligent. Scripture Press. 1991. .
- Wiersbe, Warren W. Meet yourself in the Parables. Victor Books. 1983.
- Wuest, Kenneth S. Studies in the Vocabulary of the Greek New Testament. Erdmans Publishing Company. 1955.